SEMANTIC WEB AND MODEL-DRIVEN ENGINEERING

SEMANTIC WEB AND MODEL-DRIVEN ENGINEERING

FERNANDO SILVA PARREIRAS

FUMEC University, Brazil

IEEE PRESS

A JOHN WILEY & SONS, INC., PUBLICATION

Published by John Wiley & Sons, Inc., Hoboken, New Jersey.
Published simultaneously in Canada.

For general information on our other products and services or for technical support, please contact our
Customer Care Department within the United States at (800) 762-2974, outside the United States at
(317) 572-3993 or fax (317) 572-4002.

Wiley also publishes its books in a variety of electronic formats. Some content that appears in print
may not be available in electronic formats. For more information about Wiley products, visit our web
site at www.wiley.com.

Library of Congress Cataloging-in-Publication Data is available.

ISBN: 978-1-118-00417-3

Printed in the United States of America.

10 9 8 7 6 5 4 3 2 1

To my family

CONTENTS IN BRIEF

LIST OF FIGURES

LIST OF TABLES

FOREWORD

Software modeling is in a schizophrenic situation. On the one hand, it is targeted towards the development of completely formal systems, i.e., executable code. On the other hand, the tools dominating in software modeling are typically drawing tools prepared with specific graphical icons. This dichotomy implies that the targeted meaning of a software model is limited in its use towards human understanding and communication only.

This dichotomy is reconciled when software is enriched with formulae specifying the functionality of the code. This is an exciting branch in software engineering, however, for the time being, this is a very labor-intensive exercise that can only be applied for smaller scale systems with particular value, e.g., strong safety requirements.

The above-explained dichotomy is also reduced when software models are exploited in model-driven development for the semi-automatic derivation of more formal models, e.g., executable code (stubs). In such model-driven development the meaning of a model is implicitly defined by mapping it into a (more), formal model. This (more) formal model, however, is exclusively oriented towards operational semantics, it does not bear any semantic meaning for issues like organization and modularization of software models.

Hence, what is obviously missing is a stronger notion of meaning for software models themselves. A meaning that is not only accessible to human interpretation, but that can be operationalized on the software model alone and not only on one view of a software model but on different sublanguages that together constitute a software modeling framework.

In this book, Fernando Silva Parreiras makes a major step towards realizing such meaning for software models. With his methodology TwoUSE—Transforming and Weaving Ontologies and UML for Software Engineering—he combines the established routines of current-day software modelers with the most recent technology for reasoning over large and complex models, i.e., ontology technology.

Ontology technology, based on the family of description logics dialects, has thrived over the last 15 years, coming from small formal systems where it was hardly possible to manage 102 entities in one model to systems that reason over 105 entities—and growing. It is the core target of ontology technologies to model classes, their relationships, and their instances in a versatile manner that still leads to a decidable logical language, which can (mostly) be reasoned about for models that do not appear in the worst case, but in practice. Hence, ontology technology is ideally suited to be carried over to the world of software models.

Such a step seems to be incremental at first sight. This, however, is not the case. The reason is that it is not sufficient to come up with a single mapping, e.g., from UML class diagrams to an ontology language, because the range of software models is ranging much farther and what is needed is a methodology with example cases and best practices rather than an ad hoc development.

Fernando Silva Parreiras has accomplished such a methodology with TwoUse. And this methodology has become influential even before this book could be published. First, the EU project MOST—Marrying Ontology and Software Technologies—running from Februrary 2008 to April 2011 has relied heavily on Fernando's TwoUse methodology and has taken it as a major source of inspiration for further developing best practices for using ontology technologies in software development. Second, his work has become pivotal for other researchers in our lab—and beyond-who have been building on the integration of software models and ontologies and have further refined it, most notably Tobias Walter and Gerd Gröner.

Finally, the development of TwoUse has been a major accomplishment, because its development has been off the beaten path between the software modeling and the ontology technology communities and staying within neither. At the same time, advising Fernando and charting unexplored research terrain with him has become one of my most beloved research experiences of the last years—intellectually and personally—one that I would not want to miss by any means.

Steffen Staab
Koblenz, Germany

April 2012

PREFACE

The audience for this book embraces computer science graduate students, researchers, advanced professionals, practitioners, and implementers in the areas of software engineering, knowledge engineering, and artificial intelligence, interested in knowing the possibilities of using semantic web technologies in the context of model-driven software development or in enhancing knowledge engineering process with model-driven software development.

For the knowledge engineering community, the advent of ontology engineering required adapting methodologies and technologies inherited from software engineering to an open and networked environment. With the advances provided by model-driven software development, the semantic web community is keen on learning what the benefits are of disciplines like metamodeling, domain-specific modeling, and model transformation for the semantic web field.

For software engineering, declarative specification is one of the major facets of enterprise computing. Because the Ontology Web Language (OWL) is designed for sharing terminologies, interoperability, and inconsistency detection, software engineers will welcome a technique that improves productivity and quality of software models. This book is relevant for researchers who work in the field of complex software systems using model-driven technology and for companies that build large-scale software like enterprise software offerings, data-warehousing products, and software product lines.

HOW TO READ THIS BOOK

In Part I, we present the fundamental concepts and analyze state-of-the-art approaches. Chapters 2 and 3 describe the concepts and technologies around MDE and ontologies, respectively. In Chapter 4, we present the commonalities and variations of both paradigms, analyze existing work in this area, and elicit the requirements for an integrated solution.

Part II describes the role of MDE techniques (DSL, model transformation, and metamodeling) and ontology technologies (reasoning services, query answering) in an integrated approach. In Chapters 5 and 6, we describe the conceptual architecture of our approach. Chapter 7 presents the TwoUse Toolkit—the implementation of the conceptual architecture.

We use the TwoUse Toolkit to realize case studies from the model-driven engineering and ontology engineering domains. Part III assembles case studies that use our approach at the modeling level and at the language level. Chapter 8 analyzes the application of TwoUse in software design patterns, and in Chapter 9 we present the application of TwoUse in ontology-based information systems. Chapter 10 describes the usage of TwoUse to support software developers in integrating software languages.

Part IV presents an analysis of employing our approach in ontology engineering services. We address the need for multiple languages for ontology mapping in Chapter 11. Chapter 12 presents a domain-specific language for specifying ontology APIs. Chapter 13 uses templates for encapsulating complexity of ontology design patterns.

COMMUNICATIONS OF THIS BOOK

We have communicated the research presented in this book through conference papers, a journal paper, conference tutorials, conference demonstrations, and bachelor/master theses. In the following, we list the publications according to the chapters covering the respective contributions.

Chapter 3: Silva Parreiras, F., Staab, S., Ebert, J., Pan, J.Z., Miksa, K., Kuehn, H., Zivkovic, S., Tinella, S., Assmann, U., Henriksson, J.: Semantics of Software Modeling. In: Semantic Computing. Wiley (2010) 229–248

Chapter 4: Silva Parreiras, F., Staab, S., Winter, A.: On marrying ontological and metamodeling technical spaces. In: Proceedings of the 6th joint meeting of the European Software Engineering Conference and the ACM SIGSOFT International Symposium on Foundations of Software Engineering, 2007, Dubrovnik, Croatia, September 3–7, 2007, ACM (2007) 439–448

Roadmap of This Book.

Chapters 5, 6, 9: Parreiras, F.S., Staab, S.: Using ontologies with UML class-based modeling: The TwoUse approach. Data & Knowledge Engineering 69(11) (2010) 1194–1207

Chapter 7: Silva Parreiras, F., Walter, T., Gröner, G.: Filling the gap between the semantic web and model-driven engineering: The TwoUse toolkit. In: Demo and Posters Proceedings of the 6th European Conference on Modelling Foundations and Applications, ECMFA 2010, Paris, France, June 15–18, 2010. (2010)

Chapter 8: Silva Parreiras, F., Staab, S., Winter, A.: Improving design patterns by description logics: A use case with abstract factory and strategy. In: Proceedings of Modellierung 2008, Berlin, Germany, March 12–14, 2008. Number 127 in LNI, GI (2008) 89–104

Chapter 11: Silva Parreiras, F., Staab, S., Schenk, S., Winter, A.: Model driven specification of ontology translations. In: Proceedings of Conceptual Modeling – ER 2008, 27th International Conference on Conceptual Modeling, Barcelona, Spain, October 20-24, 2008. Number 5231 in LNCS, Springer (2008) 484–497

Chapter 12: Silva Parreiras, F., Walter, T., Staab, S., Saathoff, C., Franz, T.: APIs a gogo: Automatic generation of ontology APIs. In: Proceedings of the 3rd IEEE International Conference on Semantic Computing (ICSC 2009), September 14–16, 2009, Santa Clara, CA, USA, IEEE Computer Society (2009) 342–348

Chapter 13: Silva Parreiras, F., Groener, G., Walter, T., Staab, S.: A model-driven approach for using templates in OWL ontologies. In: Knowledge Management and Engineering by the Masses, 17th International Conference, EKAW 2010, Lisbon, Portugal, October 11–15, 2010. Proceedings. Volume 6317 of LNAI, Springer (2010) 350–359

We presented parts of this work in the following tutorials:

- Silva Parreiras, F., Walter, T., Wende, C., Thomas, E.: Model-Driven Software Development with Semantic Web Technologies. In: Tutorial at the 6th European Conference on Modelling Foundations and Applications, ECMFA 2010, Paris, France, June 15–18, 2010. (2010)

- Silva Parreiras, F., Walter, T., Wende, C., Thomas, E.: Bridging Software Languages and Ontology Technologies. In: SPLASH '10: Proceedings of the ACM international conference companion on Object oriented programming systems languages and applications companion, October 17, 2010, Reno/Tahoe, NV, USA., ACM (2010) 311–315

- Gasevic, D., Silva Parreiras, F., Walter, T.: Ontologies and Software Language Engineering. In: Tutorial at Generative Programming and Component Engineering (GPCE'10) co-located with Software Language Engineering (SLE 2010), October 10, 2010, Eindhoven, The Netherlands. (2010)

- Staab, S., Walter, T., Gröner, G., Silva Parreiras, F.: Model Driven Engineering with Ontology Technologies. In: Reasoning Web. Semantic Technologies for

Software Engineering, 6th International Summer School 2010, Dresden, Germany, August 30 – September 3, 2010. Tutorial Lectures. LNCS 6325 Springer (2010) 62–98

The implementation of the approach described in this book served as basis for the following bachelor's thesis, *Studienarbeiten* or *Diplomarbeiten*:

- Saile, David: Integrating TwoUse and OCL-DL. *Studienarbeit*.
- Schneider, Mark: SPARQLAS—Implementing SPARQL Queries with OWL Syntax. *Studienarbeit*. [In German]
- Fichtner, Vitali: Developing a Semantic Environment for Analyzing Software Artifacts. Bachelor's Thesis. [In German]
- Schneider, Carsten: Towards an Eclipse Ontology Framework: Integrating OWL and the Eclipse Modeling Framework. *Diplomarbeit*. [In German]

Moreover, the implementation of the approach led to the development of a free open-source set of tools for designing models combining model-driven engineering and OWL—the TwoUse Toolkit.[1]

ACKNOWLEDGMENTS

I thank God and the Holy Mary, Mother of God, for all the blessings on my way and for giving me strength to carry on through the hard times.

I would like to thank Prof. Steffen Staab for helping in my development as a researcher. I am also indebted to Prof. Andreas Winter and Prof. Jürgen Ebert for their valuable advice and the constructive meetings through the last years.

I am grateful to Prof. Dr. Uwe Assmann and Prof. Dr. Daniel Schwabe for their time invested in reading and reviewing this book.

I am happy and thankful to have worked with Thomas Franz, Carsten Saathoff, and Simon Schenk on the applications of the work described in this book. I am also thankful to my colleagues Gerd Gröner and Tobias Walter, with whom I shared an office, for the many brainstorming hours.

I would like to thank the current and former students for their indispensable work on implementing the approach presented in this book: David Saile, Johannes Knopp, Sven Kühner, Henning Selt, Mark Schneider, Marko Scheller, and Carsten Schneider.

I am extremely grateful to my mother and father for shaping my character.

Finally, from the bottom of my heart, I thank my wife for her support and donating that time I was supposed to spend with her and my son toward writing this book.

Fernando Silva Parreiras

---

[1]http://twouse.googlecode.com/.

ACRONYMS

ABOX	Assertional Box
API	Application Program Interface
ATL	Atlas Transformation Language
BPMN	Business Process Modeling Notation
COMM	Core Ontology on Multimedia
CS	Concrete Syntax
CWA	Closed World Assumption
DL	Description Logic
DSL	Domain-Specific Language
EBNF	Extended BackusNaur Form
EMOF	Essential MOF
EU	European Union
FOL	First-Order Logic
GPML	General Purpose Modeling Language
GReTL	Graph Repository Transformation Language
HTTP	Hypertext Transfer Protocol
KAT	K-Space Annotation Tool
MDA	Model-Driven Architecture
MDE	Model-Driven Engineering
MMTS	MOF Technical Space
MOF	Meta Object Facility
NAF	Negation As Failure
OCL	Object Constraint Language
ODP	Ontology Design Pattern
OIS	Ontology-Based Information System
OMG	Object Management Group
OTS	Ontological Technical Space
OWA	Open World Assumption
OWL	Web Ontology Language
PIM	Platform Independent Model
PSM	Platform Specific Model
QVT	Query/View/Transformation Language
RDF	Resource Description Framework
RDFS	RDF Schema
SAIQL	Schema And Instance Query Language
SPARQL	SPARQL Protocol And RDF Query Language

SWRL	Semantic Web Rule Language
TBOX	Terminological Box
TS	Technical Space
UML	Unified Modeling Language
URI	Unified Resource Identifier
W3C	World Wide Web Consortium
XML	Extensible Markup Language

FUNDAMENTALS

CHAPTER 1

INTRODUCTION

1.1 MOTIVATION

Among recent attempts to improve productivity in software engineering, model-driven engineering (MDE) is an approach that focuses on the design of artifacts and on generative techniques to raise the level of abstraction of physical systems [142]. As model-driven engineering gains momentum, the transformation of artifacts and domain-specific notations become essential in the software development process.

One of the pre-existing modeling languages that boosted research on MDE is the Unified Modeling Language (UML). UML is a visual design notation [117] for designing software systems. It is a general-purpose modeling language, capable of capturing information about different views of systems, like static structure and dynamic behavior.

In addition to general-purpose modeling languages, MDE relies on domain-specific languages (DSL). Such languages provide abstractions and notations for modeling specific aspects of systems. A variety of domain-specific languages and fragments of their models is used to develop one large software system.

Among artifacts produced by multiple modeling languages, MDE faces the following challenges [57]: support for developers, interoperability among multiple artifacts, and formal semantics of modeling languages. Addressing these challenges is crucial to the success of MDE.

In contrast, issues like interoperability and formal semantics motivate the development of ontology web languages. Indeed, the World Wide Web Consortium (W3C) standard Web Ontology Language (OWL) [61], together with automated reasoning services, provides a powerful solution for formally describing domain concepts in an extensible way, thus allowing for precise specification of the semantics of concepts as well as for interoperability between ontology specifications.

Ontologies provide shared domain conceptualizations representing knowledge by a vocabulary and, typically, logical definitions [62, 161]. OWL provides a class definition language for ontologies. More specifically, OWL allows for the definition of classes by required and implied logical constraints on the properties of their members.

The strength of OWL modeling lies in disentangling conceptual hierarchies with an abundance of relationships of multiple generalization of classes (cf. [128]). For this purpose, OWL allows for *deriving* concept hierarchies from logically and

Semantic Web and Model-Driven Engineering, First Edition. Fernando Silva Parreiras.
© 2012 Institute of Electrical and Electronics Engineers. Published 2012 by John Wiley & Sons, Inc.

precisely defined class axioms stating necessary and sufficient conditions of class membership. The logics of class definitions may be validated by using corresponding automated reasoning technology.

Ontology engineers usually have to cope with W3C standard specifications and programming languages for manipulating ontologies. The gap between W3C specifications and programming language leads ontology engineers to deal with multiple languages of different natures. For instance, W3C specifications are platform independent, whereas programming languages include platform-specific constructs.

Indeed, addressing these issues has been one of the objectives of model-driven engineering. MDE allows for developing and managing abstractions of the solution domain towards the problem domain in software design, turning the focus from code-centric to transformation-centric.

Understanding the role of ontology technologies like knowledge representation, automated reasoning, dynamic classification, and consistency checking in MDE as well as the role of MDE technologies like model transformation and domain-specific modeling in ontology engineering is essential for leveraging the development of both paradigms.

For example, UML and OWL constitute modeling approaches with strengths and weaknesses that make them appropriate for specifying distinct aspects of software systems. UML provides means to express dynamic behavior, whereas OWL does not. OWL is capable of inferring generalization and specialization between classes as well as class membership of objects based on the constraints imposed on the properties of class definitions, whereas UML class diagrams do not allow for dynamic specialization/generalization of classes and class memberships or any other kind of inference *per se*.

Though schemas [111] and UML extensions (UML profiles) for OWL ontologies exist, an integrated usage of both modeling approaches in a coherent framework has been lacking so far. This book unveils research problems involving the composition of these two paradigms and presents research methods to assess the application of a novel framework integrating UML class-based models and OWL ontologies and technologies.

Investigating the composition of UML class-based modeling and ontology technologies requires a systematic procedure to address a series of research questions. Firstly, we need to characterize the fundamental concepts and technologies around UML class-based modeling and OWL ontologies and to elicit the requirements of an integrated framework. Consequently, we need to specify a framework that realizes the integration of both paradigms and fulfills the requirements previously elicited.

To analyze the impact of an integrated approach, we need to apply it in both domains: model-driven engineering and ontology engineering. In the domain of model-driven engineering, we apply the proposed framework to address shortcomings of software design and software languages. Our aim is to reduce complexity and to improve reusability and interoperability.

In the domain of ontology engineering, we tackle issues addressing the gap in clarity and accessibility of languages that operate ontologies, e.g., ontology translation languages or ontology APIs generation. Our framework is then used to support the development of platform independent models, aiming at improving maintainability and comprehensibility.

In the following subsections, we describe the motivation for investigating an integration between UML class-based modeling and OWL in Section 1.2. We presented the guidelines for reading this book and listed the previous publications covering parts of this book in the preface.

1.2   RESEARCH QUESTIONS

Over the last decade, the semantic web and the software engineering communities have investigated and promoted the use of *ontologies* and UML class-based modeling as modeling frameworks for the management of schemas. While the foci of these communities are different, the following question arises:

Question I *What are the commonalities and variations around ontology technologies and model-driven engineering?*

By identifying the main features of both paradigms, a comparison of both leads to the following sub-questions:

Question I.A *What are the scientific and technical results around ontologies, ontology languages, and their corresponding reasoning technologies that can be used in model-driven engineering?*

Question I.B *What are the scientific and technical results around UML class-based modeling that can be used in ontology engineering?*

While investigating this problem, our goal is to analyze approaches that use both UML class-based technologies and ontology technologies and to identify patterns involving both paradigms. The result of such analysis is a feature model, described in Chapter 4.

The feature model reveals the possible choices for an integrated approach of OWL ontologies and model-driven engineering and serves as a taxonomy to categorize existing approaches. Furthermore, the classification allows for eliciting requirements for a composed approach.

We carry out exploratory research by conducting a domain analysis over approaches involving UML class-based technologies and ontology technologies found in the literature. Domain analysis addresses the analysis and modeling of variabilities and commonalities of systems or concepts in a domain [32].

The research result is a descriptive model characterized by a feature model for the area of marrying UML class-based modeling and ontology technologies.

While there exist mappings between these modeling paradigms [114], an analysis of the outcome of an integrated approach for UML class-based modeling and OWL is lacking so far. The challenge of this task arises from the large number of differing properties relevant to each of the two modeling paradigms.

For example, UML modeling provides means to express dynamic behavior, whereas OWL 2 does not. OWL is capable of inferring generalization and specialization between classes as well as class membership of objects based on restrictions imposed on properties of class definitions, whereas UML class diagrams do not allow for dynamic specialization/generalization of classes and class memberships or any other kind of inference *per se*.

Contemporary software development should make use of the benefits of both approaches to overcome their restrictions. This need leads to the following question:

Question II *What are the techniques and languages used for designing integrated models?*

To address this question, we use the requirements resulting from Question I to propose a framework comprising the following building blocks: (i) an integration of the structure of UML class-based modeling and OWL; (ii) the definition of notations for denoting integrated artifacts; and (iii) the specification of a query solution for retrieving elements of integrated artifacts. Together, these building blocks constitute our original approach to Transform and Weave Ontologies and UML class-based modeling in Software Engineering—*TwoUse* (Figure 1.1).

We analyze the impact of the TwoUse approach with case studies in the domain of model-driven engineering and ontology engineering.

Applying TwoUse in Model-Driven Engineering. In UML class-based modeling, software design patterns provide elaborated, best practice solutions for commonly occurring problems in software development. However, software design patterns that manage variants delegate the decision of what variant to choose to client classes. Moreover, the inevitable usage of several software modeling languages leads to unmanageable redundancy in engineering and managing the same information

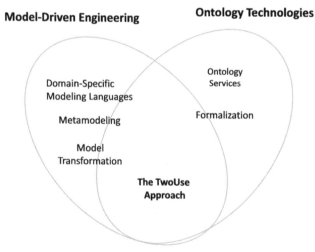

Figure 1.1 Context of the Book.

across multiple artifacts and, eventually, information inconsistency. The growing demand for networked and federated environments requires the convergence of existing web standards and software modeling standards.

In contrast, the strength of OWL modeling lies in disentangling conceptual hierarchies with multiple generalization of classes [128]. OWL allows for *deriving* concept hierarchies from logically and precisely defined class axioms stating necessary *and* sufficient conditions of class membership.

OWL provides exclusive features that distinguish it from class-based modeling languages: class expressions, individual equality, and class expression axioms. Hence, the following question arises:

> **Question III** *What is the structural impact of using OWL constructs in designing software artifacts?*

To address this problem, we work on identifying patterns at the modeling level as well as at the language level. At the modeling level, we analyze the situation where the decision of what class to instantiate typically needs to be specified at a client class. We investigate the following question:

> **Question III.A** *How does one determine the selection of classes to instantiate using only class descriptions rather than by weaving the descriptions into class operations?*

In systems that rely on ontologies, i.e., in ontology-based information systems, the question is the following:

> **Question III.B** *How does one reuse existing knowledge captured by domain ontologies in the specification of functional algorithms of ontology-based information systems?*

At the language level, to support the interrelationships of software modeling languages in distributed software modeling environments, we need to answer the following question:

> **Question III.C** *Which ontology technologies can help existing modeling languages in managing the same information across multiple artifacts and how can they do so?*

The hypothesis is that an ontology-based approach improves software quality and provides guidance to software engineers. To test the hypothesis at the modeling level, we analyze the TwoUse approach with three case studies: software design pattern, designing of ontology-based information systems, and model-driven software languages.

At the modeling level, we analyze the application of TwoUse in addressing drawbacks of software design patterns and in design ontology-based information systems. At the language level, we analyze the application of TwoUse in addressing the transformation and matching of modeling languages into OWL.

Applying TwoUse in Ontology Engineering.   In ontology engineering, the design of ontology engineering services [170] has drawn the attention of the ontology engineering community in the last years. However, as ontology engineering services become more complex, current approaches fail to provide clarity and accessibility to ontology engineers who need to see and understand the semantic as well as the lexical/syntactic part of specifying ontology engineering services. Ontology engineers use services in an intricate and disintegrated manner, which draws their attention away from the core task and into the diverging platform details.

From this scenario, the problem of supporting generative techniques in ontology engineering services emerges, adding expressiveness without going into platform specifics, i.e.,

Question IV *How does one fill the abstraction gap between specification languages and programming languages?*

We propose a representation approach for generative specification of ontology engineering services based on model-driven engineering (MDE). In order to reconcile semantics with lexical and syntactic aspects of the specification, we integrate these different layers into a representation based on a joint metamodel.

The hypothesis is that filling the gap between ontology specification languages and general purpose programming languages helps to improve productivity, since ontology engineers do not have to be aware of platform-specific details. Moreover, it simplifies the tasks of maintenance and traceability because knowledge is no longer embedded in the source code of programming languages.

We validate our approach with three case studies of three ontology engineering services: ontology mapping, ontology API generation, and ontology modeling.

For ontology mapping, we present a solution for ontology translation specification that intends to be more expressive than current ontology mapping languages and less complex and granular than programming languages to address the following question:

Question IV.A *How does one fill the abstraction gap between ontology mapping languages and programming languages?*

For ontology API generation, we present a model-driven solution for designing mappings between complex ontology descriptions and object oriented representations—the *agogo* approach—and tackle the following question:

Question IV.B *What are the results of applying MDE techniques in ontology API development?*

For ontology modeling, we present a model-driven approach for specifying and encapsulating descriptions of ontology design patterns and address the following problem:

Question IV.C *How does one allow declarative specifications of templates and tools to test these template specifications and realizations?*

CHAPTER 2

MODEL-DRIVEN ENGINEERING FOUNDATIONS

This chapter discusses the state of the art for model-driven engineering. We inspect approaches, abstractions, and techniques constituting MDE, describe them with respect to their concepts and relationships, and investigate the conceptual structure that underpins MDE in this state-of-the-art review. The result is a static structural model represented by UML class diagrams.

2.1 INTRODUCTION

Raising the level of abstraction is one of the basic principles of software engineering. It eliminates complexity that is not inherent in software artifacts. The idea is to selectively abstract away from non-fundamental aspects and to concentrate on the essential aspects of software artifacts.

Approaches that aim at reducing complexity have an impact upon software productivity. In productivity models, complexity metrics compose the cost metrics together with resources and personnel [45].

Model-driven engineering (MDE) is an approach that uses models, notations, and transformation rules to raise the level of abstraction of a physical system [142] aiming at improving productivity.

In this chapter, we present the fundamental concepts of the model-driven engineering structure. In Section 2.2, we use the concept of *megamodel* [44] to present a description of the structure of MDE. We use this structure to group concepts around ontology technologies and model-driven technologies in Section 2.3.

2.2 MODEL-DRIVEN ENGINEERING STRUCTURE

Model-driven techniques provide management, transformation, and synchronization of software artifacts. The objective is to factorize complexity into different levels of abstraction and concern, from high-level conceptual models down to the individual aspects of target platforms.

There is a consensus in the literature about the cornerstones of MDE: (i) languages comprising models that represent real-world elements, metamodels to

Semantic Web and Model-Driven Engineering, First Edition. Fernando Silva Parreiras.
© 2012 Institute of Electrical and Electronics Engineers. Published 2012 by John Wiley & Sons, Inc.

describe the structure of models, and language semantics; and (ii) transformations between languages. Schmidt [142] argues that model-driven engineering technologies should combine domain-specific modeling languages and transformation engines to address platform complexity. For Kent [88], MDE requires a family of languages, transformations between languages, and a process associated with the conception of languages and transformations. In this chapter, we concentrate on the structural specification of model-driven engineering.

An instance of MDE is the Model-Driven Architecture (MDA) [100], which is based on OMG's Meta-Object Facility. It frequently includes UML as its modeling language and a common pipeline of managing and transforming models [90]: A platform-independent model (PIM) is transformed into a platform-specific model (PSM) and eventually into an executable representation (code), being the target platform.

Favre [44] proposes a descriptive model that specifies the concepts that are the cornerstones of MDE: model, metamodel, modeling language, and model transformation. This descriptive model is called *megamodel* (Figure 2.1). We extend this model later to illustrate the relationships between MDE concepts and ontology technologies.

In the following section, we analyze and describe the concepts and relations depicted in the Figure 2.1.

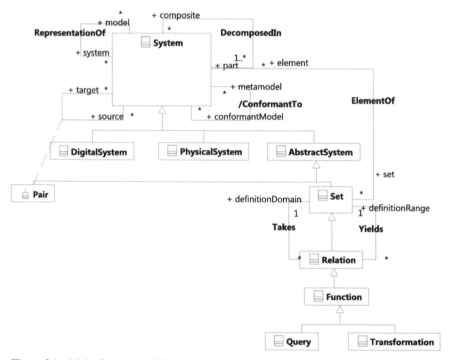

Figure 2.1   Main Concepts of Megamodel.

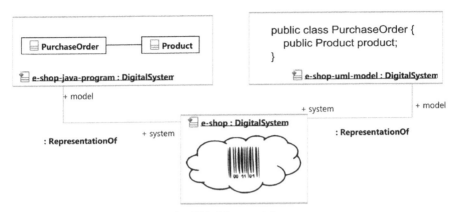

Figure 2.2   Notion of RepresentationOf in Megamodel.

2.2.1 Models

The notion of *model* accepted in MDE is that a model is a simplification of a physical system. Apostel [5] uses the word "simplification" to denote a viewpoint of a system from a certain scale where the system is controlled with a certain purpose in mind. This notion is aligned with Rothenberg's definition in which a model is a representation of the reality for a given purpose [136].

The UML specification [117] corroborates this notion describing a model as an abstraction of a physical system. Bezivin [13] and Favre [44] use the association `representedBy` or `representationOf` to connect the system under study to a model. Thus, a system can have multiple models depending on the viewpoint. For example, developers can use the UML and Java to represent different viewpoints of the real-world system `e-shop` (Figure 2.2).

Notice that Favre specifies the notion of a model as a relation to the system because a system can play the role of a model. For example, a Java program can be a model of a system and can also serve as a system for a UML model of the Java program.

2.2.2 Metamodels

While models describe a specific abstraction of reality, metamodels are models of languages used to define models [44, 145]. For example, the structure of the UML language is the metamodel of UML diagrams (Figure 2.3). Thus, we infer that a given UML class diagram conforms to the UML metamodel, i.e., a model conforms to its metamodel.

Metamodel-based approaches are based on a staged architecture of models and metamodels, where the structure of lower level models is defined by higher level metamodels. This staged architecture defines a layered structure, which is applied to define domain-specific languages and general-purpose languages, e.g., UML. Figure 2.4 illustrates a layered structure using UML as metamodeling language.

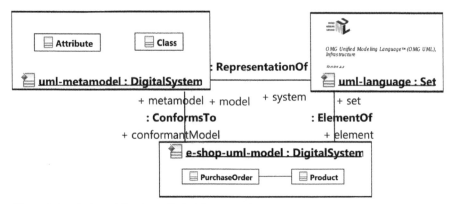

Figure 2.3   Notion of ConformsTo in Megamodel.

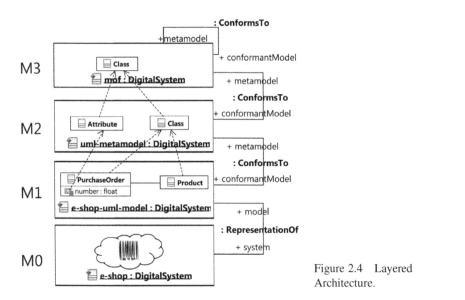

Figure 2.4   Layered Architecture.

At the top level (M3) is situated the Meta Object Facility [111] (MOF), which is a class-based modeling language that defines itself. Language specifications like the UML specification are viewed as (linguistic) instances [7] of the MOF situated on the metamodel level (M2). The model level (M1) contains concrete models defined by metamodels on M2. These models represent real-world systems situated on M0.

2.2.2.1 EMOF
Metamodeling relies on constructs like package, class, inheritance, property, and operation. Therefore, OMG reuses common core packages of UML 2.0 and MOF 2.0 to define the essential constructs of MOF—EMOF. These essential constructs are reused by multiple modeling languages, query

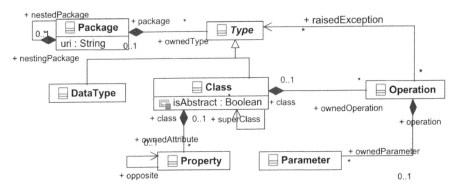

Figure 2.5   EMOF Classes.

languages, and transformation languages and comprise the core constructs for defining metamodels. Figure 2.5 shows the main classes of EMOF.

A `Package` contains `Types` or nested Packages. `DataType` and `Class` are specializations of `Type`. A class contains properties and operations. An `Operation` specifies the behavioral features of classifiers. An operation specifies a type (`Classifier`), `Parameters`, and constraints for executing a behavior.

2.2.2.2 Ecore Ecore is an implementation of EMOF defined in the Eclipse Modeling Framework [164]. Ecore addresses practical issues regarding the structure of EMOF. For example, while EMOF defines one class for defining properties, Ecore defines two types of structural features: attributes and references. The practical aspects inherent in Ecore make it more suitable for adoption.

Figure 2.6 presents the main classes of Ecore. The class `EModelElement` allows to tag model elements with names. `EPackage` is an `EModelElement` that contains classifiers and sub-packages. Properties are defined by references and attributes as structural features. An `EReference` is a type of structural feature that has as type an `EClass`. An `EAttribute` is a type of structural reference that has as type an `EDataType`.

2.2.3   Modeling Languages

Favre defines the role of a language in megamodeling as an abstract system comprising a set of elements [44] or a set of coordinated models [94].

In the realm of modeling languages, i.e., languages for defining models, we identify two categories of languages according to the purpose of usage: general-purpose modeling languages (GPML) and domain-specific modeling languages (DSML).

General-purpose modeling languages (GPML) provide constructs to represent multiple aspects of a system. For example, the Unified Modeling Language (UML) and the Extensible Markup Language (XML) are general-purpose modeling languages used to model a wide variety of systems.

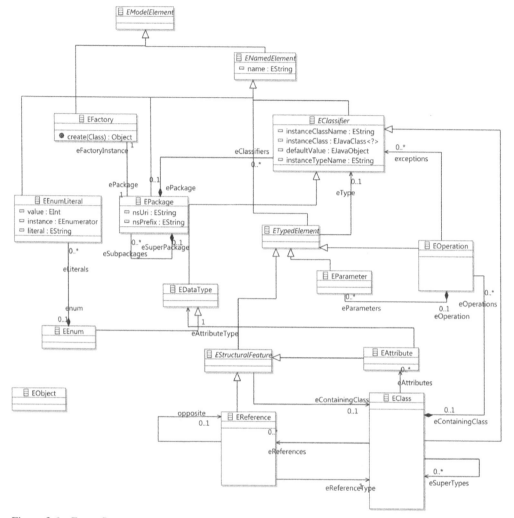

Figure 2.6   Ecore Structure.

In contrast to GPML, domain-specific modeling languages (DSML) capture the essential concepts of a limited domain. They address specific applications. An Example of DSML is the W3C HyperText Markup Language (HTML).

According to Atkinson and Kühne [7], a language definition covers four components: (i) an abstract syntax, realized by metamodels in MDE; (ii) a concrete syntax that renders the concepts defined in the metamodel; (iii) well-formedness, defined by constraints on the abstract syntax; and (iv) the semantics describing the meaning of the concepts. For Harel and Rumpe [67, 68], a modeling language consists of a syntactic notation, its semantics, and semantic mappings that relate the syntactic expressions to the semantic domain. In the next subsections, we describe these components and illustrate them with examples.

Figure 2.7 depicts the relationships and concepts for defining a modeling language using the megamodel structure. The UML metamodel defines the model of the e-shop domain. This model is the input of an injector that serializes the input e-shop UML model into a textual representation of UML (e-shop.uml.text). This textual model conforms to the EBNF grammar for UML. A mapping function connects the e-shop UML model to an equivalent representation (fol-representation) in first-order logics (FOL), giving semantics to the UML language.

2.2.3.1 Syntax   The syntax provides a structure for arranging the elements of a given language. It comprises the symbols and signs that represent the language concepts. We identify two types of syntax: textual syntax and diagrammatic syntax.

A textual syntax comprises elements in the form of sequences of characters. A textual syntax defines the valid combinations of words and sentences. Examples of textual notations are the Human-Usable Textual Notation (HUTN) [110], HTML, and XML.

A diagrammatic syntax, in contrast, comprises elements in the form of pictorial signs. Examples of diagrammatic notations are UML and the Business Process Modeling Notation (BPMN) [112].

2.2.3.2 Abstract Syntax   Model-driven engineering as promoted by the OMG is based on UML diagrams as model descriptions. UML class diagrams are a means for describing application domains and software systems in the instance-schemametaschema dimension (ISM-dimension). UML class diagrams have their roots in entity-relationship (ER) descriptions of database schemas, on the one hand, and in design notations for object-oriented programs, on the other.

The OMG Meta Object Facility (MOF) is the relevant subset of UML to describe abstract syntax during metamodeling. In other words, in model-driven engineering, metamodels serve as abstract syntax, whereas models serve as snapshots of languages.

A snapshot is the static configuration of a system or model at a given point in time [137]. It consists of objects, values, and links that represent the instances of a metamodel.

2.2.3.3 Semantics   The semantics of a modeling language allows for determining the truth value of elements in the model with respect to the system being defined. In other words, the semantics of a modeling language provides the meaning to its syntactical elements by mapping them to a meaningful representation [68, 141]. France *et al.* [48] and Harel and Rumpe [67] denominate the target of these mappings' semantic model or semantic domain. For Harel and Rumpe [67], the semantic definition of a language comprises a semantic domain and a semantic mapping from the syntax to the semantic domain.

For example, the UML specification [117] defines the semantics of the UML language by explaining each UML modeling concept using natural language. In a formal approach, Berardi [12] defines the semantics of UML class diagrams by mapping UML class diagram constructs to first-order logic (FOL) formulas and, more specifically, to its fragment description logics (see Chapter 3).

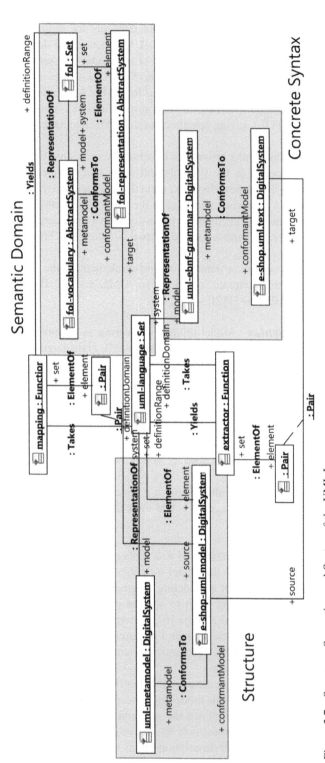

Figure 2.7   Structure, Semantics, and Syntax of the UML Language.

2.2.4 Model Transformations

A transformation definition is a set of transformation rules that together describe the conversion of one model in the source language into another related model in the target language [90].

A transformation rule is a function that takes as input one or more model elements of a language and generates one or more model elements of a target language. For example, the transformation model

$$uml : Class(?x) \rightarrow mof : Class(?x)$$

produces one MOF class for each UML class, i.e.,

$$uml : Class(Product) \rightarrow mof : Class(Product)$$

The Object Management Group (OMG) defines a standard model transformation language within the MOF metamodeling environment: Query/View/Transformation (QVT) [113]. The call for proposals of the QVT language encouraged the development of other transformation languages: AGG [167], GReTL [71], and ATL [82].

2.2.5 Query Languages

In order to manipulate models, one requires a language capable of specifying query operations. In common MOF modeling practice, the Object Constraint Language (OCL) [116] is the textual query language used to specify such queries.

Beyond querying, OCL may also be used to specify invariants on classes and types in the class model, to describe pre- and post conditions on operations and methods, and to specify initial and derived rules over a UML model.

The OCL syntax differs from SQL and SPARQL. Indeed, SQL and SPARQL do not require a starting point for query, i.e., it takes a global point of view. OCL, on the other hand, takes the object-oriented point of view, starting the queries from one given class.

In OCL, expressions are written in the context of an instance of a specific class [116]. The reserved word `self` is used to denote this instance.

OCL expressions may be used to specify the body of query operations. Since OCL is a typed language, i.e., each OCL expression is evaluated to a value, expressions may be chained to specify complex queries or invariants.

Let us consider the example of an international e-shop system. A snippet of the corresponding UML class diagram is presented in the Figure 2.8.

The class `TaskCtrl` is responsible for controlling the sales orders. A `SalesOrder` can be a `USSalesOrder` or a `CanSalesOrder`, according to the `Country` where the `Customer` lives.

The operation getSalesOrder() queries the country of the customer and returns the subclass of `SalesOrder` to be instantiated (either `CanSalesOrder` or `USSalesOrder`). Following the example mentioned above, the target operation can be denoted by the following OCL expression:

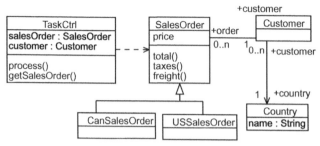

Figure 2.8   UML Class Diagram of an E-Shop System.

```
context TaskCtrl::getSalesOrder():OclType
body :
  if customer.country.name = 'USA' then
    USSalesOrder
  else
    if customer.country.name = 'Canada' then
      CanSalesOrder
    endif
  endif
```

The example above illustrates the usage of reflection in OCL to deliver the right type. The usage of OCL reflection capabilities is common in model transformations. OCL defines a predefined class called `OclAny`, which acts as a superclass for every type except for the OCL pre-defined `collection` types. Hence, features of `OclAny` are available on each object in every OCL expression, and every class in a UML model inherit all operations defined on `OclAny`. We highlight two of these operations:

- oclIsTypeOf(typespec: **OclType**): **Boolean**: evaluates to `true` if the given object is of the `type` identified by `typespec`;
- oclIsKindOf(typespec: **OclType**): **Boolean**: evaluates to `true` if the object is of the `type` identified by `typespec` or one of its subtypes.

We exemplify these operations as follows. The first one evaluates to true if we have an instance of `SalesOrder` and ask whether it is an instance of `SalesOrder`. The second one evaluates to true if we have an instance of `USSalesOrder` and ask whether it is an instance of `USSalesOrder` or if we have an instance of `USSalesOrder` and ask whether it is an instance of `SalesOrder`, *but not the opposite*.

2.2.5.1   *Semantics* The specification of OCL is given in natural language, although an informative semantics based on [134] is part of the specification. Beckert *et al.* [11] propose a translation of OCL into first-order predicate logics. Bucker presents a representation of the semantics of OCL in higher-order logic [25].

2.3   TECHNICAL SPACES

The concept of megamodel as used by Favre is platform-independent. Applying this structure into a set of technologies yields a technical space. Kurtev *et al.* [94] have coined the term *technical space* to organize concepts and to compare sets of solutions. A technical space comprises a framework for specifying models and metamodels, and a set of functions that operate on these models.

A common characteristic among several technical spaces is the organization of modeling levels. A technical space usually comprises a *metametamodel* (M3) that defines itself and defines metamodels (M2). Metamodels define models (M1) that represent systems (M0). Additionally, a technical space has a set of languages associated with it. In the context of the MDE structure presented in Section 2.2, we consider two types of languages: query languages and transformation languages.

Figure 2.9 shows the MOF Technical Space. In MOF, the metametamodel is MOF itself and an example of metamodel is UML. The query metamodel is OCL, whereas examples of transformation metamodels are ATL and QVT.

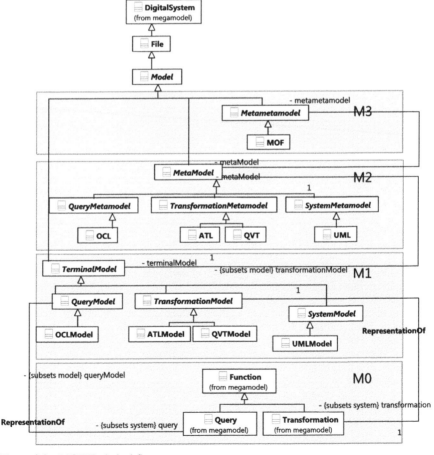

Figure 2.9   MOF Technical Space.

2.4 CONCLUSION

This chapter describes the main concepts and techniques around model-driven engineering. It provides the fundamental understanding about the role of model-driven engineering in software engineering. The contribution is a descriptive model connecting the main concepts of MDE that can be used to model further technical spaces. We use the descriptive model in further chapters for organizing the concepts and technologies presented in this book.

CHAPTER 3

ONTOLOGY FOUNDATIONS

Ontology technologies organize system knowledge in conceptual domains according to its meaning. It addresses various software engineering needs by identifying, abstracting, and rationalizing commonalities, and checking for inconsistencies across system specifications. This chapter describes the state of the art of ontology technologies. The result is an outline of the languages and services around the Web Ontology Language. Additionally, we arrange these blocks using a model-driven perspective.

3.1 INTRODUCTION

Ontologies play a fundamental role in bridging computing and human understanding. The field of artificial intelligence has been studying ontologies under multiple perspectives like knowledge engineering and natural-language processing.

Ontology languages have constructs similar to UML class-based modeling, e.g., classes, properties, and data cardinalities. Indeed, ontology languages provide various means for describing classes to the extent that explicit typing is not compulsory.

This chapter gives an overview of the scientific and technical results around ontologies, ontology languages, and their corresponding reasoning technologies used in model-driven engineering. We introduce the concept of ontology in Section 3.2.

Section 3.3 presents the W3C standard ontology language for ontology-based information systems—the Web Ontology Language. Section 3.4 describes ontology services like reasoning and querying. In Section 3.6 we describe the rule language for the semantic web.

Figure 3.1 presents the stack of technologies described in this chapter above in colored boxes. In Section 3.8, we describe the relations between these technologies using technical spaces.

Semantic Web and Model-Driven Engineering, First Edition. Fernando Silva Parreiras.
© 2012 Institute of Electrical and Electronics Engineers. Published 2012 by John Wiley & Sons, Inc.

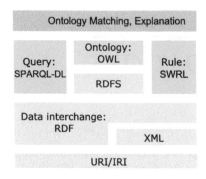

Figure 3.1 Semantic Web Stack Covered in This Chapter.

3.2 ONTOLOGY

The word *ontology* has its origin in philosophy, and it denotes the philosophical study of the nature of existence. In this sense, ontology involves identifying the fundamental categories of things. For example, ontological categories might be used to group objects as essential or existential, abstract or concrete.

Computer science took the term ontology and attributed a technical meaning to it: "An ontology is an explicit specification of a conceptualization" [62]. Studer *et al.* [166] argue that this specification is also formal, i.e., an ontology is an "explicit and formal specification of a conceptualization" [4].

In the semantic web field, ontologies provide shared domain conceptualizations representing knowledge by a vocabulary and, typically, logical definitions [62] to model the problem domain as well as the solution domain. Developers usually use ontologies as domain models for ontology-based information systems.

3.2.1 Ontology Modeling

The Web Ontology Language (OWL) [61] provides a class definition language for ontologies, i.e., OWL allows for the definition of classes by required and implied logical constraints on properties of their members.

The process of modeling ontologies exhibits a couple of overlaps with the development of conceptual models [162]. Requirements elicitation is followed by the design phase, where classes and relationships are defined similarly as in a UML class diagram. This stage, however, is followed by another step that depends on the ontology modeling paradigm and its corresponding language.

In the realm of description logic based ontologies [9], the strength of ontology modeling lies in disentangling conceptual hierarchies with an abundance of relationships of multiple generalization of classes. For this purpose, description logics allow for deriving concept hierarchies from logically, precisely defined class axioms, stating necessary and sufficient conditions of class membership.

In the realm of logic programming-based ontologies [2], the strength of ontology modeling lies in a formally integrated consideration of expressive class and rule definitions.

$$Customer \sqsubseteq \top \qquad (3.1)$$

$$Customer \sqsubseteq= 1country.Country \qquad (3.2)$$

$$\{USA, CANADA\} \sqsubseteq Country \qquad (3.3)$$

$$USSalesOrder \sqsubseteq SalesOrder \sqcap \exists customer.(Customer \sqcap$$
$$\exists country.\{USA\}) \qquad (3.4)$$

$$CanSalesOrder \sqsubseteq SalesOrder \sqcap \exists customer.(Customer \sqcap$$
$$\exists country.\{CANADA\}) \qquad (3.5)$$

$$CanSalesOrder \sqcap USSalesOrder \sqsubseteq \bot \qquad (3.6)$$

$$SalesOrder \equiv CanSalesOrder \sqcup USSalesOrder \qquad (3.7)$$

$$customer \equiv order^- \qquad (3.8)$$

$$country \equiv customer^- \qquad (3.9)$$

$$SalesOrder(ORDER1) \qquad (3.10)$$

$$Customer(HANS) \qquad (3.11)$$

$$country(HANS, CANADA) \qquad (3.12)$$

$$Customer(JOHN) \qquad (3.13)$$

$$country(JOHN, USA) \qquad (3.14)$$

$$customer(ORDER1, JOHN) \qquad (3.15)$$

Figure 3.2   E-Shop Example with Description Logic Syntax.

In both paradigms, the structure of class definitions may be validated by introspecting the model, using corresponding reasoning technology. In the first model of description logics, this is indeed the focus of its reasoning technology, while, in the second model, the focus of the corresponding reasoning technology is on reasoning with objects in a logical framework.

An ontology constitutes a formal conceptual model. Hence, its core concerns, i.e., formal definitions of classes and relationship, are germane to the software engineering community. However, ontologies have always been used differently than conceptual models in software and data engineering. Hence, the perspectives on modeling and using ontologies are slightly twisted if compared to conceptual models such as UML class diagrams.

For the sake of illustration, Figure 3.2 depicts an incomplete specification of the example presented in the Figure 2.8 using a description logic syntax. The identifier Customer is used to declare the corresponding class (3.1) as a specialization of Thing ($\top$), since classes in OWL are specializations of the reserved class Thing. The class Consumer has a restriction on property country with exactly one Country (3.2). The class Country *contains* the individuals USA and CANADA (3.3). USSalesOrder is defined as a subclass of a SalesOrder with at least one restriction on the property country, the value range must include the country USA (3.4). The description of the class CanSalesOrder is analogous. The intersection of both classes is empty ($\bot$), i.e., they are disjoint (3.6). The class SalesOrder is equal to the union of CanSalesOrder and USSalesOrder, i.e., it is a complete generalization of both classes (3.7).

3.3   THE ONTOLOGY WEB LANGUAGE

The language and reasoning paradigm that has been predominantly used and researched is the family of description logic languages covered by the W3C recommendation Web Ontology Language (OWL) [61]. Description logic languages allow for capturing the schema in the "terminological box" (T-Box) and the objects and their relationships in the "assertional box" (A-Box). The terminological box captures knowledge about the class level, i.e., independent of a given situation.

The sub-languages of OWL (or profiles) differ in the set of modeling constructs they support. Depending on the exact configuration of allowed modeling primitives, a profile requires sound and complete reasoning algorithms that are NLogSpace-Complete (OWL 2 QL), PTime-Complete (OWL 2 EL and OWL 2 RL), NExpTime-Complete (OWL DL), or 2NExpTimeComplete (OWL 2) [181].

Each OWL sub-language corresponds to a given set of constructs in description logics. For example, OWL 2 EL corresponds to the description logic language $EL++$ and OWL DL corresponds to *SHOIN(D)*. OWL 2 extends both and it corresponds to *SROIQ(D)* (see [9] for more about description logics).

3.3.1   OWL 2 Syntax

In order to save and share OWL 2 ontologies, one requires a concrete syntax for OWL 2. There are multiple concrete syntax notations for OWL 2: RDF/XML syntax, OWL/XML syntax, Manchester Syntax, Functional Syntax, and Turtle. Each of these notations is suitable for a specific purpose. In this work, we use the OWL 2 Functional Syntax due to its axiomatic nature, facilitating the analysis of the OWL 2 formal structure.

An OWL 2 Vocabulary $\mathcal{V}_O = (\mathcal{V}_{cls}, \mathcal{V}_{op}, \mathcal{V}_D, \mathcal{V}_{dp}, \mathcal{V}_{ind}, \mathcal{V}_{lt})$ is a 6-tuple consisting of the following elements:

1. $\mathcal{V}_{cls}$ is a set of named classes, class expressions, and the built-in classes `owl:Thing` and `owl:Nothing`.
2. $\mathcal{V}_{op}$ is a set of object properties, including the built-in object properties `owl:topObjectProperty` and `owl:bottomObjectProperty`.
3. $\mathcal{V}_{dp}$ is a set of data properties, including the built-in data properties `owl:topDataProperty` and `owl:bottomDataProperty`.
4. $\mathcal{V}_{ind}$ is a set of individuals.
5. $\mathcal{V}_{dt}$ is a set of datatypes.
6. $\mathcal{V}_{lt}$ is a set of literals.

Given the vocabulary $\mathcal{V}_O$, we use the following convention in Tables 3.1 to 3.4:

- `OP` indicates an object property;
- `OPE` indicates an object property expression;
- `DP` indicates a data property;
- `DPE` indicates a data property expression;
- `C` indicates a class;

- CE indicates a class expression;
- DT indicates a datatype;
- DR indicates a data range;
- a indicates an individual (named or anonymous);
- lt indicates a literal.

TABLE 3.1   Syntax of Class Expression Axioms.

OWL 2 Syntax	Description Logic Syntax
SubClassOf(CE_1 CE_2)	$CE_1 \sqsubseteq CE_2$
EquivalentClasses(CE_1 ... CE_n)	$CE_1 \equiv ... \equiv CE_n$
DisjointClasses(CE_1 ... CE_n)	$CE_1 \sqcap ... \sqcap CE_n \equiv \bot$
DisjointUnion(C CE_1 ... CE_n)	$CE_1 \sqcup ... \sqcup CE_n \equiv C$ and $CE_1 \sqcap ... \sqcap CE_n \equiv \bot$

TABLE 3.2   Syntax of Object Property Axioms.

OWL 2 Syntax	Description Logic Syntax
SubObjectPropertyOf(ObjectPropertyChain (OPE_1 ... OPE_n) OPE)	$OPE_1 \circ ... \circ OPE_n \sqsubseteq OPE$
SubObjectPropertyOf(OPE_1 OPE_2)	$OPE_1 \sqsubseteq OPE_2$
EquivalentObjectProperties(OPE_1 ... OPE_n)	$OPE_1 \equiv ... \equiv OPE_n$
DisjointObjectProperties(OPE_1 ... OPE_n)	$OPE_1 \sqcap ... \sqcap OPE_n \equiv \bot$
InverseObjectProperties(OPE_1 OPE_2)	$OPE_1 \equiv OPE_2^-$
ObjectPropertyDomain(OPE CE)	$\exists OPE. \top \sqsubseteq CE$
ObjectPropertyRange(OPE CE)	$\top \sqsubseteq \forall OPE.CE$
FunctionalObjectProperty(OPE)	$\top \sqsubseteq\, \leq 1\ OPE$
E InverseFunctionalObjectProperty(OPE)	$\top \sqsubseteq\, \leq 1\ OPE^-$
ReflexiveObjectProperty(OPE)	$\top \sqsubseteq \exists OPE.Self$
E.Self IrreflexiveObjectProperty(OPE)	$\exists OPE.Self \sqsubseteq \bot$
SymmetricObjectProperty(OPE)	$OPE \sqsubseteq OPE^-$
AsymmetricObjectProperty(OPE)	$OPE \sqsubseteq \neg OPE^-$
TransitiveObjectProperty(OPE)	OPE^+

TABLE 3.3   Syntax of Data Property Axioms.

OWL 2 Syntax	Description Logic Syntax
SubDataPropertyOf(DPE_1 DPE_2)	$DPE_1 \sqsubseteq DPE_2$
EquivalentDataProperties(DPE_1 ... DPE_n)	$DPE_1 \equiv ... \equiv DPE_n$
DisjointDataProperties(DPE_1 ... DPE_n)	$DPE_1 \sqcap ... \sqcap DPEn \equiv \bot$
DataPropertyDomain(DPE CE)	$\exists DPE.Literal \sqsubseteq DR$
DataPropertyRange(DPE DR)	$Literal \sqsubseteq \forall DPE.DR$
FunctionalDataProperty(DPE)	$Literal \sqsubseteq\, \leq 1\ DPE$
DatatypeDefinition(DT DR)	$DT \equiv DR$

TABLE 3.4 Syntax of Assertions.

OWL 2 Syntax	Description Logic Syntax
SameIndividual(a_1 ... a_n)	$a_1 \doteq ... \doteq a_n$
DifferentIndividuals(a_1 ... a_n)	$a_1 \neq ... \neq a_n$
ClassAssertion(CE a)	$CE(a)$
ObjectPropertyAssertion(OPE a_1 a_2)	$OPE(a_1, a_2)$
NegativeObjectPropertyAssertion(OPE a_1 a_2)	$\neg OPE(a_1, a_2)$
DataPropertyAssertion(DPE a lt)	$DPE(a_1, lt)$
NegativeDataPropertyAssertion(DPE a lt)	$\neg DPE(a_1, lt)$

TABLE 3.5 Syntax of Class Expressions.

OWL 2 Syntax	Description Logic Syntax
ObjectIntersectionOf(CE_1 ... CE_n)	$CE_1 \sqcap ... \sqcap CE_n$
ObjectUnionOf(CE_1 ... CE_n)	$CE_1 \sqcup ... \sqcup CE_n$
ObjectComplementOf(CE)	$\neg CE$
ObjectOneOf(a_1 ... a_n)	$\{a_1, ... , a_n\}$
ObjectSomeValuesFrom(OPE CE)	$\exists OPE.CE$
ObjectAllValuesFrom(OPE CE)	$\forall OPE.CE$
ObjectHasValue(OPE a)	$OPE.\{a\}$
ObjectHasSelf(OPE)	$\exists OPE.Self$
ObjectMinCardinality(n OPE)	$\geq n$ OPE
ObjectMaxCardinality(n OPE)	$\leq n$ OPE
ObjectExactCardinality(n OPE)	$= n$ OPE
ObjectMinCardinality(n OPE CE)	$\geq n$ $OPE.CE$
ObjectMaxCardinality(n OPE CE)	$\leq n$ $OPE.CE$
ObjectExactCardinality(n OPE CE)	$= n$ $OPE.CE$
DataSomeValuesFrom(DPE_1 ... DPE_n DR)	$\{\exists DPE_1.DR\}...\{\exists DPE_n.DR\}$
DataAllValuesFrom(DPE_1 ... DPE_n DR)	$\{\forall DPE_1.DR\}...\{\forall DPE_n.DR\}$
DataHasValue(DPE lt)	$DPE.\{lt\}$
DataMinCardinality(n DPE)	$\geq n$ DPE
DataMaxCardinality(n DPE)	$\leq DPE$
DataExactCardinality(n DPE)	$= n$ DPE
DataMinCardinality(n DPE DR)	$\geq n$ $DPE.DR$
DataMaxCardinality(n DPE DR)	$\leq n$ $DPE.DR$
DataExactCardinality(n DPE DR)	$= n$ $DPE.DR$

In order to illustrate the equivalences between OWL 2 and description logics, we present a list of OWL 2 axioms with their corresponding representation in description logics. Tables 3.1, 3.2, and 3.3 present lists of axioms for class expressions, object properties, and data properties. Table 3.4 presents the list of assertions, Table 3.5 the list of class expressions, and Table 3.6 shows the syntax of data ranges.

3.3.2 OWL 2 Semantics

OWL 2 corresponds to the description logic *SROIQ(D)* [75] and has a model-theoretic semantics defined by interpretations [105]. Model-theoretic semantics allows for interpreting unambiguously the legitimate expressions of a given language; for evaluating the truth of a language statement under a particular interpretation; and for carrying out automated reasoning with these statements [43].

An interpretation is a pair $\mathcal{I} = (\Delta^{\mathcal{I}}, \cdot^{\mathcal{I}})$, where $\Delta^{\mathcal{I}}$ is the domain and $\cdot^{\mathcal{I}}$ is the interpretation function that satisfies the conditions described in Tables 3.7–3.11. We say an interpretation $\mathcal{I}$ satisfies an ontology $\mathcal{O}$ if and only if it satisfies every axiom in $\mathcal{O}$.

3.3.3 World Assumption and Name Assumption

Analyzing the semantics of OWL, we can see that OWL does not assume unique names for individuals. For example, according to the definition of functional properties in Table 3.8 ($\forall x, y_1, y_2 : (x, y_1) \in (OPE)^{\mathcal{I}}$ and $(x, y_2) \in (OPE)^{\mathcal{I}}$ implies $y_1 = y_2$), for the two pairs of functional object property assertions $p(x, y_1)$ and $p(x, y_2)$, it is inferred that y_1 and y_2 are the same individual. The knowledge base becomes inconsistent only if it is asserted that y_1 and y_2 are different individuals ($y_1 \neq y_2$).

In contrast, according to the semantics of UML class-based modeling, the model would be inconsistent since it is assumed by default that y_1 and y_2 are different individuals.

Another important assumption is whether the set of instances is considered complete or not (world assumption). The underlying semantics of UML class-based

TABLE 3.6 Syntax of Data Ranges.

OWL 2 Syntax	Description Logic Syntax
DataIntersectionOf($DR_1 \ldots DR_n$)	$DR_1 \sqcap \ldots \sqcap DR_n$
DataUnionOf($DR_1 \ldots DR_n$)	$DR_1 \sqcap \ldots \sqcap DR_n$
DataComplementOf(DR)	$\neg DR$
DataOneOf($lt_1 \ldots lt_n$)	$\{lt_1, \ldots, lt_n\}$

TABLE 3.7 Semantics of Class Expression Axioms.

Description Logic Syntax	Semantics
$CE_1 \sqsubseteq CE_2$	$(CE_1)^{\mathcal{I}} \subseteq (CE_2)^{\mathcal{I}}$
$CE_1 \equiv \ldots \equiv CE_n$	$(CE_j)^{\mathcal{I}} = (CE_k)^{\mathcal{I}}$ for each $1 \leq j \leq n$ and each $1 \leq k \leq n$
$CE_1 \sqcap \ldots \sqcap CE_n \equiv \bot$	$(CE_j)^{\mathcal{I}} \cap (CE_k)^{\mathcal{I}} = \emptyset$ for each $1 \leq j \leq n$ and each $1 \leq k \leq n$ such that $j \neq k$
$CE_1 \sqcup \ldots \sqcup CE_n \equiv C$ and $CE_1 \sqcap \ldots \sqcap CE_n \equiv \bot$	$(CE_1)^{\mathcal{I}} \cup \ldots \cup (CE_n)^{\mathcal{I}} = (C)^{\mathcal{I}}$ and $(CE_j)^{\mathcal{I}} \cap (CE_k)^{\mathcal{I}} = \emptyset$ for each $1 \leq j \leq n$ and each $1 \leq k \leq n$ such that $j \neq k$

TABLE 3.8 Semantics of Object Property Axioms.

Description Logic Syntax	Semantics
$OPE_1 \, o \, ... \, o \, OPE_n \sqsubseteq OPE$	$\forall y_0, ... , y_n : (y_0, y_1) \in (OPE_1)^{\mathcal{I}}$ and ... and $(y_n - 1, y_n)$ $\in (OPE_n)^{\mathcal{I}}$ implies $(y_0, y_n) \subseteq (OPE)^{\mathcal{I}}$
$OPE_1 \sqsubseteq OPE_2$	$(OPE_1)^{\mathcal{I}} \subseteq (OPE_2)^{\mathcal{I}}$
$OPE_1 \equiv ... \equiv OPE_n$	$(OPE_j)^{\mathcal{I}} = (OPE_k)^{\mathcal{I}}$ for each $1 \leq j \leq n$ and each $1 \leq k \leq n$
$OPE_1 \sqcap ... \sqcap OPE_n \equiv \bot$	$(OPE_j)^{\mathcal{I}} \bigcap (OPE_k)^{\mathcal{I}} = \emptyset$ for each $1 \leq j \leq n$ and each $1 \leq k \leq n$ such that $j \neq k$
$\exists OPE. \top \sqsubseteq CE$	$\forall x,y : (x,y) \in (OPE)^{\mathcal{I}}$ implies $x \in (CE)^{\mathcal{I}}$
$\top \sqsubseteq \forall OPE.CE$	$\forall x,y : (x,y) \in (OPE)^{\mathcal{I}}$ implies $y \in (CE)^{\mathcal{I}}$
$\top \sqsubseteq \leq 1 \, OPE$	$\forall x,y_1,y_2 : (x,y_1) \in (OPE)^{\mathcal{I}}$ and $(x,y_2) \in (OPE)^{\mathcal{I}}$ implies $y_1 = y_2$
$\top \sqsubseteq \leq 1 \, OPE^-$	$\forall x_1,x_2,y, : (x_1,y) \in (OPE)^{\mathcal{I}}$ and $(x_2,y) \in (OPE)^{\mathcal{I}}$ implies $x_1 = x_2$
$\top \sqsubseteq \exists OPE.Self$	$\forall x : x \in \Delta^{\mathcal{I}}$ implies $(x,x) \in (OPE)^{\mathcal{I}}$
$\exists OPE.Self \sqsubseteq \bot$	$\forall x : x \in \Delta^{\mathcal{I}}$ implies $(x,x) \notin (OPE)^{\mathcal{I}}$
$OPE \sqsubseteq OPE^-$	$\forall x,y : (x,y) \in (OPE)^{\mathcal{I}}$ implies $(y,x) \in (CE)^{\mathcal{I}}$
$OPE \sqsubseteq \neg OPE^-$	$\forall x,y : (x,y) \in (OPE)^{\mathcal{I}}$ implies $(y,x) \notin (CE)^{\mathcal{I}}$
OPE^+	$\forall x,y,z : (x,y) \in (OPE)^{\mathcal{I}}$ and $(y,z) \in (OPE)^{\mathcal{I}}$ implies $(x,z) \in (CE)^{\mathcal{I}}$

TABLE 3.9 Semantics of Data Property Axioms.

Description Logic Syntax	Semantics
$DPE_1 \sqsubseteq DPE_2$	$(DPE_1)^{\mathcal{I}} \subseteq (DPE_2)^{\mathcal{I}}$
$DPE_1 \equiv ... \equiv DPE_n$	$(DPE_j)^{\mathcal{I}} = (DPE_k)^{\mathcal{I}}$ for each $1 \leq j \leq n$ and each $1 \leq k \leq n$
$DPE_1 \sqcap ... \sqcap DPEn \equiv \bot$	$(DPE_j)^{\mathcal{I}} \bigcap (DPE_k)^{\mathcal{I}} = \emptyset$ for each $1 \leq j \leq n$ and each $1 \leq k \leq n$ such that $j \neq k$
$\exists DPE.Literal \sqsubseteq DR$	$\forall x,y : (x,y) \in (DPE)^{\mathcal{I}}$ implies $x \in (DR)^{\mathcal{I}}$
$Literal \sqsubseteq \forall DPE. DR$	$\forall x,y : (x,y) \in (DPE)^{\mathcal{I}}$ implies $y \in (DR)^{\mathcal{I}}$
$Literal \sqsubseteq \leq 1 \, DPE$	$\forall x,y_1,y_2 : (x,y_1) \in (DPE)^{\mathcal{I}}$ and $(x,y_2) \in (OPE)^{\mathcal{I}}$ implies $y_1 = y_2$
$DT \equiv DR$	$(DT)^{\mathcal{I}} = (DR)^{\mathcal{I}}$

TABLE 3.10 Semantics of Assertions.

Description Logic Syntax	Semantics
$a_1 \doteq ... \doteq a_n$	$(a_j)^{\mathcal{I}} = (a_k)^{\mathcal{I}}$ for each $1 \leq j \leq n$ and each $1 \leq k \leq n$
$a_1 \neq ... \neq a_n$	$(a_j)^{\mathcal{I}} \neq (a_k)^{\mathcal{I}}$ for each $1 \leq j \leq n$ and each $1 \leq k \leq n$ such that $j \neq k$
$CE(a)$	$(a)^{\mathcal{I}} \in (CE)^{\mathcal{I}}$
$OPE(a_1, a_2)$	$((a_1)^{\mathcal{I}}, (a_2)^{\mathcal{I}}) \in (OPE)^{\mathcal{I}}$
$\neg OPE(a_1, a_2)$	$((a_1)^{\mathcal{I}}, (a_2)^{\mathcal{I}}) \notin (OPE)^{\mathcal{I}}$
$DPE(a_1, lt)$	$((a_1)^{\mathcal{I}}, (lt)^{\mathcal{I}}) \in (DPE)^{\mathcal{I}}$
$\neg DPE(a_1, lt)$	$((a_1)^{\mathcal{I}}, (lt)^{\mathcal{I}}) \notin (DPE)^{\mathcal{I}}$

TABLE 3.11 Semantics of Class Expression.

Description Logic Syntax	Semantics
$CE_1 \sqcap ... \sqcap CE_n$	$(CE_1)^{\mathcal{I}} \cap ... \cap (CE_n)^{\mathcal{I}}$
$CE_1 \sqcup ... \sqcup CE_n$	$(CE_1)^{\mathcal{I}} \cup ... \cup (CE_n)^{\mathcal{I}}$
$\neg CE$	$\Delta^{\mathcal{I}}(CE)^{\mathcal{I}}$
$\{a_1, ... , a_n\}$	$\{(a_1)^{\mathcal{I}}, ... , (a_n)^{\mathcal{I}}\}$
$\exists OPE.CE$	$\{x \mid \exists y : (x, y) \in (OPE)^{\mathcal{I}} \text{ and } y \in (CE)^{\mathcal{I}}\}$
$\forall OPE.CE$	$\{x \mid \forall y : (x, y) \in (OPE)^{\mathcal{I}} \text{ implies } y \in (CE)^{\mathcal{I}}\}$
$OPE.\{a\}$	$\{x \mid (x, (a)^{\mathcal{I}}) \in (OPE)^{\mathcal{I}}\}$
$\exists OPE.Self$	$\{x \mid (x, x) \in (OPE)^{\mathcal{I}}\}$
$\geq n\ OPE$	$\{x \mid \#\{y \mid (x, y) \in (OPE)^{\mathcal{I}}\} \geq n\}$
$\leq n\ OPE$	$\{x \mid \#\{y \mid (x, y) \in (OPE)^{\mathcal{I}}\} \leq n\}$
$= n\ OPE$	$\{x \mid \#\{y \mid (x, y) \in (OPE)^{\mathcal{I}}\} = n\}$
$\geq n\ OPE.CE$	$\{x \mid \#\{y \mid (x, y) \in (OPE)^{\mathcal{I}} \text{ and } y \in (CE)^{\mathcal{I}}\} \geq n\}$
$\leq n\ OPE.CE$	$\{x \mid \#\{y \mid (x, y) \in (OPE)^{\mathcal{I}} \text{ and } y \in (CE)^{\mathcal{I}}\} \leq n\}$
$= n\ OPE.CE$	$\{x \mid \#\{y \mid (x, y) \in (OPE)^{\mathcal{I}} \text{ and } y \in (CE)^{\mathcal{I}}\} = n\}$
$\{\exists DPE_1.DR\}...\{\exists DPE_n.DR\}$	$\{x \mid \exists y_1, ... , yn : (x, y_k) \in (DPE_k)^{\mathcal{I}} \text{ for each }$ $1 \leq k \leq n \text{ and } (y_1, ... , y_n) \in (DR)^{\mathcal{I}}\}$
$\{\forall DPE_1.DR\}...\{\forall DPE_n.DR\}$	$\{x \mid \forall y_1, ... , y_n : (x, y_k) \in (DPE_k)^{\mathcal{I}} \text{ for each }$ $1 \leq k \leq n \text{ and } (y_1, ... , y_n) \in (DR)^{\mathcal{I}}\}$
$DPE.\{lt\}$	$\{x \mid (x, (lt)^{\mathcal{I}}) \in (DPE)^{\mathcal{I}}\}$
$\geq n\ DPE$	$\{x \mid \#\{y \mid (x, y) \in (DPE)^{\mathcal{I}}\} \geq n\}$
$\leq n\ DPE$	$\{x \mid \#\{y \mid (x, y) \in (DPE)^{\mathcal{I}}\} \leq n\}$
$= n\ DPE$	$\{x \mid \#\{y \mid (x, y) \in (DPE)^{\mathcal{I}}\} = n\}$
$\geq n\ DPE.DR$	$\{x \mid \#\{y \mid (x, y) \in (DPE)^{\mathcal{I}} \text{ and } y \in (DR)^{\mathcal{I}}\} \geq n\}$
$\leq n\ DPE.DR$	$\{x \mid \#\{y \mid (x, y) \in (DPE)^{\mathcal{I}} \text{ and } y \in (DR)^{\mathcal{I}}\} \leq n\}$
$= n\ DPE.DR$	$\{x \mid \#\{y \mid (x, y) \in (DPE)^{\mathcal{I}} \text{ and } y \in (DR)^{\mathcal{I}}\} = n\}$

modeling assumes that the set of instances of a given model is complete, i.e., the set of instances has exactly one interpretation. In this one interpretation, the classes and relations in the model are interpreted by the objects and tuples in the instance. Therefore, the lack of information in the set of objects and values that are an instance of a UML based-class model is interpreted as negative information, since there is only one interpretation and everything that does not belong to this interpretation belongs to its complement (closed-world assumption).

In contrast, OWL assumes incomplete knowledge by default. The set of individuals, literals, and property assertions has many different interpretations. Therefore, the absence of information in this set is only the evidence of lack of knowledge (open-world assumption).

Each of these approaches (OWA and CWA) has its proper place. OWA serves to describe knowledge in an extensible way, since OWL is monotonic. The OWA is suitable to represent the core knowledge of a domain.

$$\{HANS, JOHN, ORDER1, USA, CANADA\} \equiv \top \qquad (3.16)$$

$$HANS \neq JOHN \neq ORDER1 \neq USA \neq CANADA \qquad (3.17)$$

$$SalesOrder \sqcap Customer \sqcap Country \equiv \bot \qquad (3.18)$$

$$CanSalesOrder \sqcap USSalesOrder \equiv \bot \qquad (3.19)$$

Figure 3.3   Closing the Domain of E-Shop with OWL Axioms.

Closed-world assumption is appropriate for defining integrity constraints and validation based on negation as failure (NAF). The negation as failure inference allows for deriving the negation of a proposition if it is not possible to obtain the affirmation of this proposition.

Let us use the example depicted in Table 3.2. We consider the following instances and property assertions: country(JOHN, USA), country(HANS, CANADA). Under the CWA, querying the ontology for customers who *are not* American (*Customer* $\sqcap \neg country.\{USA\}$?) produces HANS. Since there is no fact about HANS being American, it is derived that he is not. The same query under OWA would produce no results, since there are no facts asserting that HANS is not American. To achieve the same result, we need to close the domain.

There are OWL constructs that can be used to constrain the interpretation to a defined set of individuals, i.e., to *close the domain* (closed-domain assumption). Figure 3.3 shows axioms used to close the domain of the ontology presented in the Figure 3.2. One may declare that the set of all existing individuals comprises {HANS, JOHN, ORDER1, USA, CANADA} (Line 3.16). Moreover, because of the non-unique name assumption, we have to assert that all individuals are different from each other (Line 3.17). Additionally, we declare that the classes SalesOrder, Customer and Country are disjoint from each other (Line 3.18) as well as the subclasses of SalesOrder are (Line 3.19).

By adding these axioms, we can also deliver the same results of CWA using OWA in the query aforementioned. We can infer that HANS does not live in USA, since HANS is a Customer, a Customer must live in exactly one country (3.2), HANS lives in CANADA, and CANADA is different from USA.

However, closing the domain does not imply CWA because NAF is not in place. For example, if we remove the object property assertion Country (HANS, CANADA) and ask the same query, using CWA, the result is still HANS because the lack of information about HANS. By using OWA, there are no results, since the lack of information about HANS is not enough to infer that he is not American.

Research in the field of combining description logics and logic programming [103] provides solutions to support OWL reasoning with CWA. Different strategies have been explored like adopting an epistemic operator [35, 87] or extending OWL with the specification of external predicates that implements the idea of negation as failure [131].

The CWA and OWA are not contradictory. Recent results [104] show that it is possible to control the degree of incompleteness in an ontology obtaining a more versatile formalism. Such "under-specification" can be used to allow reuse and extension and does not mean insufficiency. Again using our example, suppose we define an incomplete list of countries part of the North American Free Trade Agreement (NAFTA) comprising only Canada and USA, because these are the countries the store ships to, and we do not need to know the others. If the store starts shipping to Mexico at some point in time, a query about whether Mexico is a member of NAFTA returns *undefined*, which is reasonable, providing that our list of NAFTA countries is incomplete and does not include Mexico.

3.4 ONTOLOGY SERVICES

Ontology-Based Information Systems [170] provide users with a set of functionalities to manage ontologies—ontology services.

Tran *et al.* [170] described a set of ontology services for supporting ontology engineering. In this book, we concentrate on the following services: reasoning and querying.

3.4.1 Reasoning Services

Reasoning services are services provided by reasoning systems with respect to the ontology. Standard reasoning services are services available in all reasoning systems, whereas non-standard reasoning services are extensions of basic reasoning services.

The standard reasoning services for TBox are satisfiability and subsumption. A class C is unsatisfiable ($C \sqsubseteq \perp$) with respect to an ontology $\mathcal{O}$ if C is empty (does not have any instances) in all models of $\mathcal{O}$. Satisfiability checking is useful for verifying whether an ontology is meaningful, i.e., whether all classes are instantiable.

Subsumption is useful to hierarchically organize classes according to their generality. A class C is subsumed by another class D with respect to an ontology $\mathcal{O}$ if the set denoted by C is a subset of the subset denoted by D for every model of $\mathcal{O}$.

The standard reasoning services for ABox are instance checking, consistency, realization, and retrieval. *Instance checking* proves whether a given individual i belongs to the set described by the class C. An ontology is *consistent* if every individual i is an instance of only satisfiable classes. The *realization* service identifies the most specific class a given individual belongs to. Finally, the `retrieval` service identifies the individuals that belong to a given concept.

3.4.2 Querying

Querying ontologies is a research field that comprises multiple techniques and languages. We limit the scope of our analysis to two languages, conjunctive query and the SPARQL-like language SPARQL-DL. We address conjunctive queries because they have been the querying mechanism for description logic-based knowledge bases. The reason for using SPARQL is that it is a W3C standard query language [69], and it includes the definition of graph pattern matching for OWL 2 Entailment Regime [55].

3.4.2.1 Conjunctive Query Conjunctive queries correspond to the conjunctive existential subset of first-order logic formulas, i.e., disjunction ($\vee$), negation ($\neg$), or universal quantification ($\forall$) are not allowed. The body of a conjunctive query consists of one or more atoms binding variables or literal values to class expressions or property expressions in the ontology [77].

For example, the query

$$Q(x, y) : -Customer(x) \wedge hasOrder(x, y)$$

is a query for any instance of the concept Customer (x is a distinguished variable) that have some order (y is a non-distinguished variable).

Let $\mathcal{V}_O = (\mathcal{V}_{cls}, \mathcal{V}_{op}, \mathcal{V}_{dp}, \mathcal{V}_{ind}, \mathcal{V}_D, \mathcal{V}_{lit})$ be an OWL vocabulary. Let $\mathbf{x} \equiv \{y_1, \ldots, y_n\}$ and $\mathbf{y} \equiv \{x_1, \ldots, x_n\}$ be sets of distinguished and non-distinguished variables. A conjunctive query $Q(s_i)$ is a conjunction of atoms in the form:

$$Q(s_i) \leftarrow \wedge \, P_i(s_i) \bigcup \wedge \, P_i(c_i)$$

where

- $P \in \mathcal{V}_{cls} \cup \mathcal{V}_{op} \cup \mathcal{V}_{dp} \cup \mathcal{V}_D$
- $s \equiv \mathbf{y} \cup \mathbf{x}$
- $c \in \mathcal{V}_{ind} \cup \mathcal{V}_{lit}$

An answer of a conjunctive query Q w.r.t. ontology is an assignment σ of individuals to distinguished variables, such that $\mathcal{I} \models Q(x\sigma, y)$.

3.4.2.2 SPARQL SPARQL 1.0 [69] is the triple-based W3C standard query language for RDF graphs. The semantics of SPARQL 1.0 is based on graph pattern matching and does not take into account OWL, although the specification allows for extending the SPARQL basic graph matching. SPARQL 1.1 [69] will address this problem by specifying an OWL entailment regime for SPARQL [55].

Sirin and Parsia [154] have done preliminary work on answering full SPARQL queries on top of OWL ontologies on SPARQL-DL. Next, we describe the abstract syntax of SPARQL-DL and its semantics.

SPARQL-DL Abstract Syntax. The abstract syntax of SPARQL-DL comprises basically the extension of the OWL abstract syntax to cover the usage of variables and blank nodes for classes, properties, individuals, and literals. Let $\mathcal{V}_O = (\mathcal{V}_{cls}, \mathcal{V}_{op}, \mathcal{V}_{dp}, \mathcal{V}_{ap}, \mathcal{V}_{ind}, \mathcal{V}_D, \mathcal{V}_{lit})$ be an OWL vocabulary. Let $\mathcal{V}_{bnode}$ and $\mathcal{V}_{var}$ be the set of blank nodes and set of variables. A SPARQL-DL query atom q is of the form:

```
q ← Type(a, C) | PropertyValue(a, p, v) | SameAs(a, b) |
DifferentFrom(a, b) |
    ClassExpressionAxioms(CE₁, . . . , CEₙ) |
    ObjectPropertyAxioms(OPE₁, . . . , OPEₙ) |
    DataPropertyAxioms(DPE) | Annotation(s, pₐ,o)
```

where $a, b \in \mathcal{V}_{ind} \cup \mathcal{V}_{bnode} \cup \mathcal{V}_{var}$, $v \in \mathcal{V}_{ind} \cup \mathcal{V}_{lit} \cup \mathcal{V}_{bnode} \cup \mathcal{V}_{var}$, $p \in \mathcal{V}_{op} \cup \mathcal{V}_{dp} \cup \mathcal{V}_{var}$, $CE \in \mathcal{V}_{cls} \cup \mathcal{V}_{var}, s \in \mathcal{V}_{cls} \cup \mathcal{V}_{op} \cup \mathcal{V}_{dp} \cup \mathcal{V}_{ap} \cup \mathcal{V}_{ind} \cup \mathcal{V}_D$,

$p_a \in \mathcal{V}_{ap}$, $o \in \mathcal{V}_{cls} \cup \mathcal{V}_{op} \cup \mathcal{V}_{dp} \cup \mathcal{V}_{ap} \cup \mathcal{V}_{ind} \cup \mathcal{V}_D \cup \mathcal{V}_{lit}$. A SPARQL-DL query Q is a finite set of SPARQL-DL query atoms and the query is interpreted as the conjunction of the elements in the set.

For example, the query

```
Type(?x, ObjectHasValue(country, USA))
```

returns all individuals that have the individual USA as value of the property country.

The semantics of SPARQL-DL extends the semantics of OWL to provide query evaluation. We say that there is a model of the query $Q = q_1 \wedge \ldots \wedge q_n$ ($\mathcal{I} \models \sigma Q$) with respect to an evaluation σ iff $\mathcal{I} \models \sigma q_i$ for every $i = 1, \ldots, n$.

A solution to a SPARQL-DL query Q with respect to an OWL ontology $\mathcal{O}$ is a *variable mapping* $\mu : \mathcal{V}_{var} \rightarrow \mathcal{V}_{uri} \cup \mathcal{V}_{lit}$ such that $\mathcal{O} \models \mu(Q)$.

3.5   ONTOLOGY ENGINEERING SERVICES

On top of core ontology services, ontology engineers count on functionalities to support the ontology development life cycle [170]. Two ontology engineering services are particular useful for application in UML class-based modeling: explanation and ontology matching.

3.5.1   Explanation

Users rely on reasoning services for classification and consistency checking. However, in case of inconsistencies in ontologies with a large amount of classes, users need to identify which constructs are causing the inconsistencies. Therefore, research on explanations of inferred assertions is gaining attention.

Explanations can be seen as a form of *debugging* ontologies. It consists of identifying and computing justifications, i.e., the set of axioms causing the subsumption.

There are distinguishing methods for computing a simple justification or all justifications [83, 84].

3.5.1.1   *Black Box Method for Single Justification*   The algorithm of a black-box technique for computing a justification comprises two steps. Firstly, axioms of an ontology $\mathcal{O}$ are inserted into a new ontology $\mathcal{O}'$ until a class C becomes unsatisfiable with regard to $\mathcal{O}'$. Secondly, irrelevant axioms are pruned until concept C becomes satisfiable, i.e., a single minimal justification is achieved.

3.5.1.2   *Computing All Justifications*   Once a single justification is achieved, one requires other techniques to compute the remaining justifications. Please refer to Kalyanpur *et al.* [84] for a description of a variation of the Hitting Set Tree (HST) algorithm [129] for finding all justifications.

3.5.2   Ontology Matching

Ontology matching is the discipline responsible for studying techniques for reconciling multiple resources on the web. It comprises two steps: matching and determining alignments and the generation of a processor for merging and transforming [38]. Matching identifies the correspondences. A correspondence for two ontologies A and B is a quintuple, including an id, an entity of ontology A, an entity of ontology B, a relation (equivalence, more general, disjointness), and a confidence measure. A set of correspondences forms an alignment. Correspondences can be done at the schema-level (metamodel) and at the instance-level (model).

Matchings can be based on different criteria: name of entities, structure (relations between entities, cardinality), or background knowledge like existing ontologies or wordnet. Techniques can be string-based or rely on linguistic resources like wordnet.

Furthermore, matchings are established according to the different structures that are compared. There are three techniques for comparing structures: internal structure comparison, relational structure comparison, and extensional techniques. Internal structure comparison includes the comparison of property, key, datatype, domain, and multiplicities. Relational structure comparison comprises the comparison of the taxonomic structure between the ontologies.

Finally, the extensional techniques cover the usage of extensional information, e.g., formal concept analysis for comparison.

3.6   RULES

Efforts in extending the expressiveness of the OWL language has led to the combination of OWL with the unary/binary Datalog sublanguages of RuleML [18]: The Semantic Web Rule Language (SWRL) [76].

A drawback of SWRL rules is that they are undecidable in general. Nevertheless, Motik *et al.* have identified the decidable subset of OWL, usually called description logic safe rules [107]. Although a syntax for description logic safe rules is not part of the OWL 2, standard existing work [54] defines such a syntax which is supported by the de facto standard OWL application program interface (OWL API) [72]. Thus, engineers can use description logic safe rules over reasoners that implement the tableau algorithm for description logic safe rules extension to OWL.

A rule comprises an antecedent and a consequent. Antecedents and consequents are composed by a set of atoms. An atom has the form $P(x)$ where P can be a class expression, data range, object property expression, data property expression, sameAs construct, differentFrom construct, or built-ins and x are variables or named individuals.

The model-theoretic semantics for SWRL extends the semantics of OWL [105] to define extensions of OWL interpretations that map variables to elements of the ontology (bindings). Hence, an interpretation satisfies a rule *iff* every binding that satisfies the antecedent also satisfies the consequent [76].

3.7   METAMODELS FOR ONTOLOGY TECHNOLOGIES

The definition of metamodel for ontology technologies enables the specification of model transformations of software engineering artifacts into OWL-related languages. For example, the transformation of UML class diagrams into OWL uses transformation rules based on the metamodel of both languages. In the next subsections, we give an overview of existing metamodels for OWL-related specifications.

3.7.1   OWL Metamodels

The following section presents a short description of the most prominent OWL metamodels, namely the *OMG OWL Metamodel* [114], the *NeOn OWL Metamodel* [23], and the *W3C OWL 2 Metamodel* [106].

We do not to describe these metamodels completely. Instead, we concentrate on two central constructs: classes and properties. Please refer to the citations for more details.

OMG OWL Metamodel.   The *OMG OWL Metamodel* is part of the OMG *Ontology Definition Metamodel* [114]. It has a large number of classes, since it imports the *OMG RDFS Metamodel*. Thus, some relations between classes are described in the RDFS Metamodel and reused in the OWL Metamodel.

For example, Figures 3.4 and 3.5 depict the class description diagram and the properties diagram, respectively. The domain and range of properties are specified in the RDFS Metamodel, depicted in Figure 3.6.

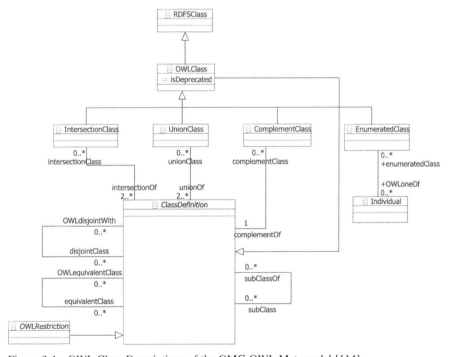

Figure 3.4   OWL Class Descriptions of the OMG OWL Metamodel [114].

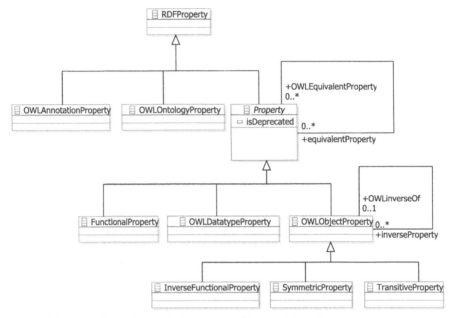

Figure 3.5   OWL Properties of the OMG OWL Metamodel [114].

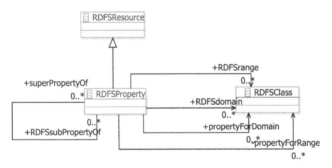

Figure 3.6   RDFS Properties of the OMG OWL Metamodel [114].

The OMG Metamodel has public acceptance as standard and popularity. Nevertheless, the OMG Metamodel introduces unnecessary complexity in dealing with RDF without any gain. Furthermore, the OMG Metamodel does not provide support for OWL 2.

NeOn OWL Metamodel.   The *NeOn Metamodel* [23] is a concise metamodel able to cover the OWL-DL functional syntax. Figures 3.7 and 3.8 depict the OWL class hierarchy and the property diagram, respectively. The relationship between Class and Property is direct, since the NeOn OWL Metamodel does not provide support for RDFS.

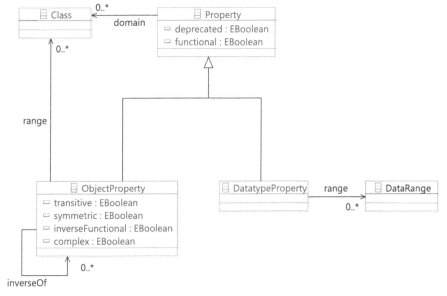

Figure 3.7   OWL Class Descriptions of the NeOn Metamodel.

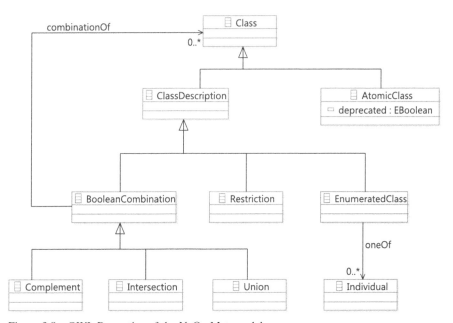

Figure 3.8   OWL Properties of the NeOn Metamodel.

The NeOn OWL Metamodel is smaller on the number of classes and simpler, since it is not attached to the RDF Metamodel. However, the NeOn Metamodel does not cover OWL 2 constructs.

W3C OWL 2 Metamodel. Improvements in the OWL language led the W3C OWL Working Group to publish working drafts of a new version of OWL: *OWL 2* [106]. OWL 2 is fully compatible with OWL-DL and extends the latter with limited complex role inclusion axioms, reflexivity and irreflexivity, role disjointness, and qualified cardinality restrictions.

The OWL 2 Metamodel is considerably different from the aforementioned metamodels for OWL. Constructs like Axiom and OWLEntity play central roles and associations between classes and properties are done by axioms. Figures 3.9 and 3.10 exemplify such constructs.

SWRL Metamodel. The SRWL Metamodel (Figure 3.11) is an extension of the OWL 2 Metamodel to provide support for OWL Rules. Brockmans *et al.* [21] have defined a Metamodel for SWRL rules.

In the SWRL Metamodel, a `Rule` is a subclass of `OWLAxiom`, which is defined as an element of an `Ontology`. A `Rule` contains an `Antecedent` and a `Conse-quent`, and those contain atoms. An `Atom` factors out OWL 2 axioms that can be used in SWRL rules like OWLClass and ObjectProperty.

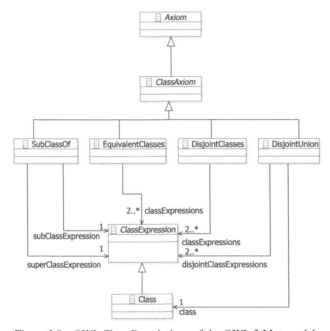

Figure 3.9   OWL Class Descriptions of the OWL 2 Metamodel.

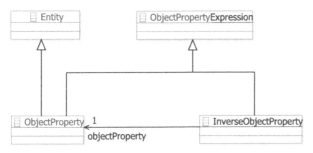

Figure 3.10   OWL Properties of the OWL 2 Metamodel.

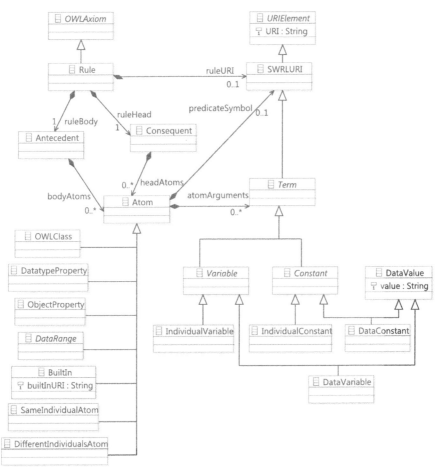

Figure 3.11   Snippets of the SWRL Metamodel and the Connections with the OWL Metamodel.

3.7.2   SPARQL Metamodel

In addition to OWL and SWRL, we capture the structure of the SPARQL language using a metamodel. Since the SPARQL specification does not recommend a structural specification of the SPARQL language, we have designed the SPARQL Metamodel based on the SPARQL EBNF Syntax.

Figure 3.12 presents the main classes of the SPARQL Metamodel. A SPARQL query comprises a prologue, where namespaces are declared, and the query body. There are multiple types of SPARQL queries: DESCRIBE, CONSTRUCT, SELECT, and ASK.

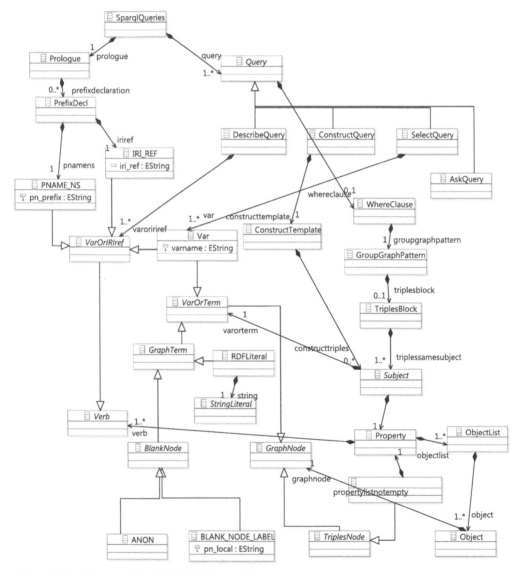

Figure 3.12   Snippets of the SPARQL Metamodel.

SPARQL queries have a WHERE clause, where the conditions are defined in the form of graph pattern. A graph pattern contains a triple block of subjects, properties, and objects. In SPARQL queries, variables and blank nodes may occur in any position of the triples.

3.8 ONTOLOGICAL TECHNICAL SPACES

In order to organize the concepts presented in this chapter, we use the notion of technical spaces presented in Chapter 2. Figure 3.13 presents the description logics technical space.

The description logics technical space uses the description logic terminology as schema for defining knowledge bases as well as the SPARQL-DL or the conjunctive query vocabulary for defining queries. Query models are representations of evaluation functions that map variables into elements of a knowledge base.

The description logics technical space is an abstract technical space which is realized by the serialization of text files. OWL includes a set of concrete syntax notations for modeling OWL ontologies underpinned by description logics. Figure 3.14 depicts the relationships between OWL and description logics under the

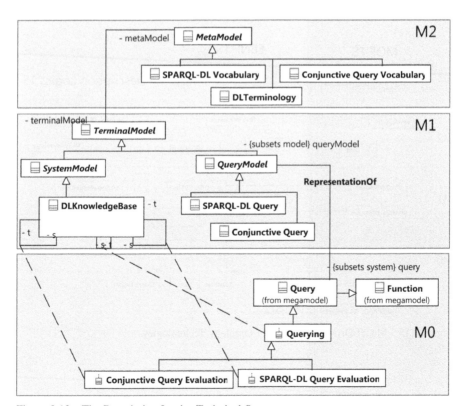

Figure 3.13 The Description Logics Technical Space.

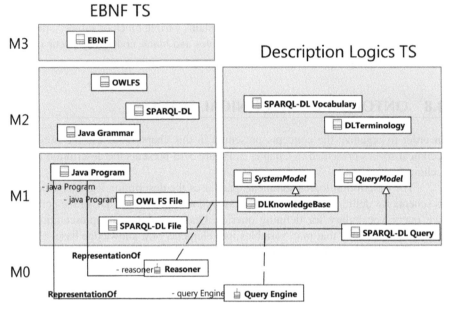

Figure 3.14   Relation between the EBNF Technical Space and the Description Logics Technical Space.

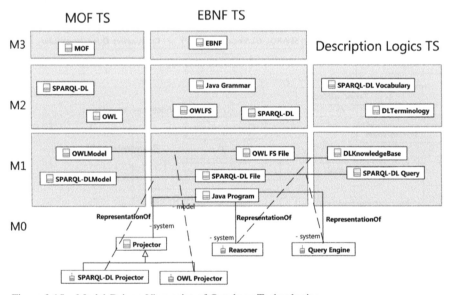

Figure 3.15   Model-Driven Viewpoint of Ontology Technologies.

model-driven structure. The Java language is used to create Java programs that realize the idea of a reasoner and of a query engine. OWL reasoners take as input an OWL ontology written using, e.g., the OWL 2 Functional Syntax and generate a knowledge base in memory for applying description logic algorithms. The same principles apply to query engines.

As defined in Section 3.7, there exist multiple MOF Metamodels for ontology technologies and these are the main artifacts for model-driven engineering. Figure 3.15 depicts ontology technologies defined based on three technical spaces: MOF, EBNF, and description logics technical space. MOF-based models of OWL ontologies and queries are defined using ontology-related MOF Metamodels. These models are serialized using projectors that generate textual representations of ontologies and queries. The textual file is the input artifact for reasoners, query engines, and ontology services.

3.9   CONCLUSION

This chapter describes the main technologies of the semantic web stack related to ontology technologies. Additionally, we group languages and techniques according to the model-driven engineering structure. The contribution is a model-driven viewpoint of ontology technologies. We refer to these concepts and techniques later as we describe the integration with model-driven engineering.

CHAPTER 4

MARRYING ONTOLOGY AND MODEL-DRIVEN ENGINEERING

In this chapter, we present a literature review and describe a domain analysis of ontological technical spaces and MOF technical space, explaining the features of the different paradigms. We analyze their similarities and describe frequently used patterns for transformations between instantiations of metamodeling technical spaces and ontological technical spaces.[1]

4.1 INTRODUCTION

Ontology technologies and model-driven engineering have distinct foci. For example, MOF targets automating the management and interchange of metadata, whereas knowledge representation focuses on semantics of the content and on automated reasoning over that content [49].

While the focus of these communities is somewhat different, the following question arises: What are the commonalities and variations around ontology technologies and model-driven engineering?

MDE can be based on the *MOF Technical Space* (MMTS) (cf. Section 2.3) as well as on the *Ontological Technical Space* (OTS) (cf. Section 3.8). Figure 4.1 illustrates an example indicating the use of OTSs in the MDE process. The classical MDE transformations, residing in the MOF technical space, are extended by further transformations, making use of OTSs.

Further transformation into other technical spaces may provide additional analysis and implementation support that is not as efficiently available in metamodeling technical spaces. Current MDE uses semi-formal metamodels instead of formal specification languages as support for describing models [168]. In Figure 4.1, EMOF is transformed into an ontological representation in OWL, e.g., for model checking. The resulting ontology describes a submodel of EMOF that enables logic-based model analysis and serves as knowledge base for a reasoner.

---

[1]This chapter contains work from the paper "On Marrying Ontological and Metamodeling Technical Spaces" presented at ESEC-FSE'07 [150] and EU STReP MOST Deliverable D1.1 "Report on Transformation Patterns" [152].

Semantic Web and Model-Driven Engineering, First Edition. Fernando Silva Parreiras.
© 2012 Institute of Electrical and Electronics Engineers. Published 2012 by John Wiley & Sons, Inc.

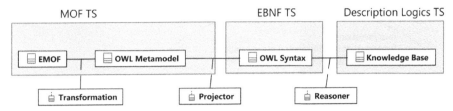

Figure 4.1   Marrying MMTS and OTS.

TABLE 4.1   OTS and MMTS: Comparable Features.

UML Class-Based Modeling	OWL
Package	Ontology
Class	Class
Instances and attribute values	Individuals and data values
Association, attribute	Property
Datatypes	Datatypes
Subclass, generalization	Subclass, sub-property
Enumeration	Enumeration
Navigable, non-navigable	Domain, range
Disjointness, cover	Disjointness, disjoint union
Multiplicity	Cardinality

In order to improve the understanding of the space composed by MMTS and OTS (MMTS+OTS), we compare MMTS+OTS approaches using a feature model and validate the model offering a survey and categorization of a number of existing approaches.

The chapter is organized as follows: Section 4.2 defines basic similar concepts between UML class-based modeling and OWL modeling. Section 4.3 presents an understanding of the domain in the form of a feature model. In Section 4.4, the model categorizing related approaches is applied.

4.2   SIMILARITIES BETWEEN OWL MODELING AND UML CLASS-BASED MODELING

Despite having distinct purposes, OTS and MMTS share similar constructs. Recent approaches presented similarities between MOF and RDF [53], between OWL/RDF and Object-Oriented Languages [92], and between UML and OWL [114, 42]. The features are summarized in Table 4.1. For the subtleties, please refer to the cited papers.

These similarities allow for translating UML class-based modeling into description logics, which gives UML class-based modeling a model-theoretic semantics. For example, the work of Berardi *et al.* [12] investigates the translation of UML class diagrams into $\mathcal{DLR}_{ifd}$, an expressive yet decidable description logic.

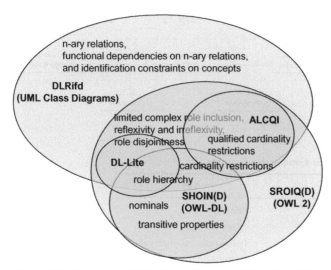

Figure 4.2   Comparing UML Class Diagrams, OWL-DL, OWL 2, and DL-Lite.

Figure 4.2 depicts distinguishing features of UML class diagrams ($\mathcal{DLR}_{ifd}$), OWL-DL ($\mathcal{SHOIQ}$ (D)), OWL 2 ($\mathcal{SROIQ}$(D)), and $\mathcal{ALCQI}$, a fragment supported by state-of-the-art reasoning services that $\mathcal{DLR}_{ifd}$ has in common with $\mathcal{SROIQ}$(D). Considering Figure 4.2, UML class diagrams ($\mathcal{DLR}_{ifd}$) differentiate from OWL-DL ($\mathcal{SHOIQ}$ (D)) by representing n-ary relations, functional dependencies on n-ary relations, identification constraints on concepts [27, 26], limited complex role inclusion axioms, and role disjointness.

State-of-the-art automated reasoning systems do not support all constructs of UML class diagrams ($\mathcal{DLR}_{ifd}$). However, by dropping functional dependencies and identification constraints, one achieves $\mathcal{ALCQI}$. $\mathcal{ALCQI}$ is the most expressive fragment in common between UML class diagrams ($\mathcal{DLR}_{ifd}$) and OWL 2 ($\mathcal{SROIQ}$(D)). Automated reasoning systems [155] support constructs of OWL-DL ($\mathcal{SHOIN}$ (D)), OWL 2($\mathcal{SROIQ}$(D)), and, consequently, $\mathcal{ALCQI}$.

Notice that we compare the language constructs and we do not consider OCL. Rahmani *et al.* [127] described an adjustable transformation from OWL to Ecore and identified that it is possible to represent most OWL constructs with Ecore and OCL invariants. However, such a transformation has the purpose of aligning OWL constraints with OCL invariants and does not cover OWL reasoning services like realization and instance checking.

4.3   COMMONALITIES AND VARIATIONS

In this section, we present a domain analysis of MMTS+OTS approaches. Domain analysis is concerned with analyzing and modeling the variabilities and commonalities of systems or concepts in a domain [32].

The product of such analysis is a feature model, described in this section. A feature model comprises a feature diagram, depicted in the Figure 4.3, the description of the features, and examples. The feature model reveals the possible choices for a MMTS+OTS approach and also serves as a taxonomy to categorize approaches involving both paradigms. We describe the features in Figure 4.3 in the next sections.

4.3.1 Language

The choice of a language shapes the message exchange between agents. A language is defined based on:

1. A concrete syntax describing the way in which the language elements appear in a human-readable form. Extended BNF is frequently used to describe the concrete syntax of lexical notations. In the case of graphical notations, natural language and symbols are used to describe how graphical symbols represent information, and how these symbols are laid out. A particular case of concrete syntax is a serialization syntax, which allows the language expressions to be made persistent or interchanged between tools. XML can be used as serialization syntax. Syntactical variations may co-exist for one given language.

2. An abstract syntax of a language portraying the elements that compose the language, and the possible combination of these elements. Abstract syntax graphs, metamodels, and Extended BNF are commonly used to represent the abstract syntax of a language.

3. The semantics of a language attributes meaning to the language primitives and its vocabulary. This attribution can be done by means of a formal language, using mathematics, or an informal language, using natural language. The relevant formal semantics for MMTS+OTS are [156]:

   • *Model-theoretic semantics.* Model-theoretic semantics assigns meaning to a set of logical sentences by considering *all* possible interpretations that may be given to its atomic elements. Such a set of logical sentences is then satisfiable if there is an interpretation that will render all the sentences to become true (refer to Section 3.3.2).

   • *Axiomatic semantics.* Axiomatic semantics is based on methods of logical deduction from predicate logic. The semantic meaning of a program is based on assertions about relationships that remain the same each time the program executes.

   • *Translational semantics.* Another way of giving a semantics to a language is translating expressions from one language into another language that has a defined semantics.

The abstract syntax characterizes the primitives of a language. The concrete syntax realizes the primitives by a concrete notation. The semantics assigns meaning to the primitives, and the models constructed using these primitives.

Let us consider three examples: UML is a modeling language with a graphical notation, an informal semantics described in natural language (there exist

48

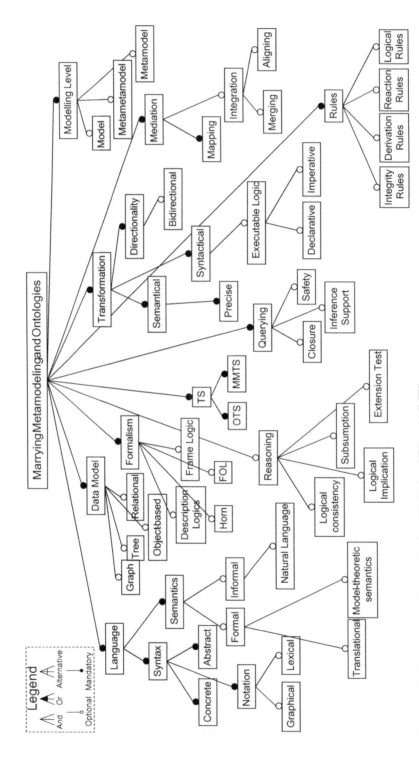

Figure 4.3   Snippet of the Feature Model of Bridging OTS and MMTS.

translational semantics approaches for UML) that uses a metamodeling approach to describe its abstract syntax, as well as natural language and symbols to describe the concrete syntax.

OWL is an ontology modeling language with a lexical notation, formalized by description logics. It is a subset of first-order predicate logics with a model-theoretic semantics. OWL's concrete and abstract syntax are specified by Extended BNF.

RDF(S) is a language based on triples as the abstract syntax graph, with a concrete lexical notation and a formal axiomatic semantics [47].

4.3.2   Formalism

We define the term "formalism" as formal language used to precisely define concepts of the world. A formalism is the basis for reasoning over models. We distinguish between four formalisms applicable to MMTS+OTS:

- *First-Order Logic.* First-order logic is a logical language able to express relations between individuals using predicates and quantifiers [157].

- *Description Logics.* Description logics is a family of knowledge representation formalisms aimed at unifying and giving a logical basis to frame-based systems, semantic networks, object-oriented representations, semantic data models, and type systems [9]. Core to each language from this family is its capability to express class definitions by restrictions on relationships to other classes and by inheritance relations. Though the exact expressiveness varies, all description logic languages are subsets of first-order predicate logics.

- *Horn Rules.* Horn rules restrict first-order predicate logics to axioms of a particular form. Though horn rules are in general Turing powerful, in a practical situation it is possible to oversee deductive consequences and to reason efficiently with terms (i.e., kind of objects).

  While horn rules can be given a model-theoretic semantics, e.g., first-order predicate logics, in order to handle negation efficiently, most approaches select specific interpretation functions in order to decide upon satisfiability (or inconsistency).

- *Frame Logic.* Frame logic is a syntactically more expressive variant of horn rules. It constitutes a deductive, object-oriented database language combining declarative semantics and the expressiveness of deductive database languages with the data modeling capabilities supported by the object-oriented data model [2].

Ontologies and models written in a given language, e.g., OWL, are usually translated to one or more formalisms, e.g., $\mathcal{SHOIN}$ (D), a member of the family of description logic languages, to realize reasoning.

4.3.3   Data Model

A data model is an underlying structure mandating how data is represented. The data model provides a basis for organizing the primitive elements of a language. This organization is used by the abstract syntax of the language to relate the primitives. We differentiate four data models:

1. *Graph*: consisting of (hyper-)edges and nodes.
2. *Tree*: constituting a restricted graph data model having a hierarchical organization of the data.
3. *Object-based*: organizing data according to the object-oriented paradigm.
4. *Relational*: organizing data in relations.

A modeling approach can be seen from the point of view of data models. For instance, the UML class diagram is commonly seen either as a graph data model or as an object data model.

OWL is primarily based on unary relations (i.e., logically defined classes) and binary relations (i.e., relationships between objects), but there are alternative access methods, e.g., via Java object APIs or querying through the SPARQL graph data model query language.

RDF(S) constitutes a graph data model, but it can also be seen as a kind of object model or a constrained relational model.

4.3.4 Reasoning

Each type of reasoning is based on a formalism, typically a logical language, to deduce (infer) conclusions from a given set of facts (also called assertions) encoded in a model. Standard reasoning services include:

1. *Logical consistency.* Logical consistency checks whether a set of logical sentences, i.e., a logical theory, has an interpretation, i.e., admits a model.
2. *Logical implication.* Given a set of logical sentences as a premise (i.e., a "theory"), another set of logical sentences may be implied as a conclusion because every model of the premise is also a model of the conclusion.
3. *Subsumption.* Subsumption is a special case of checking logical implications. Subsumption tests whether one class definition is more specific than another one—given a set of logical sentences as background theory. Subsumption tests can be used to generate a sound and complete classification of a set of class definitions.
4. *Extension test.* An extension test checks whether a tuple is contained in a logical relation. Specifically, it tests whether an instance belongs to the extension of a class, which is a unary relation.

Indeed, all standard reasoning services in first-order predicate logics (and in description logics, specifically) that are illustrated here can be based on consistency checking.

In horn rules formalisms, reasoning is defined either based on resolution or on naïve bottom-up evaluation.

4.3.5   Querying

Querying plays an important role for accessing and bridging between technical spaces. The work by Haase *et al.* [64] comparing aspects of query languages for ontologies has been used to identify features of querying:

1. *Inference support.* A query engine may access only explicitly available data (e.g., SPARQL [69]), or it may include facts derived by using a reasoner (e.g., OWL-QL [46] or SAIQL [93]).

2. *Closure.* A query language may represent the results of a query on a model (i.e., a kind of database) either in the same format as the model itself (usual) or in a different paradigm. For instance, the earliest RDF query languages returned results as variable bindings, i.e., as relations rather than graphs, while SPARQL may return results in its native paradigm, i.e., as a graph.

3. *Safety.* A query language is considered safe, iff a syntactically correct query returns a finite set of results.

Queries are expressed in a language, over a data model, in a modeling level, and can use a reasoning service. For example, OCL can be used as a query language with lexical notation over a UML object data model.

SPARQL is a query language with lexical notation over RDF graph data model without reasoning support (according to the version 1.0 of SPARQL specification [126]) and with results being either represented as relations or as graphs.

4.3.6   Rules

Rules are present inside technical spaces as well as in transformations between them. Rule languages can be considered to include a querying mechanism over a data model. The term "rules" is ambiguous and includes in its range:

1. *Integrity constraints.* Integrity constraints restrict the number of possible interpretations. They do not add inferences, but they signal exceptions.

2. *Derivation rules.* Integrity constraints comprise one or more conditions from which a fact is derived as conclusion iff the rule holds.

3. *Reaction rules.* Reaction rules have as a core feature their reactivity. They comprise a triggering event and a condition that carries out a triggered action iff the rule holds.

4. *Logical rules.* Logical rules describe a logical axiom that holds.

For example, OCL is a language with lexical notation, uses metamodeling to represent its abstract syntax, and has translational semantics into first-order logics. It serves to write integrity constraints and derivation rules as well. Part of the UML specification called action semantics can be used to specify reaction rules.

F-logic rules [2] are logical rules can be considered to constitute derivation rules and can be configured to model integrity constraints.

DL-safe rules [107] are a logical rule mechanism for a subset of OWL allowing for sound and complete reasoning with class definitions and a restricted rule language that defines specific logical axioms.

ATL [82] and QVT [113] are languages with lexical notation, metamodeling abstract syntax and they can be used to write transformation rules.

4.3.7 Transformation

A transformation definition is a set of transformation rules that together describe the conversion of one model in the source language into another related model in the target language [90]. Concerning MMTS+OTS, we distinguish between three aspects of transformations:

1. *Semantic.* The semantic aspect of a transformation differs between precise transformation and approximative transformations. Approximative transformations give up on soundness (rarely) or completeness (more often) in order to speed up subsequent querying or reasoning. Precise transformations are sound and complete.

2. *Syntactic.* We distinguish between (i) graph-based syntactic transformation, which draws on the theoretical work on graph transformations, operating on typed, attributed, labeled graphs (e.g., UMLX [179] and GReTL [71]); and (ii) hybrid syntactic transformations, which involve declarative and prescriptive notations. ATL [82] is an example of a hybrid language.

3. *Directionality.* Directionality concerns the generation of models in different directions based on the definition of a transformation. Bidirectional transformations are sufficient to transform forward and backward between source and target models. Examples include QVT and UMLX [179]. Unidirectional transformations allow for transformations in exactly one direction, such as ATL, in general.

A transformation language requires querying over a data model and transformation rules to manipulate the source and target metamodels. For example, an ATL transformation has a lexical notation, precise semantics, and hybrid syntax, and is composed by transformation rules using OCL as a query language over UML object models.

4.3.8 Mediation

Mediation is the process of reconciling differences between heterogeneous models. Mediation plays a central role in MMTS+OTS, as models in different languages must coexist. A mediation consists of:

1. *Integration.* Integration focuses on interoperability between models so that they work together effectively. It comprises:

   - *Aligning.* Aligning preserves the source models and produces a new model containing additional axioms to describe the relationship between the concepts from the source models.

   - *Merging.* Merging refers to the creation of one new merged model from two or more source models. The merging process can involve aligning as a step.

2. *Mapping.* Mappings are declarative specifications of the correspondences between elements of the two models. In the transformation process, the mapping specification precedes the transformation definition.

3. *Composition.* Composition comprises the combination of elements that conform to overlapping concepts in different source models. Usually, each source model handles a different dimension of the overlapping elements. A weaving process does not necessarily produce a merged mediation, but it can produce a model with new knowledge based on the source models.

Both integration and composition make use of mappings to specify overlaps. A transformation usually takes as input the source models and the mappings to generate the target models.

4.3.9 Modeling Level

Considering that "everything is a model" in model-driven engineering, these models are organized according to their conformance. Such an organization is defined by [13] as follows:

1. *System*: corresponding to the executable system, the runtime instances.

2. *Model*: defining the circumstances under which a system operates and evolves.

3. *Metamodel*: defining the constructs to design models.

4. *Metametamodel*: defining the constructs to design metamodels.

This organization corresponds to the OMG layered metamodel architecture: the metametamodel level (M3), the metamodel level (M2), the model level (M1), and the runtime instances (M0). Each modeling level is described using a language and is organized according to a data model (refer to Section 11.3.2 for an example of the OMG layered metamodel architecture).

Figure 4.4 shows a layered architecture of the features presented in this section according to the abstraction level. Each layer exploits facilities of the layers below. It shows how the features are organized to realize each of the technical spaces.

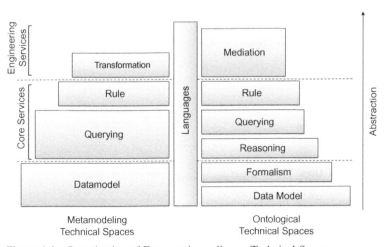

Figure 4.4 Organization of Features According to Technical Space.

4.4 THE STATE OF THE ART OF INTEGRATED APPROACHES

In this section, we apply the model presented in Section 4.3 to MMTS+OTS approaches found in the literature. As an example, we identify major categories that group related work. Each category corresponds to one configuration of our feature model.

4.4.1 Model Validation

This category assembles the works that use automated reasoning techniques for checking and validation of models in formal languages. It implies aligning the source model and the target model by a mapping. A *unidirectional transformation* approach takes the mapping and uses transformation rules to generate the models. Queries against a reasoner serve to verify the models.

Approaches for validating models verify specification against design. The description logics technical spaces, however, have specifically been defined to validate the *internal* consistency of a set of class definitions. To exploit this model of validation, one may transform a part of a given MDE-based model, e.g., a UML class diagram, into a set of OWL class definitions (cf. [12]) and one may check class hierarchy relationships, property hierarchies and the logical consistency of instantiating classes.

Berardi *et al.* [12] provide automated reasoning support for detecting relevant properties of UML class diagrams, e.g., implicit consequences, refinement of properties, and class equivalence. This work consists of aligning a UML class diagram (independent of modeling level) and a DL $\mathcal{ALCQI}$ knowledge base. A precise automatic unidirectional transformation generates an $\mathcal{ALCQI}$ knowledge base that corresponds to the UML class diagram.

We illustrate this process using the simple diagram depicted in the Figure 4.5. The diagram shows that a `WebPortalAccount` is a particular kind of `UserAccount` and that each `UserAccount` is owned by one and only one `User`. Additionally, there exist two types of users: `Researcher` and `Student`. A `Researcher` can have only one `WebPortalAccount`. The association class `Uses` specializes the association class Owns.

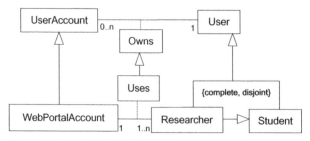

Figure 4.5   Checking Consistency of UML Models.

After applying the transformation from UML into a description logic model, such as OWL (more specifically, Berardi *et al.* [12] mapped it into $\mathcal{ALCQI}$), we ask the reasoner to verify the model. By reasoning over such a diagram, we discover undesirable characteristics. For instance, the class Researcher must be empty and, hence, cannot be instantiated. The reason is that the disjointness constraint asserts that there is no Researcher that is also Student. Furthermore, since the class User is made up by the union of classes Researcher and Student, and since Researcher is empty, the classes User and Student are equivalent, implying redundancy.

By dropping the generalization Student-Researcher, we arrive at a valid model. If we invoke the reasoner one more time, we can refine the multiplicity of the role Researcher in the association uses to *1*. Owns is a generalization of Uses, hence every link of Uses is a linkof Owns, and because Account is owned by exactly one User, necessarily every WebPortalAccount is used by at most one Researcher, since WebPortalAccount is a subclass of Account.

Straeten [165] proposes an approach to detect and resolve inconsistencies between versions of UML models, specified as a collection of class diagrams, sequence diagrams, and state diagrams. She presents a UML profile able to describe the evolution of the models.

Ren *et al.* [130] propose an approach for validating refinements of BPMN diagrams with OWL based on the execution set semantics. The OWL ontology serves to identify the invalid execution set in the refined BPMN diagram according to the abstract BPMN diagram.

The configuration of this category uses the following features (Figure 4.6): (i) a model at a given modeling level (model, metamodel, or metametamodel), written

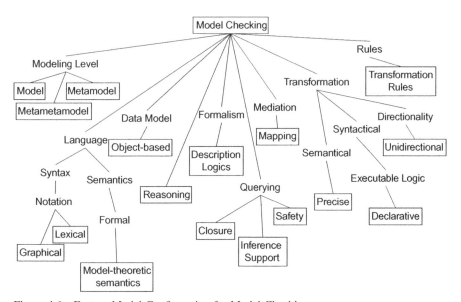

Figure 4.6   Feature Model Configuration for Model Checking.

in a graphical language, using an object data model; (ii) a target model, written in a language with model-theoretic semantics and lexical notation, including one formalism, reasoning capability, querying with closure, inference support, and safety; (iii) a mapping specification describing the links between the models; (iv) a unidirectional, declarative, and precise transformation definition, which includes transformation rules and querying.

4.4.2   Model Enrichment

This category comprises the approaches that make use of ontologies to infer knowledge from the MMTS models and convert these inferences back as facts in the new MMTS models. The main difference between this category and the former is the bidirectional transformation and the application of transformation rules and reasoning on the OTS side. First, the MMTS model is transformed into an OTS model. On the OTS side, inference services and transformation rules are used to make explicit the assertions that are implicit in the MMTS. Then, the resulting OTS model is transformed back.

Let us illustrate this process with an example of mappings between two MMTS models, depicted in the Figure 4.7. Let us assume that we have two models capturing bibliographical references. On the left side, we have the model Ma with the class Publication, which generalizes Article and Thesis, which generalizes MScThesis and PhDThesis. On the right side, we have the model Mb with the classes Entry and Thesis. At the center, we have the mapping Mab with the association

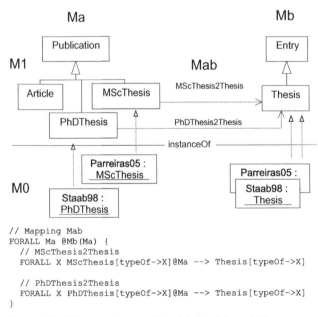

```
// Mapping Mab
FORALL Ma @Mb(Ma) {
  // MScThesis2Thesis
  FORALL X MScThesis[typeOf->X]@Ma --> Thesis[typeOf->X]

  // PhDThesis2Thesis
  FORALL X PhDThesis[typeOf->X]@Ma --> Thesis[typeOf->X]
}
```

Figure 4.7   Mapping between Two Models Ma and Mb.

class `MScThesis2Thesis`, mapping a `MScThesis` onto a `Thesis`, and the association class `PhDThesis2Thesis`, mapping a `PhDThesis` onto a `Thesis`.

After translating both models into RDF models, we can use TRIPLE [33], a RDF query, inference, and transformation language, to apply the transformation rules depicted in Figure 4.7, corresponding to the `MScThesis2Thesis` and `PhDThesis2Thesis` labels. This resulting query is translated back into MMTS model Mb.

The works that fit in this category have different facets. Billig *et al.* [15] use TRIPLE to generate mappings between a PIM and a PSM using a feature model that describes user requirements as input. It comprises a transformation from MMTS into OTS (TRIPLE), the generation of the mappings, the transformation into a PSM under OTS, and the transformation OTS to MMTS of the PSM. Roser and Bauer [135] propose a framework to automatically generate model transformations inside a MMTS using the OTS; Kappel *et al.* [86] provide an approach for model-based tool integration; it consists of transforming two MMTS metamodels into ontologies, using reasoning services and generating mapping between the two MMTS.

The configuration of features in this category includes (Figure 4.8): (i) a model at a given modeling level (model, metamodel, or metametamodel), written in a given language, using an object data model; (ii) a target model, written in a given logical language, reasoning capability, querying with closure, inference support, and safety; (iii) a mapping specification describing the links between the models; (iv) a bidirectional declarative transformation definition, which includes transformation rules and querying; and (v) logical rules and reasoning to make the knowledge explicit on the OTS side.

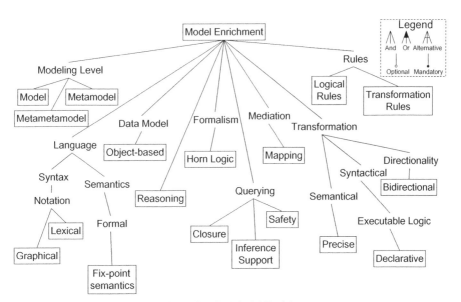

Figure 4.8   Feature Model Configuration for Model Enrichment.

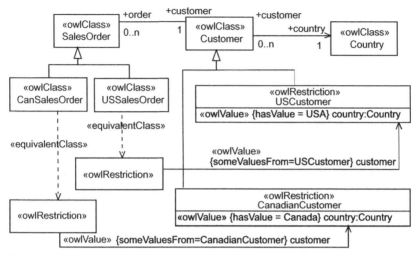

Figure 4.9   Ontology Modeling with UML Profile.

4.4.3   Ontology Modeling

This category assembles the efforts into giving a graphical notation to ontology modeling. Referring to our feature model, this category embraces the usage of MMTS graphical notations to design OTS ontologies. It requires integration, bidirectional transformation, the model level, transformation rules, and querying. It is the only one that does not involve reasoning.

Cranefield and Purvis [31] and Falkovych *et al.* [42] advocate the usage of UML without extensions as Ontology Representation Language capable of representing ontologies.

Extensions of the Unified Modeling Language for ontology development were proposed [10], culminating in a new metamodel into the MDA family of modeling languages – the Ontology Definition Metamodel [23, 114, 34]. These approaches use UML extension mechanisms (UML profile) to represent the ontology, a mapping onto the ODM, and a transformation from the ODM into the serialization syntax of the OWL ontology language. Figure 4.9 depicts the example of a UML class diagram representing an OWL ontology using the ODM UML profile for OWL.

The configuration of this category includes (Figure 4.10): (i) a model written in a given language with graphical notation from MMTS; (ii) a target model written in a given language and including one formalism from OTS; and (iii) a mapping specification describing the links between the models.

4.5   EXISTING WORK ON CLASSIFYING INTEGRATED APPROACHES

Research on the understanding of the large number of possible relations between OTS and MMTS is not new. Uschold and Jasper [171] propose a framework for understanding the ontology application scenarios outside the artificial intelligence

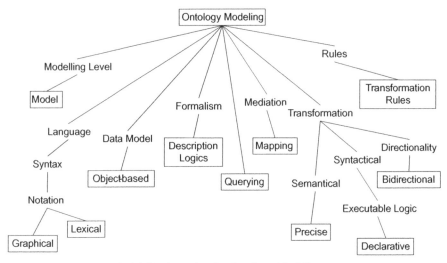

Figure 4.10   Feature Model Configuration for Ontology Modeling.

community. Despite presenting application scenarios of ontologies in software development, the work does not explore the domain modeling community within software engineering.

Tetlow *et al.* [168] propose ideas based on how semantic web technologies can be applied in systems and software engineering and examples of these ideas. Such work does not present a framework pointing out ways of integration. It serves as a research agenda instead, involving applications in the software engineering process.

Happel *et al.* [66] categorize ontologies in software engineering, distinguishing between four groups: ontology-driven development (ODD), ontology-enabled development (OED), ontology-based architectures (OBA), and ontology-enabled architectures (OEA). Our work takes a more detailed look at the ODD and OBA groups.

Bézivin *et al.* [14] bridge model engineering and ontology engineering using a M3-neutral infrastructure. They consider software engineering and ontology engineering as two similarly organized areas, based on different metametamodels (M3-level).

4.6   CONCLUSION

In this chapter, we have illustrated commonalities and variations of using metamodeling technical spaces (MMTS) with ontological technical spaces (OTS). The basic pattern is that, next to existing technical spaces of established metamodeling frameworks, new technical spaces are positioned that either enrich or exploit the software engineering capabilities by or for ontology technologies. We have identified the main characteristics of such approaches and designed a feature model to enlighten the possible conceptual choices. We have applied our model illustrating the usage of ontology technologies.

CONCLUSION OF PART I

In this part, we have used the concept of megamodeling to provide a descriptive model for specifying the structure of MDE approaches (research question I). We use this model to describe the relationship between concepts of MDE and ontologies. Moreover, we use the approach to specify the relations between metamodeling technical spaces and ontological technical spaces.

Additionally, we propose a classification for existing approaches that use MDE and ontologies and identify patterns for transformations between both paradigms, addressing the Research Questions I.A and I.B from Section 1.2. The analysis of existing work resulted in the identification of requirements for the integration of MDE and ontology technologies.

PART II

THE TWOUSE APPROACH

CHAPTER 5

THE TWOUSE CONCEPTUAL ARCHITECTURE

The next software engineering era will rely on the synergy between both model-driven engineering and ontology technologies. However, an approach that allows for exploiting the uniqueness of each paradigm has been missing so far. This chapter defines an integration between OWL and UML class-based modeling. It comprises an integration of existing metamodels and UML profiles, including relevant (sub) standards such as OCL. The result is a model-driven architecture for specifying integrated systems[1].

5.1 INTRODUCTION

UML class-based modeling and OWL comprise similar constituents: classes, associations, properties, packages, types, generalization, and instances [114]. Despite the similarities, both approaches come with restrictions that may be overcome by an integration.

On the one hand, a key limitation of UML class-based modeling is that it allows only for static specification of specialization and generalization of classes and relationships, whereas OWL provides mechanisms to define these in a dynamic fashion. In other words, OWL allows for recognition of generalization and specialization between classes as well as class membership of objects based on conditions imposed on the properties of class definitions.

On the other hand, UML provides means to specify dynamic behavior, whereas OWL does not. The Object Constraint Language (OCL) [116] complements UML by allowing the specification of query operations, derived values, constraints, and pre and post conditions.

Since both approaches provide complementary benefits, contemporary software development should make use of both. The benefits of an integration are twofold. Firstly, it provides software developers with additional modeling facilities.

---

[1]This chapter contains work from the paper "Using Ontologies with UML Class-based Modeling: The TwoUse Approach" published in the Journal Data & Knowledge Engineering [122].

Semantic Web and Model-Driven Engineering, First Edition. Fernando Silva Parreiras.
© 2012 Institute of Electrical and Electronics Engineers. Published 2012 by John Wiley & Sons, Inc.

Secondly, it enables semantic software developers to use object-oriented concepts like operation and polymorphism together with ontologies in a platform independent way. These considerations have led us to investigate the following challenge: How can we develop and denote models that benefit from advantages of the two modeling paradigms?

We present TwoUse in this chapter as follows: Section 5.2 describes the requirements for integrating ontology technologies and model-driven engineering. Section 5.3 presents and explains the building blocks of TwoUse. In Section 5.4 we present the metamodeling infrastructure for UML class-based models and OWL. In Section 5.5, we describe the notations for designing TwoUse models.

5.2 REQUIREMENTS FOR INTEGRATING ONTOLOGY TECHNOLOGIES AND MODEL-DRIVEN ENGINEERING

Section 4.4 presents in the state-of-the-art research and MDE approaches that use OWL technologies and *vice versa*. However, the relationships between the two paradigms are still under exploration. In this section, we present the requirements for an integrated framework. These requirements are extended and refined in Part III and Part IV, where we present the case studies.

5.2.1 Usage of Ontology Services in MDE

In addition to model validation and model enrichment, ontology technologies have more to offer. The integration between MDE and ontology technologies enables extending UML class-based modeling with OWL constructs and using ontology services to support the MDE process.

5.2.1.1 *Integrate OWL Constructs in UML Class-Based Modeling* While mappings from one modeling paradigm to the other one were established a while ago (see Section 4.4.1), the task of an integrated language for UML class-based modeling and OWL models is missing so far.

Such an approach simplifies the modeling task by introducing intuitive constructs that require complex OCL expressions otherwise, and it enables the definition of domain models enriched by formal class descriptions. Moreover, the usage of OWL class expressions allows decoupling class selection from the definition of query operations in client classes.

Such an integration is not only intriguing because of the heterogeneity of the two modeling approaches, but it is now a strict requirement to allow for the development of software with thousands of ontology classes and multiple dozens of complex software modules in the realms of medical informatics [108], multimedia [159], or engineering applications [160].

5.2.1.2 *Usage of Ontology Services in UML Class-Based Modeling* In addition to integrating OWL constructs in UML class-based modeling, the usage of ontology services (see Section 3.4) is essential for realizing the potential of ontology

technologies. Therefore, one requires model transformations that transform integrated models into OWL ontologies.

Moreover, the integration between UML class-based modeling and OWL needs to cover the usage of ontology services at runtime as well as in design time. Thus, developers specify queries that use ontology services over the OWL representation. These queries are the interface between users and ontology services. The results generated by ontology services should be compatible with existing languages used to operate UML class-based models, e.g., OCL.

The intended benefit is that developers will not have to program by having to enumerate actions class-by-class. Instead they will rely on the ontology engine to perform generic operations to retrieve classes that satisfy ontological relationships with other classes, so that developers can focus only on the application specific actions.

5.2.2   Usage of MDE Techniques in OWL Ontology Engineering

5.2.2.1   *MDE Support for Ontology Modeling*   Research on ontology engineering has been inspired by the advances in software engineering over the years. For example, current approaches (see 4.4.3) use the graphical notation of UML to design OWL ontologies to support the ontology development life cycle. Moreover, as in software engineering, the usage of design patterns in ontology engineering is an established practice [52].

As new modeling techniques in model-driven engineering emerge, it is desirable to analyze the application of MDE techniques in ontology modeling. For example, the usage of domain-specific modeling is a promising approach for improving the usability of the OWL language by providing users with syntactical shortcuts. Moreover, the usage of templates in UML class-based modeling for reusing pieces of models is an accepted practice for improving reusability.

5.2.2.2   *Usage of Domain Specific Modeling for Ontology Engineering Services*   Currently, the development of ontology engineering services needs to manage multiple languages for defining services. For example, modelers of ontology matching services need to manage different languages: (1) an ontology translation language to specify translation rules and (2) a programming language to specify built-ins, when the ontology translation language does not provide constructs to completely specify a given translation rule. This intricate and disintegrated manner draws their attention away from the alignment task proper down into diverging technical details of the translation model.

Addressing this issue allows developers to concentrate on constructs related to the problem domain, raising the abstraction level. Moreover, by defining domain concepts as first-class citizens, developers may reuse these domain concepts in different situations. This helps to improve productivity, since modelers will not have to be aware of platform-specific details and will be able to exchange translation models even when they use different ontology translation platforms.

5.3 ADDRESSING THE REQUIREMENTS WITH THE TWOUSE APPROACH

We build the TwoUse approach based on four core ideas:

1. As abstract syntax, it provides an integrated *MOF-based metamodel* as a common backbone for UML class-based modeling and OWL modeling (Section 5.4).

2. As concrete syntax, it uses pure UML, Ecore, a *UML profile* supporting standard UML2 extension mechanisms, and a textual concrete syntax to write integrated models (Section 5.5).

3. It provides a canonical *set of transformation rules* in order to deal with integration at the semantic level.

4. It provides a novel SPARQL-like language to write queries and constraints over OWL ontologies, SPARQLAS (Chapter 6).

To give an idea of the target integration, let us consider the simple example of E-Shop (see Figure 2.8). Instead of defining the operation getTypes() in the class SalesOrder using OCL, a more transparent and maintainable solution will use the expressiveness of the OWL language. Using the querying service, a query retrieves the OWL subclasses of SalesOrder according to the logical requirements of a given instance. The body of the getTypes() operation will then be specified by:

```
context SalesOrder
  def getTypes():Set(Class)
    ?self type ?T
    ?T subClassOf SalesOrder
```

As specified above, to identify which subclasses are applicable, we use the variable ?T to get all types of ?self that are subclasses of SalesOrder. We explain these and other expressions in Section 6.3.

The usage of the variable ?self means that at the implementation level, we consistently correlate class instances with individuals in the ontology. That is, for every object in the system, we generate a corresponding individual in the ontology. As the classification of these individuals depends on structural relationships between objects, we need to update the individual information whenever changes in the object state occur.

The advantage of this integrated formulation of getTypes() lies in separating two sources of specification complexity. First, the classification of complex classes remains in an OWL model. The classification is re-useable for specifying other operations, and it may be maintained using diagram visualizations as well as decidable, yet rigorous reasoning models. Second, the specification of the business logic itself remains in OCL specifications. It becomes smaller, more understandable, and easier to maintain.

Figure 5.1 presents a model-driven view of the TwoUse approach. TwoUse uses UML profiles for class diagrams and textual notations for designing combined

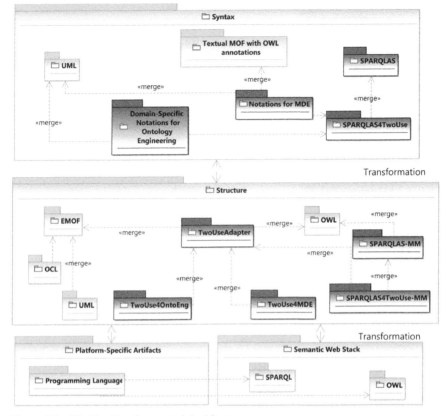

Figure 5.1   The TwoUse Conceptual Architecture.

models (Syntax). These notations are input for model transformations that generate TwoUse models conforming to the TwoUse metamodel (Structure). The TwoUse metamodel provides the abstract syntax for the TwoUse approach. Further model transformations take TwoUse models and generate the OWL ontology and Java code (Platform-Specific Artifacts and the Semantic Web Stack).

We correlate the building blocks in Figure 5.1 with the requirements presented in Section 5.2 to show how TwoUse realizes the integration of MDE and ontology technologies. Table 5.1 depicts a traceability matrix and correlates the requirements (columns) with the building blocks (rows).

Extended languages for MDE (syntax and structure) and the TwoUse adapter allow for using OWL constructs in UML class-based modeling, whereas the SPARQLAS language enables the usage of ontology services. Domain-specific languages and the TwoUse adapter realizes the usage of MDE techniques for supporting ontology engineering.

TABLE 5.1 Correlating Building Blocks with Requirements.

Requirements vs. Building Blocks	OWL Constructs in UML Class-Based Modeling (5.2.1.1)	Ontology Services in UML Class-based Modeling (5.2.1.2)	MDE Support for Ontology Modeling (5.2.2.1)	Domain Modeling for Ontology Engineering Services (5.2.2.2)
Notations for MDE	X			
Domain-Specific Notations for Ontology Engineering				X
SPARQLAS		X		
SPARQLAS4TwoUse		X		
TwoUseAdapter	X	X	X	X
TwoUse4OntoEng			X	X
TwoUse4MDE	X	X		
SPARQLAS-MM		X	X	
SPARQLAS4TwoUse-MM		X	X	

5.4 METAMODELING ARCHITECTURE

In this section, we describe the concepts with respect to the integration of UML class-based modeling and OWL in the form of metamodels. The advantages of having an integrated metamodel are threefold:

- It enables the verification of well-formed models integrating both paradigms.
- It provides a common structure for supporting multiple notations.
- It realizes the mapping between UML class-based constructs and OWL constructs.

5.4.1 The TwoUse Metamodel

The TwoUse metamodel provides the abstract syntax integrating UML class-based modeling, OWL, and a SPARQL-like query language. The abstract syntax provides an abstraction over the concrete syntax notations used in TwoUse.

The TwoUse metamodel provides the integration between common constructs in OWL and UML class-based modeling: package, class, property, instance, and datatype. Basically, we compose classes from the Ecore metamodel with classes from the OWL metamodel.

We use model adaptation as a composition technique to integrate the OWL metamodel and the Ecore metamodel. This consists of applying the Object Adapter

Pattern [51] to *adapt* classes of the OWL metamodel to corresponding classes of the Ecore metamodel (see Table 4.2 for common features between UML class-based modeling and OWL). The Object Adapter Pattern allows us to compose objects within *Adapters*, called TwoUse classes.

Following the nomenclature of Gamma *et al.* [51], *Target* classes represent the interfaces from the Ecore metamodel (EPackage, EClass, EDatatype, EAttribute, EReference, EEnum, EEnumLiteral, and EObject). *Adapter* classes are prefixed with TU and suffixed with Adapter (TUPackageAdapter, TUClassAdapter, TU-DatatypeAdapter, TUAttributeAdapter, TUReferenceAdapter, TUEnumAdapter, TUEnumLiteralAdapter, and TUObjectAdapter). *Adaptee* classes are classes of the OWL 2 metamodel.

Figure 5.2 illustrates the principle of model adaptation. We adapt the class Class from the OWL 2 metamodel for the class EClass from the Ecore metamodel. In the class TUClassAdapter, we implement the operations defined in the class Ecore::EClass.

For example, the class Ecore::EClass defines the operation addAttribute for inserting attributes into a class. The class TUClassAdapter implements this

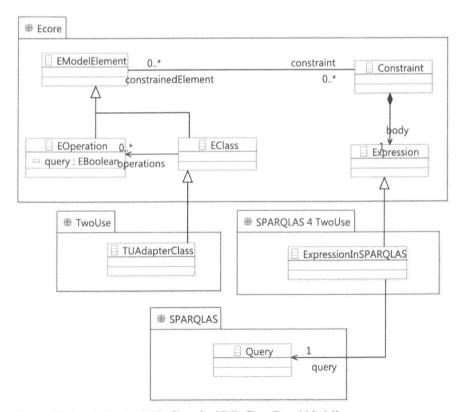

Figure 5.2   Adapting the OWL Class for UML Class-Based Modeling.

LISTING 5.1 Implementing the Operation `addAttribute` in the Class `TUClassAdapter`.

```
1 public Void addAttribute(Attribute attribute) {
        // DataPropertyDomain
        DataPropertyDomain dpd = owl2fsFactory
                        .createDataPropertyDomain();
5       dpd.setDataPropertyExpression(attribute.getName());
        dpd.setDomain(eclass.getName());
        ...
        // DataPropertyRange
10      DataPropertyRange dpr = owl2fsFactory
                        .createDataPropertyRange();
        dpr.setDataPropertyExpression(attribute.getName());
        dpr.setRange(attribute.getEAttributeType().getName());
        ...
15
      attributes.add(attribute);
  }
```

operation as described in Listing 5.1. The implementation creates instances of the OWL 2 metamodel corresponding to the mappings between UML class-based modeling and OWL. In this example, for the addition of an attribute in a class in UML class-based modeling, we need to create two OWL axioms: one asserting the domain of the dataproperty and another asserting the range of the dataproperty.

Figure 5.3 depicts the mappings for the TwoUse metamodel using a simplified notation that associates the interfaces in the UML class-based metamodel to the corresponding concepts in the OWL 2 metamodel. As we have mentioned, this integration is independent of metamodeling level, i.e., it works for MOF, UML, and any UML-class based modeling systems.

5.5 SYNTAX

5.5.1 UML Profile for OWL

The TwoUse approach provides developers with UML profiling as concrete syntax for simultaneous design of UML models and OWL ontologies, exploiting the full expressiveness of OWL ($\mathcal{SROIQ}$(D)) and allowing usage of existing UML2 tools. We reuse the UML profile for OWL proposed by OMG [114] and introduce stereotypes to label integrated classes.

We use the UML profile for OWL proposed by OMG [114] for designing OWL ontologies using UML notation. We call the UML class diagram with elements

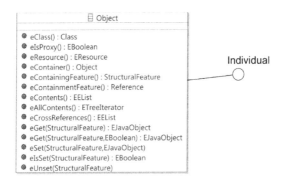

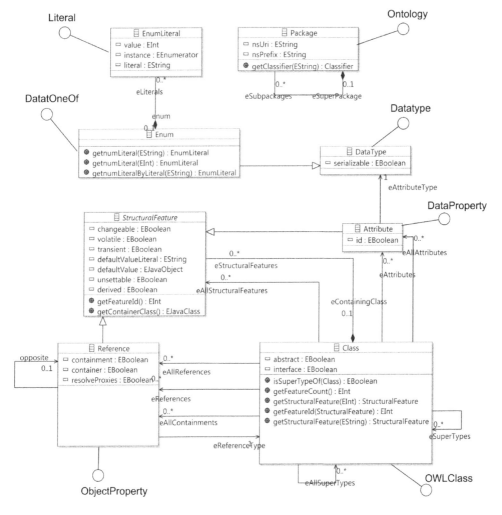

Figure 5.3   The OWL 2 Metamodel Adapted for the UML Class-Based Metamodel—the TwoUse Metamodel.

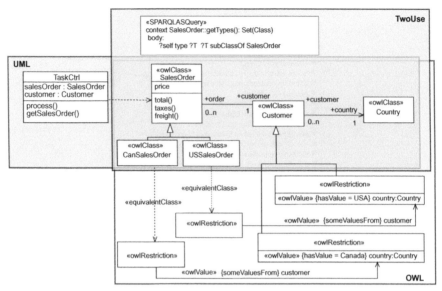

Figure 5.4   UML Class Diagram Profiled with UML Profile for OWL and TwoUse Profile.

stereotyped by a UML profile for OWL a *hybrid diagram*. The hybrid diagram comprises three viewpoints, illustrated in the Figure 5.4: (1) the UML view, including OCL, (2) the OWL view and its logical class definitions, and (3) the TwoUse view, which integrates UML classes and OWL classes and, relying on SPARQLAS, defines query operations that use ontology services (Chapter 6).

Considering the example of E-Shop (Figure 5.4), the OWL view consists of nine classes, five of which are named classes and four are unnamed classes. The restriction classes are required for reasoning on the subclasses USSalesOrder and CanSalesOrder. The UML View comprises six classes. The TwoUse view will contain five classes and the SPARQLAS query operation.

A TwoUse class is the bridge that links OWL elements with SPARQLAS expressions. To be compatible with tools that support UML2 extension mechanisms, developers annotate the UML element OpaqueBehavior with the stereotype ≪SPARQLASQuery≫ and define the SPARQLAS query as the body of the opaque behavior.

Table 5.2 illustrates the mappings between the UML profile for OWL (hybrid diagram) and the TwoUse metamodel. Any class that has the stereotype ≪owlClass≫ in the hybrid diagram is mapped onto a TwoUse class. Any class with the stereotype ≪owlRestriction≫ and its properties ≪datatypeProperty≫ or ≪objectProperty≫ are mapped onto OWL classes and properties. Any class without any stereotype results in a regular class (Ecore::EClass). A TwoUse package is any package that has TwoUse classes. The UML Opaque behaviors stereotyped as ≪SPARQLASQuery≫ are mapped onto SPARQLAS.

TABLE 5.2 Mapping between the UML Profile for OWL (Hybrid Diagram) and the TwoUse Metamodel.

UML Class Diagram	TwoUse Metamodel
UML Package	TUPackageAdapter
UML Class	Ecore::Class
(owlClass)UMLClass	TUClassAdapter
(owlRestriction)UMLClass	OWL::Class
(owlRestriction)UMLClass.(datatypePropert) UMLProperty	OWL::DataProperty
(owlRestriction)UMLClass.(objectProperty) UMLProperty	OWL::ObjectProperty
(owlClass)UMLClass.(owlDataProperty)UMLProperty	TUAttributeAdapter
(owlClass)UMLClass.(owlObjectProperty) UMLProperty	TUReferenceAdapter
(owlIndividual)InstanceSpecification	TUObjectAdapter
(dataRange)Enumeration	TUEnumAdapter

5.5.2 Pure UML Class Diagrams

We have explored additional notations with increasing expressiveness, presented next. In addition to the UML Profile for TwoUse, one may use the pure UML class diagram notation to model OWL ontologies with SPARQLAS expressions at class operations or use a textual syntax to design class-based models with OWL descriptions.

To let UML2 users develop ontology-based information systems, pure UML class diagrams may be used. Developers who do not need the full expressiveness of OWL can use this approach without having to handle the OWL syntax.

Model transformations transform the UML class diagram into a TwoUse model to support SPARQLAS expressions over the OWL translation of the UML class diagram. In this case, developers attach SPARQLAS expressions to the body of opaque behavior of class operations. Each UML class will be a TUClassAdapter. For transforming UML class diagrams into ontologies, we follow the rules defined in [114].[2]

5.5.3 Textual Notation

As an alternative to graphical languages, we have defined a textual notation for specifying UML class-based models together with OWL. This approach is useful

---

[2]In this case, the expressiveness of the generated OWL ontology is limited to the description logic $\mathcal{ALCOIQ}(\mathcal{D})$, since $\mathcal{DLR}_{ifd}$ is not supported by state-of-the-art DL-based reasoning systems [12].

for experienced developers who work more productively with textual languages than visual languages.

In the following, we illustrate the textual notation with our running example. Again, each class is a TUClassAdapter. In this case, the textual notation allows for exploring the full expressiveness of OWL. The textual notation is a combination of the Java-like syntax and the OWL Manchester Syntax [74] (see Appendix A.1 for the EBNF grammar).

```
1  package PurchaseOrder // package name
           PurchaseOrder // namespace prefix
           "http://org.example/PurchaseOrder. ecore" //
   namespace URI
           {
5
           class TaskCtrl {
                   reference SalesOrder salesOrder (0..-1);
                   reference Customer customer (0..-1);

10                 operation process();
           }
           class SalesOrder {
                   attribute EFloat price (0..1);
15
                   reference Customer customer (1..1) opposite orders;
                   operation EClass (0..-1) getTypes();
                   operation EFloat total();
20                 operation EFloat taxes();
                   operation EFloat freight();
               }
           class CanSalesOrder extends SalesOrder [equivalentTo
               [SalesOrder and [customer some [country value CANADA]]]
                   {}
25
           class USSalesOrder extends SalesOrder [equivalentTo
               [SalesOrder and [customer some [country value USA]]]] {}

           class Customer {
               reference SalesOrder orders (0..-1) opposite
                   customer;
30             reference Country country (1..1);
           }
           enum Country {
                   1 : USA = "USA";
35                 2 : Canada = "Canada";
           }
       }
```

The textual notation uses constructs familiar to programmers and enables developers to write class descriptions in a human readable way.

5.6 CONCLUSION

In this chapter, we have introduced a technique for integrating existing UML class-based metamodels and OWL metamodels. We describe the usage of the adapter design pattern to compose similar constructs between the OWL 2 metamodel and the Ecore metamodel. Moreover, we have defined notations for creating integrated models. As we apply our approach in Parts III and IV, we will extend the integrated metamodel according to application requirements.

CHAPTER 6

QUERY LANGUAGES FOR INTEGRATED MODELS

After providing a unified view of metamodels and addressing the integration of modeling languages in the previous chapter, this chapter describes a querying approach to support developers in querying integrated models. We examine a combination of existing approaches and introduce our solution for querying integrated models.[1]

6.1 INTRODUCTION

To exploit integrated models, it is important to enable engineers with the proper tools to manage and understand models. An important service for developers to gain insight into their models and to manage models is integrated querying.

In order to be able to query integrated models, a query framework needs to be integrated on the metamodeling level. A querying framework provides engineers with support for using existing approaches and for addressing modeling decisions.

In this chapter, we investigate the possibilities for querying elements of the combined metamodel in a flexible manner using or combining existing languages.

The chapter is structured as follows: in Section 6.2, we analyze the combination of existing query languages for UML class-based modeling and OWL. In Section 6.3, we present a concise query language for querying OWL ontologies: SPARQLAS. We extend SPARQLAS for supporting integrated models in Section 6.4: SPARQLAS4TwoUse.

6.2 COMBINING EXISTING APPROACHES

The OCL language provides the definition of functions and the usage of built-in functions for defining query operations in UML class diagrams, whereas SPARQLDL provides a powerful language to query resources in OWL ontologies, allowing for retrieval of concepts, properties, and individuals. While OCL assumes Unique Name Assumption (UNA) OWL may mimic it using constructs like `owl:AllDifferent` and `owl:distinctMembers`.

---

[1]This chapter contains work from EU STReP MOST Deliverable D1.2 "Report on Querying the Combined Metamodel" [81] and of the paper "Using Ontologies with UML Class-Based Modeling: The TwoUse Approach" published in the Data & Knowledge Engineering Journal [122].

Semantic Web and Model-Driven Engineering, First Edition. Fernando Silva Parreiras.

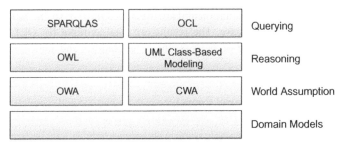

Figure 6.1   Existing Approaches for Querying Models.

A combination of existing languages reflects configurations for querying integrated models. Figure 6.1 presents an architecture for querying integrated models. These configurations can be realized by adopting current approaches or combining different assumptions and reasoning services. We describe these configurations in the following sections.

Using SPARQL over OWL with OWA.   Among existing RDF-based query languages for the semantic web, SPARQL is the W3C recommendation. It is based on triples patterns and allows for querying the vocabulary and the assertions of a given domain.

Restrictions on the SPARQL language, i.e., entailment regimes, allow for querying OWL ontologies, including TBox, RBox, and ABox. One implementation is SPARQL-DL [154] (see Section 3.4.2.2 for a description of SPARQL-DL).

SPARQL-DL enables querying OWL ontologies using the Open World Assumption. It is currently available with the Pellet Reasoner [155].

Using SPARQL over OWL with CWA.   Polleres et al. [124] have explored the usage of the SPARQL language in combination with closed-world reasoning in SPARQL++. SPARQL++ extends SPARQL by supporting aggregate functions and built-ins. SPARQL++ queries can be formalized in HEX Programs or description logic programs. However, SPARQL++ covers only a subset of RDF(S) and how it can be extended towards OWL is still an open issue.

Using OCL over UML Class-Based Modeling with CWA.   This is the standard application of OCL as a query language. Query operations may be defined and used as helpers for OCL queries and constraints. Default values as well as initial and derived values can be defined by using UML and OCL.

Using OCL and SPARQL over OWA and UML Class-Based Modeling.   In some cases, a combination of UML class-based modeling and OWL is desired, e.g., for defining complex class descriptions or reusing existing ones. To make use of behavioral features like query operations, helpers, and built-ins, UML class-based modeling comes into play.

In the next section, we present our approach for such a combination. Our approach allows for describing query operations using SPARQL-like syntax. Query operations are written in SPARQL-like notation and are translated into SPARQL and executed against an OWL knowledge base. The results are used as input for OCL query operations that allows the usage of helpers, query operations and built-ins defined in OCL.

6.3 QUERYING ONTOLOGIES USING OWL SYNTAX: SPARQLAS

Writing SPARQL queries for OWL can be time-consuming for those who work with OWL ontologies, since OWL is not triple-based and requires reification of axioms when using a triple-based language.

Therefore, we propose SPARQLAS, a language that allows for specifying queries over OWL ontologies with the OWL syntax [143]. SPARQLAS uses the OWL Functional Syntax as well as OWL 2 Manchester Syntax and allows using variables wherever an entity (`Class`, `ObjectProperty`, `DataProperty`, `NamedIndividual`) or a literal is allowed.

We will illustrate the SPARQLAS concrete syntax with examples in Section 6.3.1, present the main classes of the SPARQLAS metamodel in Section 6.3.2, and exemplify the transformation of SPARQLAS into SPARQL in Section 6.3.3.

6.3.1 SPARQLAS Concrete Syntax

For creating SPARQLAS queries, we adopt the existing standard concrete syntax notations for OWL 2. Users can write SPARQLAS queries using the OWL 2 Functional Syntax [106] or the OWL 2 Manchester-like Syntax [74]. Appendix A.3 and Appendix A.2 specify the EBNF grammar for both notations.

Listing 6.1 and Listing 6.2 present the same query using the two different notations. The query results in all subclasses of a class that have, as the value of the property `customer`, a customer who lives in `USA`.

LISTING 6.1 Example of SPARQLAS Query with Functional Syntax.

```
 1 Namespace ( = <http://www.example.org/customer#> )
   Select ?x
   Where (
     SubClassOf (
 5      ?x
        ObjectSomeValuesFrom(
            customer
            ObjectIntersectionOf(
              Customer
10            ObjectHasValue(country USA)
            )
        )
     )
   )
```

LISTING 6.2   Example of SPARQLAS Query with Manchester-like Syntax.

```
1 Namespace: <http://www.example.org/customer#>
  Select ?x
  Where: ?x subClassOf (customer some (Customer and (country value
         USA)))
```

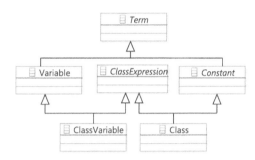

Figure 6.2   Variables in the SPARQLAS Metamodel.

Since SPARQLAS copes with the OWL 2 syntax, it does not provide support for SPARQL solution sequences and modifiers (ORDER BY, OFFSET) or optional values (OPTIONAL). Schneider [143] presents an analysis of these constructs and the details about the mappings between SPARQLAS and SPARQL.

6.3.2   SPARQLAS Metamodel

The SPARQLAS metamodel extends the OWL 2 metamodel [106] for including support for variables. Figure 6.2 depicts the additional classes in the SPARQLAS metamodel used for supporting the usage of variables. In the appendix, Figure A.1 depicts the complete SPARQLAS metamodel.

The class Variable is a term that has a symbol as property, which represents the variable (e.g., ?x). Specializations of the class Variable define the existing variable types: ClassVariable, ObjectPropertyVariable, DataPropertyVariable, IndividualVariable and LiteralVariable. All these classes extend the class Variable and the corresponding class in the OWL 2 metamodel. For example, the class ClassVariable extends the class Variable as well as the class ClassExpression. Therefore, users can use variables whenever class expressions fit.

6.3.3   Transformation from SPARQLAS to SPARQL

SPARQLAS queries are translated into SPARQL queries to be executed by SPARQL engines that support graph pattern matching for OWL 2 entailment regime [55]. The

LISTING 6.3 SPARQL Query Generated from the SPARQLAS Query.

```
1  PREFIX rdf: <http://www.w3.org/1999/02/22-rdf-syntax-ns#>
   PREFIX rdfs: <http://www.w3.org/2000/01/rdf-schema#>
   PREFIX owl: <http://www.w3.org/2002/07/owl#>
   PREFIX xsd: <http://www.w3.org/2001/XMLSchema#>
5  PREFIX : <http://www.example.org/customer#>
   SELECT DISTINCT ?x
   WHERE {
       ?x rdfs:subClassOf [
10           rdf:type owl:Restriction ;
             owl:onProperty :customer ;
             owl:someValuesFrom [
                   rdf:type owl:Class ;
                   owl:intersectionOf [
15                      rdf:first :Customer ;
                        rdf:rest [
                           rdf:first [
                                rdf:type owl:Restriction ;
                                owl:onProperty :country ;
20                              owl:hasValue :USA
                                ];
                           rdf:rest rdf:nil
                           ]
                        ]
25                  ]
                ]
         }
```

model transformation comprises the implementation of the mappings from the OWL 2 structural specification to RDF Graphs (please consult [123] for the list of mappings).

For the sake of illustration, Listing 6.3 presents the corresponding SPARQL query for the SPARQLAS query defined in Listing 6.1 and 6.2. The SPARQL syntax uses triples to reify class expressions defined in the SPARQLAS queries.

6.4 QUERYING INTEGRATED MODELS: SPARQLAS4TWOUSE

An adaptation of SPARQLAS allows for defining the body of query operations in integrated models using an OWL-like language. Such an approach enables users to use ontology services integrated with UML class-based modeling, as depicted in the Figure 5.4.

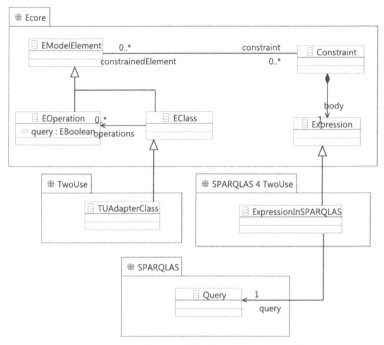

Figure 6.3   Composing the SPARQLAS Metamodel and the TwoUse Metamodel.

LISTING 6.4   Example of SPARQLAS Query with Manchester-like Syntax.

```
1 context SalesOrder::getCustomer() : Customer
  Namespace: <http://www.example.org/customer#>
  Select ?c
  Where: ?self :customer ?c
```

For this purpose, we need first to compose the TwoUse metamodel with the SPARQLAS metamodel. Figure 6.3 depicts the navigation from the class TU-AdapterClass to the query definition SPARQLAS::Query. The TUAdapterClass extends the EClass, which contains operations. An operation extends a model element that contains constraints. A constraint contains a body as an expression. The ExpressionInSPARQLAS defines a SPARQLAS Query.

The Variable **?self**.   Unlike in SPARQLAS, the expressions are written in the context of an instance of a specific class in SPARQLAS4TwoUse. We use the same rationale as OCL and reserve the variable ?self for referring to the contextual instance. For example, the SPARQLAS4TwoUse query in Listing 6.4 evaluates to John if the contextual instance of the class SalesOrder is ORDER1 (see Table 3.2 for the running example).

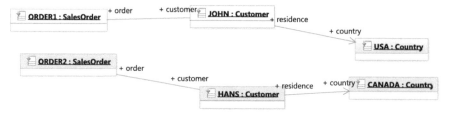

Figure 6.4   Snapshot of the Running Example.

TABLE 6.1   Evaluation of SPARQLAS Expressions According to the Running Example Snapshot.

	ORDER1	ORDER2
?self type SalesOrder	true	true
?self type USSalesOrder	true	false
?self type ?C	SalesOrder, USSalesOrder	SalesOrder, CanSalesOrder
?self inverse order ?c	John	Hans
?self directType ?C	USSalesOrder	CanSalesOrder

SPARQLAS queries operate on the modeling layer (M) as well as on the snapshot layer (M-1). In the Figure 6.4, we present an object diagram representing a possible snapshot for the running example.

The result of SPARQLAS queries is mapped from OWL onto UML class-based modeling, i.e., although all OWL expressions like property chains and universal quantification can be used to write SPARQLAS queries, only classes, instances, and literals can be delivered as the result.

Table 6.1 presents results of evaluating SPARQLAS expressions considering the snapshot depicted in Figure 6.4. We take two objects of the snapshot (ORDER1, ORDER2) and bind them to the predefined variable self. For example, for the expression ?self type SalesOrder where ?self is bound to ORDER1, the result is true.

Since the results of SPARQLAS4TwoUse queries are transformed back from OWL into UML class-based modeling, the results can be used by OCL expressions that utilize query operations defined in SPARQLAS4TwoUse. For example, the OCL expression self.getTypes().size(); evaluates to 3 if the contextual instances are ORDER1 (Thing, SalesOrder, USSalesOrder). Consequently, OCL expressions can use query operations defined in SPARQLAS4TwoUse as input (see Figure 6.5).

6.5   CONCLUSION

This chapter analyzes how current approaches can serve to query UML class-based modeling and OWL and possible combinations. The query languages SPARQLAS

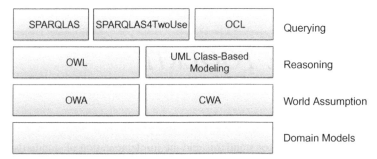

Figure 6.5   Positioning SPARQLAS4TwoUse among Existing Approaches.

and OCL may be used according to different requirements to query OWL and UML class-based modeling, respectively.

The adaptation of SPARQLAS, SPARQLAS4TwoUse, allows the definition of query operations for TwoUse classes that rely on ontology reasoning services. The combination of OCL and SPARQLAS4TwoUse allows for using the results of ontology reasoning services as input of OCL queries.

CHAPTER 7

THE TWOUSE TOOLKIT

The gap between the specification of standards and the implementation of standards in a programming language leads to adaptation penalties when new versions are available. Among the possible solutions for raising the level of abstraction from code to standard specification, a framework that allows the integration of multiple standards at the design level is so far lacking. This chapter presents a generic architecture for designing artifacts using multiple standard languages, turning the focus from code-centric to transformation-centric. We test this architecture by instantiating its conceptual blocks in an integrated development environment—the TwoUse Toolkit.[1]

7.1 INTRODUCTION

Although integrating ontology technologies and software engineering has gained more attention, practitioners still lack tool support. And though guidelines for model transformations and implementations of these transformations exist, these still is not a comprehensive framework dedicated to fill the gap between model-driven engineering and ontology technologies. Ontology engineering environments [101] exclusively support ontology development and do not provide support for OMG standards.

Providing a framework for integrating MDE and ontology technologies requires dealing with the following challenges:

- Seamless integration between UML class-based modeling languages and OWL. Developers should be able to design models seamlessly in different formats like Ecore, UML, XML, and OWL.

- Modeling design patterns. Integrated frameworks should provide developers with capabilities for reusing existing knowledge from other projects in the form of design patterns.

- Integration with existing standard and recommendations such as SWRL [76] and OCL [116]. Developers should be able to work with semantic web languages (OWL, SWRL, and SPARQL) as well as with software languages (UML and OCL).

---

[1]This chapter contains work from the tool demonstration "Filling the Gap between the Semantic Web and Model-Driven Engineering: The TwoUse Toolkit" at ECMFA2010 [147].

Semantic Web and Model-Driven Engineering, First Edition. Fernando Silva Parreiras.

In this chapter, we present a generic architecture to implement OWL-related standard specifications and model-driven techniques in an integrated engineering tool, turning the focus from code-centric to transformation-centric. It comprises a set of model transformations, graphical and textual editors, and reasoning services.

We organize this chapter as follows. In Section 7.2, we describe the use cases for such an architecture based on the requirements specified in Section 5.2 and correlate use cases and requirements in Section B.2. We describe the generic architecture in Section 7.3. In Section 7.4, we describe an instantiation of the generic architecture for development of model-driven applications and ontology-based information systems—the TwoUse Toolkit.

7.2   USE CASE DESCRIPTIONS

In Section 5.2, we present the requirements for an integrated approach. Figure 7.1 depicts the use cases (UC) to address those requirements. It gives an overview of actors and their relation to the use cases. Appendix B.1 presents the description of these use-cases.

Designing integrated UML class diagrams or integrated Ecore models (UC Design Integrated Model) enables the integration of OWL constructs in UML class-based modeling. By specifying SPARQLAS4TwoUse query operations at classes (UC Specify Query Operations), software engineers can define queries over ontologies and thus use classification and realization to improve software quality (see case studies 8 and 9). Moreover, when ontology engineers transform Ecore-based models and metamodels into OWL (UC Transform to OWL), it allows the usage of explanation (UC Explain Axiom), querying (UC Query UML class-based models) and ontology matching (UC Compute Alignments) for supporting software engineers in debugging and maintenance.

The Usage of SPARQLAS for querying OWL ontologies applies the principles of MDE (domain-specific modeling and model transformation) to enable ontology engineers to write SPARQL queries without having to deal with the reification of OWL axiom in RDF triples (UC Query OWL ontologies). Moreover, the design and generation of ontology engineering services (UC Design Ontology Engineering Service) counts on domain-specific modeling and model transformation to generate platform-specific artifacts and raises the level of abstraction (see case studies 11, 12, and 13).

7.3   A GENERIC ARCHITECTURE FOR MDE AND ONTOLOGY ENGINEERING

The architecture of an integrated environment for OWL modeling and UML class-based modeling serves as a guideline for the development of artifacts for ontology engineering that use model-driven technologies and artifacts for model-driven engineering that use ontology technologies. It comprises a layered view according to the

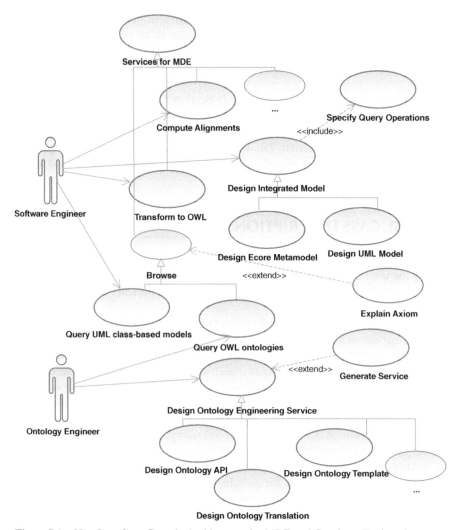

Figure 7.1   Use Case for a Generic Architecture for MDE and Ontology Engineering.

degree of abstraction of the components. Components of higher layers invoke components of lower layers.

Figure 7.2 depicts the generic architecture for developing integrated artifacts. It comprises a set of core services, services for ontology engineering, services for MDE, and a front-end layer.

7.3.1   Core Services

The core services comprise the core ontology services and the model management services. The core ontology services correspond to the ontology services described in Section 3.4 and cover querying and reasoning.

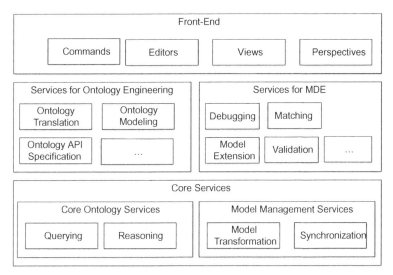

Figure 7.2   A Generic Architecture for MDE and Ontology Engineering.

The model management services involve model transformations and the synchronization of the source and target model. For example, when transforming a UML class diagram into OWL, one requires that the generated OWL ontology remains synchronized with changes on the source model.

7.3.2   Engineering Services

Services for Ontology Engineering.   Engineering services assemble the services for ontology engineering and the services for MDE. Among the services for ontology engineering, we highlight three services that use model-driven technologies to support ontology engineering: ontology translation, ontology modeling, and ontology API specification. Further ontology engineering services are described in [170].

The ontology modeling service provides the structure for designing ontologies. It covers the support for ontology design patterns and the validation and verification of well-formedness constraints.

Ontology translation enables the translation of a source ontology into target formalisms. It adopts a dedicated language for defining mappings of multiple natures: semantic, syntactic, and lexical.

Ontologies require dedicated APIs to encapsulate the complexity of concepts and relations. Therefore, to facilitate the adoption of these ontologies, ontology engineers specify which ontological concepts and roles require operations for creation, update, and deletion. The ontology API service supports this task.

Services for Model-Driven Engineering.   Among the services for MDE, we have identified the following services that use ontology technologies to support

MDE: debugging, matching, validation, and extension. Debugging allows for supporting software engineers in identifying the model elements that underpin a logical conclusion. For example, it consists of pointing out the assertions that support a given statement.

The matching services consist of applying ontology matching techniques [38] to identify similar concepts or relations in multiple models (see Section 3.5.2 for ontology matching techniques).

Finally, the model extension service controls the integration between OWL and UML class-based modeling. It manages the extension of UML class diagrams and textual Ecore notation with OWL axioms and the specification of a SPARQLAS4TwoUse query as the body of query operations.

7.3.3 Front-End

The layer `Front-End` is the interface between services and ontology engineers / software engineers. It comprises editors, views, commands, and perspectives.

The editors enable engineers to create and update artifacts written in ontology languages as well as in software languages. For example, the OWL2FS editor enables ontology engineers to create OWL ontologies using the OWL 2 functional syntax.

Commands comprise the actions that engineers execute to manipulate artifacts. For example, to evaluate a given query operation, ontology engineers execute the command `evaluate` that requests the instance specifications to be used as the snapshot and invokes the model extension to control the applicable model transformations.

The component `View` provides engineers with multiple types of visualizations of artifacts. For example, engineers require the visualization of classes in a class hierarchy or the results of a query in a grid.

Perspectives arrange views and editors in the workbench. It consists of supporting the organization of the front-end services according to engineers needs.

7.4 INSTANTIATING THE GENERIC MODEL-DRIVEN ARCHITECTURE: THE TWOUSE TOOLKIT

TwoUse toolkit is an open source tool that implements the research presented in this book. It is an instantiation of the generic architecture and an implementation of current OMG and W3C standards for designing ontology-based information systems and model-based OWL ontologies. It is a model-driven tool to bridge the gap between semantic web and model-driven engineering.

TwoUse toolkit building blocks are (Figure 7.3):

- A set of textual and graphical editors. TwoUse relies on textual and graphical editors for editing and parsing W3C standard languages (OWL 2 and SPARQL), OMG standards (UML, MOF and OCL), and other domain-specific languages.

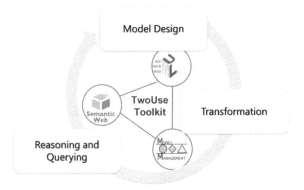

Figure 7.3   The TwoUse Toolkit.

- A set of model transformations. Generic transformations like "Ecore to OWL" allow developers to transform any software language into OWL. Specific transformations like "UML to OWL" and "BPMN to OWL" allow developers to create ad hoc OWL representations of software models.
- A set of ontology services like reasoning, query answering and explanation.

Figure 7.4 depicts the TwoUse instantiation of the generic architecture depicted previously in Figure 7.2. It comprises core services, services for ontology engineering and model-driven engineering, and a front-end.

Core Services.   The TwoUse toolkit uses the implementation of SPARQL-DL and the OWL 2 reasoner provided by the Pellet reasoner [155] as components for realizing the core ontology services. The model transformation component consists of a set of model transformations implemented using the Java language [56] as well as the model transformation language ATL [82]. The synchronization service maintains the dependencies between the source artifacts and the target artifacts. For example, when engineers use a SPARQLAS query, a corresponding SPARQL query is generated and executed. The synchronization service maintains the generated SPARQL query updated in case of changes on the SPARQLAS query. It basically implements the observer pattern [51] to notify state changes on the source model.

Services for Engineering.   The services for ontology engineering cover concrete applications of the TwoUse toolkit. We detail each of these applications in Part IV.

The services for model-driven engineering cover explanation, ontology matching, and the TwoUse metamodel. The explanation service uses ontology services to help software engineers in pinpointing statements. The TwoUse toolkit covers the following types of explanation: unsatisfiability, class subsumption, instantiation, and property assertion. The matching service uses the Ontology Alignment API [40] to support engineers in identifying similar constructs over multiple metamodels. We illustrate the application of these services in Chapter 10.

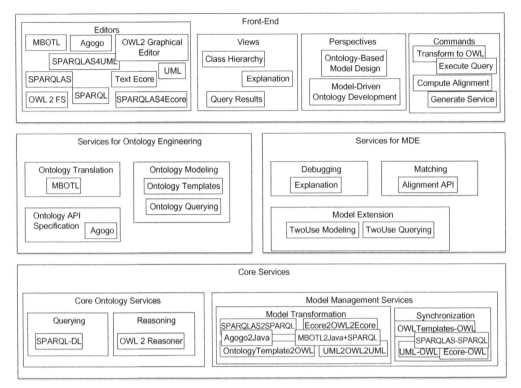

Figure 7.4   Instantiation of the Generic Architecture: The TwoUse Toolkit.

Figure 7.5 depicts a snapshot of the TwoUse Toolkit showing the view Expla-nation. The result of the explanation is showed in the console with links to the class on the UML class diagram.

Front-End.   The front-end is the interface of the TwoUse toolkit to engineers. It comprises multiple editors that implement W3C standard languages and OMG standards as well as other domain-specific languages. We define three views to help engineers in visualizing models: a hierarchy of the inferred classes (Figure 7.6), a user interface for explanation and an interface for query results. The commands involve transforming models into OWL, executing queries, and generating services and code. We group the editors, views, and commands under two perspectives: ontology-based model design and model-driven ontology development.

We implement the TwoUse toolkit on top of the Eclipse Rich Client Platform [97] as an open-source tool under the eclipse public license. It is available for down-load on the Project Website.[2]

---

[2]http://twouse.googlecode.com/.

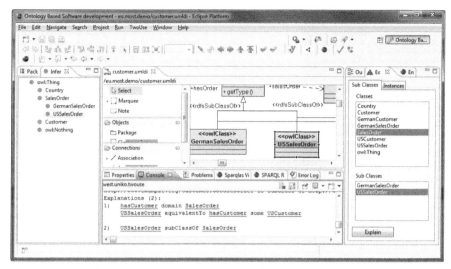

Figure 7.5   TwoUse Toolkit Snapshot: Explanation Service.

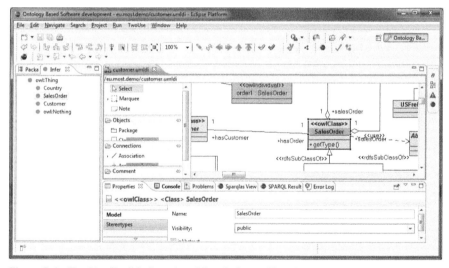

Figure 7.6   TwoUse Toolkit Snapshot: View Inferred Class Hierarchy.

7.5   CONCLUSION

In this chapter, we have specified a generic architecture for integrated approaches. The architecture fulfills the requirements defined in Section 5.2. We validated the architecture by instantiating it as an implementation of the conceptual architecture—the TwoUse Toolkit.

CONCLUSION OF PART II

This part presented TwoUse as a solution for developing and denoting models that benefit from the advantages of UML class-based modeling and OWL modeling (Research Question II from Section 1.2). We described the main building blocks of a conceptual architecture covering an integration of UML class-based modeling, OWL, and a query language for OWL. Moreover, we specify a generic architecture for implementing the conceptual architecture and describe an instantiation of the generic architecture—the TwoUse Toolkit.

PART III

APPLICATIONS IN MODEL-DRIVEN ENGINEERING

CHAPTER 8

IMPROVING SOFTWARE DESIGN PATTERNS WITH OWL

This chapter tackles problems in common design patterns and proposes OWL modeling to remedy these issues. We exploit the TwoUse approach and integrate OWL with UML class-based modeling to overcome drawbacks of the strategy pattern, which are also extensible to the abstract factory pattern. The results are ontology-based software design patterns to be used with software design patterns.[1]

8.1 INTRODUCTION

Design patterns [51] provide elaborated, best practice solutions for commonly occurring problems in software development. During the last years, design patterns were established as general means to ensure quality of software systems by applying reference templates containing software models and their appropriate implementation to describe and realize software systems.

In addition to their advantages, Gamma *et al.* [51] characterize software design patterns by their consequences including side effects and disadvantages caused by their use. In this chapter, we address the drawbacks associated with pattern-based solutions for variant management [169]. Design patterns rely on basic principles of reusable object design like manipulation of objects through the interface defined by abstract classes, and by favoring delegation and object composition over direct class inheritance in order to deal with variation in the problem domain.

However, the decision of what variation to choose typically needs to be specified at a client class. For example, solutions based on the strategy design pattern embed the treatment of variants into the client's code, leading to an unnecessarily tight coupling of classes. Gamma [51] identifies this issue as a drawback of pattern-based solutions, e.g., when discussing the strategy pattern and its combination with the abstract factory pattern. Hence, the question arises of how the selection of specific classes could be determined using only their descriptions rather than by weaving the descriptions into client classes.

---

[1]This chapter contains work from the paper "Improving Design Patterns by Description Logics: A Use Case with Abstract Factory and Strategy" presented at Modellierung'08 [151].

Semantic Web and Model-Driven Engineering, First Edition. Fernando Silva Parreiras.
© 2012 Institute of Electrical and Electronics Engineers. Published 2012 by John Wiley & Sons, Inc.

Here, *description logics* come into play. Description logics, in general, and OWL as a specific expressive yet pragmatically usable W3C recommendation [61] allow for specifying classes by rich, precise logical definitions [9]. Based on these definitions, OWL reasoners dynamically infer class subsumption and object classification.

The basic idea of this chapter lies in decoupling class selection from the definition of client classes at runtime by exploiting OWL modeling and reasoning. We explore a slight modification of the strategy pattern and the abstract factory pattern that includes OWL modeling and leads to a minor, but powerful variation of existing practices: the *Selector Pattern*. To realize the *Selector Pattern*, we apply the TwoUse approach.

This chapter is organized as follows. Section 8.2 presents an example demonstrating the application of the strategy and abstract factory patterns to solve a typical implementation problem. The example illustrates the known drawbacks of the state-of-the-art straightforward adoption of these patterns. Section 8.3 presents a solution extending the existing patterns by OWL modeling. We explain how our revision modifies the prior example and how it addresses the issues raised in the example. Section 8.4 describes an abstraction of the modified example, i.e., the selector pattern. We present its structure, guidelines for adoption, consequences, and related works. A short discussion of open issues concludes this chapter in Section 8.6.

8.2 CASE STUDY

This section presents a typical case study of design patterns involving the strategy and abstract factory patterns. To illustrate an application of such patterns, we take the example of an order-processing system for an international e-commerce company in the United States [146]. This system must be able to process sales orders in different countries, e.g., the US and Germany, and handle different tax calculations.

Design patterns rely on principles of reusable object-oriented design [51]. In order to isolate *variations*, we identify the *concepts* (commonalities) and concrete implementations (variants) present in the problem domain. The `concept` generalizes common aspects of `variants` by an abstract class. If several variations are required, the variations are subsumed to contextual classes, which delegate behavior to the appropriate variants. These variants are used by *clients*.

8.2.1 Applying the Strategy Pattern

Considering the principles above, we identify the class `SalesOrder` as a *context*, `Tax` as a *concept*, and the classes `USTax` and `GermanTax` as the *variants* of tax calculation. Since tax calculation varies according to the country, the strategy pattern allows for encapsulating the tax calculation and letting them vary independently of the *context*. The resulting class diagram is depicted in the Figure 8.1.

To specify operations, we use the Object Constraint Language (OCL) [116]. The `TaskController` requires the operation `getRulesForCountry`, which returns the concrete strategy to be used. The specification must include criteria to

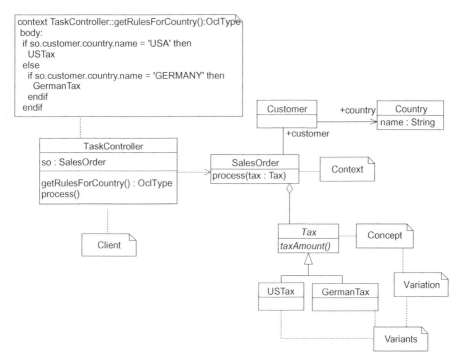

```
context TaskController::getRulesForCountry():OclType
body:
  if so.customer.country.name = 'USA' then
    USTax
  else
    if so.customer.country.name = 'GERMANY' then
      GermanTax
    endif
  endif
```

Figure 8.1   Application of the Strategy Pattern in the Running Example.

select from the strategies. In our example, the criterion is the country where the customer of a sales order lives.

The drawback of this solution is that, at runtime, the *client* TaskController must decide on the *variant* of the *concept* Tax to be used, achieved by the operation getRulesForCountry. Nevertheless, it requires the *client* to understand the differences between the variants, which increases the coupling between these classes.

Indeed, the decision of whether a given object of SalesOrder will use the class GermanTax to calculate the tax depends on whether the corresponding Customer lives in Germany. Although this condition refers to the class GermanTax, it is specified in the class TaskController. Any change in this condition will require a change in the specification of the class TaskController, which is not intuitive and implies an undesirably tight coupling between the classes GermanTax, Country, and TaskController (Figure 8.2).

8.2.2   Extending to the Abstract Factory

When the company additionally needs to calculate the freight, new requirements must be handled. Therefore, we apply again the strategy pattern for freight calculation. As for the tax calculation, the *context* SalesOrder aggregates the *variation* of freight calculation, USFreight and GermanFreight generalized by the *concept* Freight (Figure 8.3).

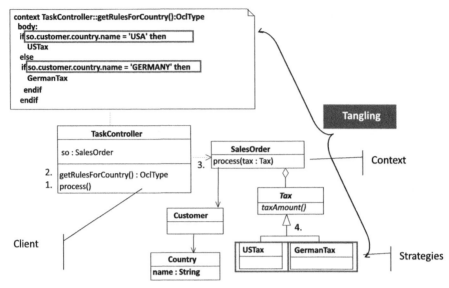

Figure 8.2   Drawbacks of the Strategy Pattern.

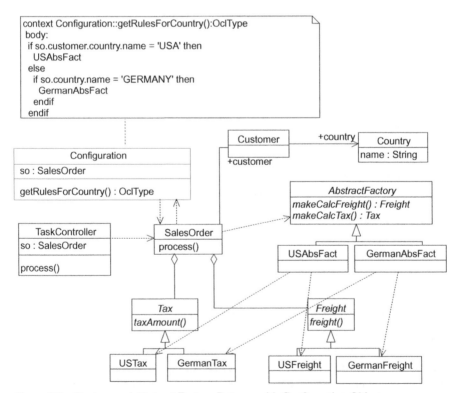

Figure 8.3   Strategy and Abstract Factory Patterns with Configuration Object.

As we now have families of objects related to the US and Germany, we apply the abstract factory pattern to handle these families. The abstract factory pattern provides an interface for creating groups of related *variants* [51].

As one possible adaptation of the design patterns, the *client* (TaskController) remains responsible for selecting the *variants* of the *concept* AbstractFactory to be used, i.e., the family of strategies, and passes the concrete factory as a parameter to the class SalesOrder. The class SalesOrder is associated with the class AbstractFactory, which interfaces the creation of the strategies Tax and Freight. The concrete factories USAbsFact and GermanAbsFact implement the operations to create concrete strategies USFreight, GermanFreight, GermanTax, and USTax.

The adaptation of the design patterns used as the example introduces a Configuration object [146] to shift the responsibility for selecting variants from one or several clients to a Configuration class, as depicted in the Figure 8.3. The class Configuration decides which variant to use. The class SalesOrder invokes the operation getRulesForCountry in the class Configuration to get the variant. These interactions are also depicted in a sequence chart in Figure 8.4.

8.2.3 Drawbacks

In general, the strategy pattern solves the problem of dealing with variations. However, as documented by Gamma [51], the strategy pattern has a drawback. The clients must be aware of variations and of the criteria to select between them at runtime, as described at the end of Section 8.2.1.

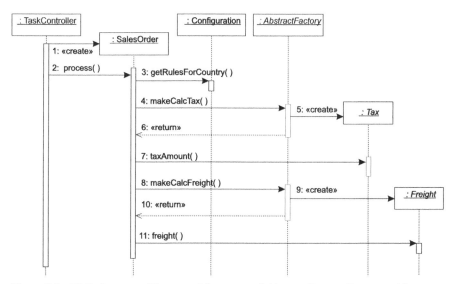

Figure 8.4   UML Sequence Diagram of Strategy and Abstract Factory Patterns with Configuration Object.

When combining the strategy and abstract factory patterns, the problem of choosing among the variants of the `AbstractFactory` remains almost the same. Indeed, the abstract factory pattern assembles the families of strategies. Hence, the client must still be aware of variations.

The solution using the class `Configuration` does not solve this problem either, i.e., the coupling migrates. As the `Configuration` must understand how the variants differ, the selection is transferred from the client `TaskController` to the class `Configuration`.

Furthermore, each occurrence of the strategy and the abstract factory patterns increases the number of operations that the class `Configuration` must be able to handle. It makes the specification of such a class complex, decreasing class cohesion.

Thus, a solution that reuses the understanding of the variations without increasing the complexity is desirable. Furthermore, such a solution should allow one to decide on the appropriate variants as late as possible. Separating the base of the decision from the decision itself will provide an evolvable and more modular software design. In the next section, we describe how TwoUse provides such a mechanism.

8.3 APPLICATION OF THE TWOUSE APPROACH

A solution for the drawbacks presented at the end of Section 8.2 is to dynamically classify the *context*, and verify whether it satisfies the set of requirements of a given `variant`. To do so, one requires a logical class definition language that is more expressive than UML, e.g., the Web Ontology Language (OWL) [61].

To benefit from the expressiveness of OWL and UML modeling it is necessary to weave both paradigms into an integrated model-based approach, e.g., by using the TwoUse modeling approach (see Chapter 5).

8.3.1 OWL for Conceptual Modeling

OWL provides various means for expressing classes, which may also be nested into each other. One may denote a class by a class identifier, an exhaustive enumeration of individuals, a property restriction, an intersection of class descriptions, a union of class descriptions, or the complement of a class description.

For the sake of illustration, an incomplete specification of the E-Shop example using a description logic syntax repeated here. The identifier `Customer` is used to declare the corresponding class (8.1) as a specialization of `Thing` ($\top$), since all classes in OWL are specializations of the reserved class `Thing`. The class `Country` *contains* the individuals USA and GERMANY (8.2). The class `USCustomer` is defined by a restriction on the property `hasCountry`; the value range must include the country USA (8.3). The description of the class `GermanCustomer` is analogous (8.5). `USSalesOrder` is defined as a subclass of a `SalesOrder` with at least one `USCustomer` (8.4). The intersection of both classes is empty ($\perp$), i.e., they are disjoint (8.7). The class `SalesOrder` is equal to the union of

`GermanSalesOrder` and `USSalesOrder`, i.e., it is a complete generalization of both classes (8.8).

$$Customer \sqsubseteq \top \tag{8.1}$$

$$\{USA, GERMANY\} \sqsubseteq Country \tag{8.2}$$

$$USCustomer \sqsubseteq Customer \sqcap \exists hasCountry\{USA\} \tag{8.3}$$

$$USSalesOrder \sqsubseteq SalesOrder \sqcap \exists hasCustomer.USCustomer \tag{8.4}$$

$$GermanCustomer \sqsubseteq Customer \sqcap \exists hasCountry\{GERMANY\} \tag{8.5}$$

$$GermanSalesOrder \sqsubseteq SalesOrder \sqcap \exists hasCustomer.GermanCustomer \tag{8.6}$$

$$GermanSalesOrder \sqcap USSalesOrder \sqsubseteq \bot \tag{8.7}$$

$$SalesOrder \equiv GermanSalesOrder \sqcup USSalesOrder \tag{8.8}$$

Notations for OWL modeling have been developed, resulting in lexical notations (cf. [73, 61]) and in UML as visual notation (cf. [21, 34, 114]). When modeling the problem domain of our running example using a UML profile for OWL [114], the diagram looks as depicted in the Figure 8.5. The number relates the list of DL statements above to the corresponding visual notation.

8.3.2   TwoUse for Software Design Patterns: The Selector Pattern

To integrate the UML class diagram with patterns (Figure 8.3) and the OWL profiled class diagram (Figure 8.5), we rely on the TwoUse approach. We use UML profiles

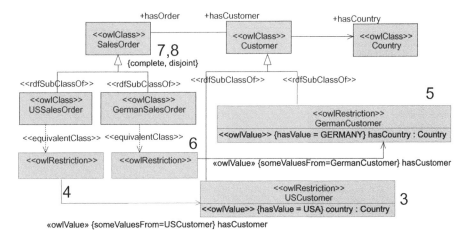

Figure 8.5   Domain Design by a UML Class Diagram Using a UML Profile for OWL.

as concrete syntax, and allow for specifying UML entities and OWL entities using one hybrid diagram. These entities are connected using the UML profile and SPARQLAS queries. This hybrid diagram, i.e., a UML class diagram with profiles for OWL and TwoUse, is mapped later onto the TwoUse abstract syntax.

The approach enables the modeler to use SPARQLAS4TwoUse expressions to describe the query operations of classes that have both semantics of an OWL class and a UML class in the *same* diagram. Moreover, this operation can query the OWL model, i.e., invoke a reasoning service at runtime that uses the same OWL model.

Hence, we can achieve dynamic classification writing SPARQLAS4TwoUse query operations in the *context* to classify the *variation* in the OWL model in runtime. The result is returned as a common object-oriented class.

8.3.2.1 Structure The hybrid diagram is depicted in Figure 8.6 and in Figure 8.7. The classes `Customer` and `Country` are OWL classes and UML classes, i.e.,

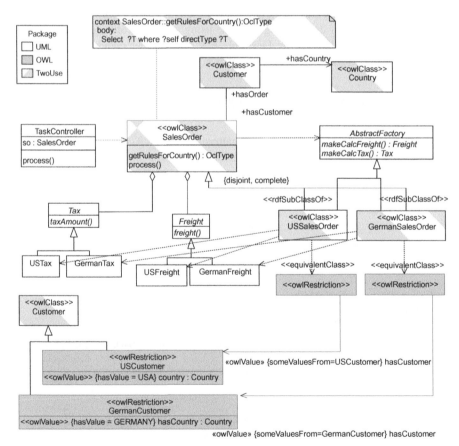

Figure 8.6   Profiled UML Class Diagram of an Ontology-Based Solution.

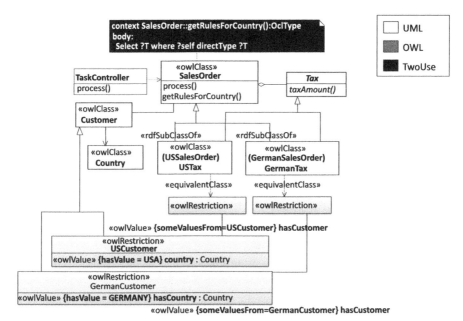

Figure 8.7   Profiled UML Class Diagram with the Strategy Pattern.

they are hybrid TwoUse classes. They are used in the OWL part of the model to describe the variations of the context `SalesOrder`. The TwoUse profile provides a mapping between the names in OWL and in UML in such a way that class names in both OWL and UML are preserved.

The concrete factories, i.e., the variants to be instantiated by the client `Task-Controller` are TwoUse classes as well. The concrete factories are described based on the restrictions on the class `SalesOrder` which must also exist in both paradigms. In the OWL part of the model, the concrete factories specialize the `Sales-Order`, but in UML, they specialize the class `AbstractFactory`. Hence, they do not inherit the methods of the class `SalesOrder`, because the associations between the variants and the context happen only in OWL part of the model.

8.3.2.2   *Participants and Collaborations*   The TwoUse approach preserves the signature and behavior of existing pattern implementations, as only the body of the operation `getRulesForCountry` is affected. The class `Configuration` is no longer needed, as the selection is moved to querying the OWL part of the model (cf. the query in Figure 8.6).

As depicted in Figure 8.8, the class `TaskController` invokes the operation `process` in the class `SalesOrder` (2), which invokes the operation `getRulesFor-Country` (3). This operation calls SPARQLAS4TwoUse query operations. The SPARQLAS4TwoUse operations use reasoning services to classify dynamically the object `SalesOrder` to the appropriate subclass. The resulting OWL class, i.e.,

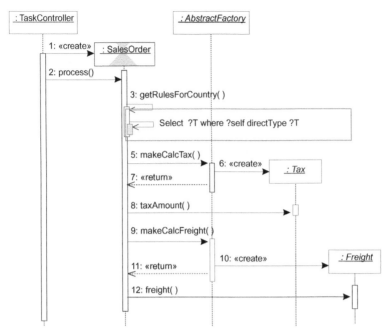

Figure 8.8   Sequence Diagram of an OWL-Based Solution.

US-SalesOrder or GermanSalesOrder, is mapped onto a UML class and is returned. The remaining sequence (5-12) remains unchanged.

For instance, let ORDER1 be a SalesOrder with the property customer being HANS with the property country being GERMANY. The call ORDER1.getRules-ForCountry() results in an object of type GermanSalesOrder.

8.3.2.3   *Comparison*
In the strategy and abstract factory solution, the decision of which *variant* to use is left to the *client* or to the Configuration object. It requires associations from these classes (TaskController and Configuration, respectively) with the concepts (Tax and AbstractFactory, respectively). Furthermore, the conditions are hard-coded in the client's operations.

The TwoUse-based solution cuts these couplings, as the selection is done at the OWL concept level, without any impact on the UML level, allowing the OWL part of the model to be extended independently.

The descriptions of the classes USSalesOrder and GermanSalesOrder are used for the Reasoner to classify the object dynamically. As the classification occurs at the OWL level, resulting OWL classes are transformed into UML classes. Hence, the conditions are specified as logical descriptions.

When evolving from Figure 8.1 to Figure 8.3, the OWL part of the model does not change. Thus, new patterns can be applied without additional effort in modeling the OWL domain.

8.4   VALIDATION

After analyzing the case study of composing OWL and design patterns in Section 8.3, we abstract repeatable arrangements of entities and propose a design pattern supported by OWL to address decision of variations—*the selector pattern.*

The selector pattern provides an interface for handling variations of context. It enables the context to select the appropriated variants based on their descriptions. Selections in the selector pattern are encapsulated in appropriate SPARQLAS-queries against the concept, facilitating a clear separation between the base of the decision and the decision itself.

8.4.1   Participants and Collaborations

The selector pattern is composed by a *context* (e.g., SalesOrder in Figure 8.6), the specific *variants* (e.g., USAbsFact and GermanAbsFact in Figure 8.6) of this context and their respective descriptions, and the *concept* (e.g., AbstractFactory in Figure 8.6), which provides a common interface for the variations (Figure 8.9). Its participants are:

- Context maintains a reference to the Concept object.
- Concept declares an abstract method behavior common to all variants.
- Variants implement the method behavior of the class Concept.

The *Context* has the operation select, which uses SPARQLAS operations to call the reasoner and dynamically classify the object according to the logical descriptions of the variants. A *Variant* is returned as the result (Figure 8.9). Then, the *Context* establishes an association with the *Concept*, which interfaces the variation.

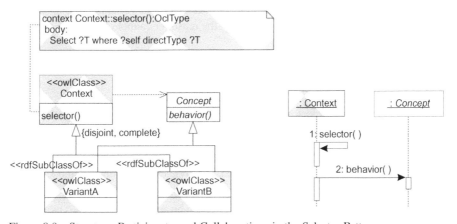

Figure 8.9   Structure, Participants, and Collaborations in the Selector Pattern.

8.4.2   Applicability

The selector pattern is applicable:

- when the strategy pattern is applicable (cf. [51]);
- when the decision of what variant to use appears as multiple conditional statements in the operations;
- when exposing complex and case-specific data structures must be avoided.

The selector pattern preserves the interactions of the strategy and abstract factory patterns, studied in this chapter. The following steps guide the application of the selector pattern:

1. Design the OWL part of the model using a UML profile for OWL, identifying the concept and logically describing the variations;
2. Map the overlapping classes in UML and in OWL using a UML profile;
3. Write the operation in the Context class corresponding to the operation selector using SPARQLAS expressions.

8.4.3   Drawbacks

The proposed solution may seem complex for practitioners. Indeed, applying the selector pattern requires sufficiently deep understanding by developers of topics like open and closed world assumption, class expressions, and satisfiability, in addition to knowledge of SPARQLAS4TwoUse. Moreover, the diagram presented by Figure 8.6 is visibly more complex than the corresponding version without patterns, although applying aspect-oriented techniques can minimize this problem.

Further, calls from OCL to SPARQLAS4TwoUse may return OWL classes that are not part of the TwoUse model. This implies a dynamic diffusion of OWL classes into the UML model and either they must be accommodated dynamically into it or an exception needs to be raised.

Therefore, class descriptions must be sufficient for the reasoner to classify the variant, i.e., classes and properties needed to describe the variants must also exist at the OWL level. When this is not possible, the reasoner cannot classify the variants correctly.

8.4.4   Advantages

The application of the selector pattern presents the following consequences:

Reuse. The knowledge represented in OWL can be reused independently of platform or programming language.

Flexibility. The knowledge encoded in OWL can be modeled and evolved independently of the execution logic.

Testability. The OWL part of the model can be automatically tested by logical unit tests, independently of the UML development.

Easy Adoption. Expanding Figure 8.3 with Figure 8.6 and Figure 8.4 with Figure 8.8 in the motivating example, shows that the changes required by applying the selector pattern in existing practices are indeed minor.

UML Paradigm Dominance. The concrete cases are bound to the context only in OWL. It has no impact on the UML part of the model. The programmer freely specifies the SPARQLAS operation calls when applicable.

8.5 RELATED WORK

State-of-the-art approaches require hard-coding the conditions of selecting a particular variant [146]. Our approach relies on OWL modeling and reasoning to dynamically subclassify an object when required.

The composition of OWL with object-oriented software has been addressed by [91] and [119]. We address this composition at the modeling level in a platform-independent manner [90].

8.6 CONCLUSION

We have proposed a novel way of reducing coupling in important design patterns by including OWL modeling. We have proposed an ontology-based software design pattern called selector pattern and discuss the impact of adopting the new approach.

The application of TwoUse can be extended to other design patterns concerning variant management and control of execution and method selection. Software design patterns that factor out commonality of related objects, e.g., prototype, factory method and template method, are good candidates.

CHAPTER 9

MODELING ONTOLOGY-BASED INFORMATION SYSTEMS

Developers of ontology-based information systems have to deal with domain knowledge represented in ontologies and domain logic represented by algorithms. An approach that allows developers to reuse knowledge embedded in ontologies for modeling algorithms is lacking so far. In this chapter, we apply the TwoUse approach for enabling developers of ontology-based information systems to reuse domain knowledge for modeling domain logic. This results in improvements in maintainability, reusability, and extensibility.[1]

9.1 INTRODUCTION

The development of ontology-based information systems has gained momentum as users increasingly consume applications relying on semantic web technologies. For example, a core ontology-based information system for the Semantic Web is the semantic annotation of formulas, text, or image, which transforms human-understandable content into a machine-understandable form.

The development of these applications requires software engineers to handle software artifacts and the ontologies separately. For instance, software engineers cannot use OWL class expressions in the body of operations that rely on information contained in the ontology. Therefore, software engineers have to define the conditions for selecting classes twice, first in the ontology and second in the body of operations. This process is error prone and requires the synchronization of both definitions in case of changes.

In this chapter, we analyze the application of the TwoUse approach for integrating the ontologies in the development of ontology-based information systems. TwoUse enables ontology engineers to specify conditions reusing the knowledge encoded in the ontology.

---

[1]This chapter contains work from the paper "Using Ontologies with UML Class-based Modeling: The TwoUse Approach" published in the Data & Knowledge Engineering Journal [122].

Semantic Web and Model-Driven Engineering, First Edition. Fernando Silva Parreiras.
© 2012 Institute of Electrical and Electronics Engineers. Published 2012 by John Wiley & Sons, Inc.

This chapter is structured as follows: Section 9.2 describes the domain of the case study and analyzes current modeling techniques. In Section 9.3, we apply the TwoUse approach for integrating domain ontologies and software specification. Section 9.4 analyzes the application of the TwoUse approach according to ISO 9126 non-functional software requirements, and it describes the limitations.

9.2   CASE STUDY

We describe the case study in the context of the semantic multimedia tools in this chapter. The K-Space Annotation Tool (KAT) [138] is a framework for semi-automatic and efficient annotation of multimedia content that provides a plug-in infrastructure (analysis plug-ins and visual plug-ins) and a formal model based on the Core Ontology for Multimedia (COMM) [6].

Analysis plug-ins provide functionalities to analyze content, e.g., to semi-automatically annotate multimedia data like images or videos, or to detect structure within multimedia data. However, as the number of available plug-ins increases, it becomes difficult for KAT end-users to choose appropriate plug-ins.

For example, semantic multimedia developers provide machine learning–based classifies, e.g., support vector machines (SVM), for pattern recognition. There are different recognizers (object recognizers, face detectors, and speaker identifiers) for different themes (sport, politics, and art), for different types of multimedia data (image, audio, and video), and for different formats (JPEG, GIF, and MPEG). Moreover, the list of recognizers is continuously extended and, like the list of multimedia formats, it is not closed but, by sheer principle, it needs to be open.

Therefore, the objective is to provide KAT end-users with the functionality of automatically selecting and running the most appropriate plug-in(s) according to the multimedia data captured by the ontology. Such improvement enhances user satisfaction, since it prevents KAT end-users from employing unsuitable recognizers over multimedia data.

In the following, we consider three recognizers that work over soccer videos: highlight recognizer, jubilation recognizer, and goal shots detector. A highlight recognizer works on detecting sets of frames in videos with high changing rates, e.g., intervals where the camera view changes frequently in a soccer game. A jubilation recognizer analyzes the video and audio, searching for shouts of jubilation. Finally, a goal shots detector works on matching shouts of jubilation with changes in camera view to characterize goal shots.

9.2.1   UML Class-Based Software Development

We apply an extensible approach to model recognizer variations, namely an adaptation of the strategy pattern [51]. The strategy pattern allows for encapsulating recognizers uniformly, as depicted in Figure 9.1.

Figure 9.1 depicts the KAT domain in the UML class diagram. It is a complex domain since KAT uses the COMM ontology that comprises multiple occurrences of ontology design patterns, e.g., *semantic annotation* used in the running example.

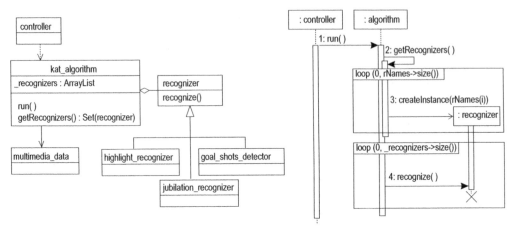

Figure 9.1   UML Class Diagram and Sequence Diagram of KAT Algorithms.

Users select KAT algorithms for SVM recognition and, consequently, the class `controller` invokes the method `run()` in the class `kat_algorithm` (Figure 9.1). The method `run()` invokes the method `getRecognizers()`, which uses reflection to get a collection (`rNames()`) of the recognizers (`_r`) applicable to a given multimedia content (multimedia_data). Then, the method `recognize()` of each recognizer is invoked, which adds further annotations to multimedia data to refine the description.

Nevertheless, applying the strategy design pattern opens the problem of strategy selection. To solve it, one needs to model how to select the appropriate recognizer(s) for a given item of multimedia content. Listing 9.1 illustrates a solution using OCL. It shows the description of the query operation `rNames()` in OCL. This operation is used in the guard expression of the loop combined fragment in the sequence diagram (Figure 9.1).

The operation `rNames()` collects the classes of recognizers to be created. The OCL expression `Set(OclType)` (Line 4) is used here as a reflection mechanism to get a list of the classes to be created. This is required to iterate through the instances of `kat_algorithm` (Line 4) and test whether it satisfies the requirements of a given recognizer. If it does, the recognizer is added into a collection of recognizers to be created (Line 17).

In fact, the OCL expressions in Listing 9.1 contain class descriptions in some sense. For example, the classes `highlight_recognizer` and `jubilation_recognizer` need a `kat_algorithm` with some `annotated_data_role` with some `video_data` (Lines 19–24). The description of a `goal_shots_detector` is complicated (Lines 7–15), since it needs a `soccer_video`, that is a subclass of `video_data`, with some `semantic_annotation` with some `highlight`, and with some `semantic_annotation` with some `jubilation`.

LISTING 9.1   OCL Expressions for the UML Sequence Diagram of Figure 9.1.

```
 1  context kat_algorithm
      def rNames() : Set(OclType)
      = kat_algorithm.allInstances ()
          ->iterate    ( _i : kat_algorithm;
 5                            _r : Set(OclType) = Set{} |
            if
               _i.annotated_data_role->exists ( adr |
                  adr.video_data->exists ( v |
                     v.oclIsTypeOf (soccer_video) and
10                   v.semantic_annotation->exists (sa |
                        sa.kat_thing->exists ( g |
                           g.oclIsTypeOf (highlight) ) ) and
                     v.semantic_annotation->exists (sa |
                        sa.kat_thing->exists ( j |
15                         j.oclIsTypeOf (jubilation) ) )
                  ) )
            then
               _r->including(goal_shots_detector)
            else if
20             _i.annotated_data_role->exists ( adr |
                  adr.video_data->exists ( v |
                     v.oclIsTypeOf(video_data) ) )
               then
                  _r->including(highlight_recognizer)->union(
25                _r->including(jubilation_recognizer))
               else
                  _r
               endif
            endif)->asSet()
```

Indeed, the UML/OCL approach has limitations:

• It restricts information that can be known about objects to object types, i.e., known information about objects is limited by information in object types (or in object states when using OCL).

• Class descriptions, e.g., goal_shots_detector (Lines 7–16), are embedded within conditional statements that are hard to maintain and reuse. In scenarios with thousands of classes, it becomes difficult to find those descriptions, achievable only by text search.

• OCL lacks of support for transitive closure of relations [165, 17]. It makes expressions including properties like part-of more complex.

9.2.2   Ontology-Based Software Development

OWL Modeling.   Instead of hard-coding class descriptions using OCL expressions, a more expressive and extensible manner of modeling data provides flexible ways to describe classes and, based on such descriptions, it enables type inference.

Therefore, one requires a logical class definition language that is more expressive than UML class-based modeling. Indeed, OWL provides various means for describing classes. One may denote a class by a class identifier, an exhaustive enumeration of individuals, property restrictions, an intersection of class descriptions, a union of class descriptions, or the complement of a class description.

For the sake of illustration, we use description logic syntax to specify the KAT domain as follows (Table 9.1). KAT uses the COMM ontology [6] as a conceptually sound model of MPEG-7 and as a common but extensible denominator for different plug-ins exchanging data.

For example, the classes `jubilation` and `highlight` are subclasses of `kat_thing` (1). A `soccer_video` is a subclass of `video_data` (2). A `highlight_annotation` is a `semantic_annotation` that `setting_for` some `highlight` (3). A `highlight_video` is equivalent to a `video_data` that `setting` some `highlight_annotation` (4). A `jubilation_video` is similarly described (5). A `highlight_recognizer` is a subclass of a `kat_algorithm` and is equivalent to a `kat_algorithm` that `defines` some `annotated_data_role` that is `played_by` some `video_data` (7).

OWL is compositional, i.e., OWL allows for reusing class descriptions to create new ones. A look at the class `soccer_jub_hl_video` (6) shows that it is equivalent to an intersection of `soccer_video`, `highlight_video`, and `jubilation_video`, i.e., a soccer video with highlight and jubilation. Thus, it becomes easier to describe the class `goal_shots_detector` (8), which is a subclass of a `kat_algorithm` and is equivalent to a `kat_algorithm` that defines

TABLE 9.1   Specifying KAT with Description Logic Syntax.

$$jubilation, highlight \sqsubseteq kat\_thing \tag{9.1}$$

$$soccer\_video \sqsubseteq video\_data \tag{9.2}$$

$$highlight\_annotation \equiv semantic\_annotation \sqcap \exists setting\_for.highlight \tag{9.3}$$

$$highlight\_video \equiv video\_data \sqcap \exists setting.highlight\_annotation \tag{9.4}$$

$$jubilation\_video \equiv video\_data \sqcap \exists setting.jubilation\_annotation \tag{9.5}$$

$$soccer\_jub\_hl\_video \equiv soccer\_video \sqcap highlight\_video \sqcap jubilation\_video \tag{9.6}$$

$$highlight\_recognizer \equiv kat\_algorithm$$
$$\sqcap \exists defines(annotated\_data\_role \sqcap \exists played\_by.video\_data) \tag{9.7}$$

$$goal\_shots\_detector \equiv kat\_algorithm$$
$$\sqcap \exists defines(annotated\_data\_role \sqcap \exists played\_by.soccer\_jub\_hl\_video) \tag{9.8}$$

some `annotated_data_role` that is `played_by` some `soccer_jub_hl_video`. Moreover, OWL allows for defining properties as transitive, simplifying query expressions. The reader may compare these reusable class definitions against the involved and useable implicit definition of distinctions provided in Listing 9.1 (Lines 6–25).

OWL Reasoning.   OWL ontologies can be operated on by reasoners providing consistency checking, concept satisfiability, instance classification, and concept classification. The reasoner performs model checking to the extent that entailments of the Tarski-style model theory of OWL are fulfilled. For instance, it is possible to verify whether it is possible to apply `goal_shots_detector` to images (consistency checking) (the answer is "no" if `goal_shots_detector` is disjoint from image recognizers) or whether a given instance is a `soccer_jub_hl_video` (instance classification). It is possible to ask a reasoner to classify the concepts of the ontology and find that `highlight_video` and `jubilation_video` are both superclasses of `soccer_jub_hl_video` (concept classification).

More specifically, given that we know an object to be an instance of `highlight_video`, we can infer that this object has the property `setting` and the value of `setting` is an individual of `highlight_annotation`. Conversely, if we have an object of `video_data`, which has the property `setting` and the value of `setting` associated with such an individual is a `highlight_annotation`, we can infer that the prior individual is an instance of `highlight_video`. This example illustrates how to define OWL classes like `highlight_video` by necessary and sufficient conditions.

To sum up, OWL provides important features complementary to UML and OCL that improve software modeling: it provides multiple ways of describing classes; it handles these descriptions as first-class entities; it provides additional constructs like transitive closure for properties; and it enables dynamic classification of objects based upon class descriptions.

The need for an integration emerges since OWL is a purely declarative and logical language and not suitable to describe, e.g., dynamic aspects of software systems such as states or message passing. Thus, to benefit from inference, one must decide at which state or given which trigger one should call the reasoner. In the next section, we address this issue among others, proposing ways of integrating both paradigms using the TwoUse approach.

9.3   APPLICATION OF THE TWOUSE APPROACH

We apply the TwoUse approach described in Part II to enable engineers to design and integrate UML models and OWL ontologies, exploiting the full expressiveness of OWL($\mathcal{SROIQ}$(D)) and allowing usage of existing UML2 tools.

To give an idea of the integration, we use the example of the E-Shop domain. Instead of defining the query operation `rNames` using UML/OCL expressions, we use the expressiveness of the OWL language together with SPARQLAS4TwoUse. Querying an *OWL reasoning service*, it is possible to ask which OWL subclasses of kat_algorithm describe a given instance, enabling dynamic classification. Such expression will then be specified by:

```
1 context kat_algorithm
  def rNames(): Set(Class)
    ?self type ?T
    ?T subClassOf kat_algorithm
```

As specified above, to identify which subclasses are applicable, we use the variable ?T to get all types of ?self that are subclasses of kat_algorithm.

The advantage of this integrated formulation of rNames lies in separating two sources of specification complexity. First, the classification of complex classes remains in an OWL model. The classification reuses the COMM model and it is reuseable for specifying other operations; it is maintainable using graphical notations; and it is a decidable, yet rigorous reasoning model (see Figure 9.2). Second, the specification of the execution logic remains in the UML specification (sequence diagram in the Figure 9.1).

9.3.1 Concrete Syntax

Figure 9.2 shows a snippet of the UML class diagram for the case study. In this snippet, the OWL view consists of five classes. The UML view comprises the seven classes depicted in the Figure 2.8 and the TwoUse view contains six classes and a SPARQLAS query expression.

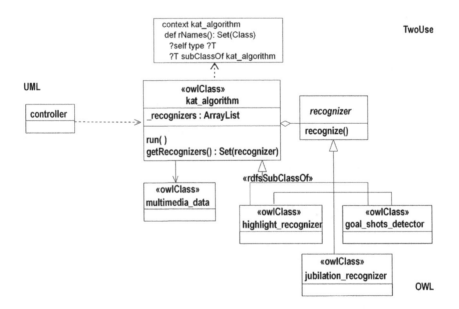

Figure 9.2   UML Class Diagram of KAT.

LISTING 9.2   Modeling KAT Using the Textual Language.

```
1    class controller {}
     class kat_algorithm extends core:algorithm {
        attribute recognizer recognizers (0.. -1);
        operation void run();
5       operation recognizer (0.. -1) getRecognizers ();
        operation rNames(): Set(OclType)
            Select ?T where ?self type ?T ?T subClassOf kat_algorithm;
     }
     . . .
10   abstract class recognizer{
        operation void recognize();
     }
     class highlight_annotation [equivalentTo [core:semantic_annotation
        and [dsn:setting_for some highlight]]] {}
     class highlight_video [equivalentTo [core:video_data and
        [dsn:setting some highlight_annotation]]] {}
15   class jubilation_video [equivalentTo [core:video_data and
        [dsn:setting some jubilation_annotation]]] {}
     class soccer_jub_hl_video [equivalentTo [soccer_video and
        highlight_video and jubilation_video]] {}
     class highlight_recognizer extends kat_algorithm, [subClassOf
        [dns:defines some [core:annotated_data_role and [played_by some
        core:video data]]]] {}
     class jubilation_recognizer extends kat_algorithm, [subClassOf
        [dns:defines some [core:annotated_data_role and [dns:played_by
        some core:video_data]]]] {}
     class goal_shots_detector extends kat_algorithm, [subClassOf
        [dns:defines some [core:annotated_data_role and [dns:played_
        by some soccer_jub_hl_video]]]] {}
```

Another way or integrating ontologies in the development of ontology-based information systems is using the textual syntax. Listing 9.2 presents the equivalent of the UML class diagram defined using the textual syntax for Ecore and includes the OWL class expressions (between brackets).

9.3.2   Abstract Syntax

The TwoUse abstract model is generated as output of model transformations that take as input models defined using any of the notations supported by TwoUse. Figure 9.3 depicts an excerpt of the abstract model for the running example.

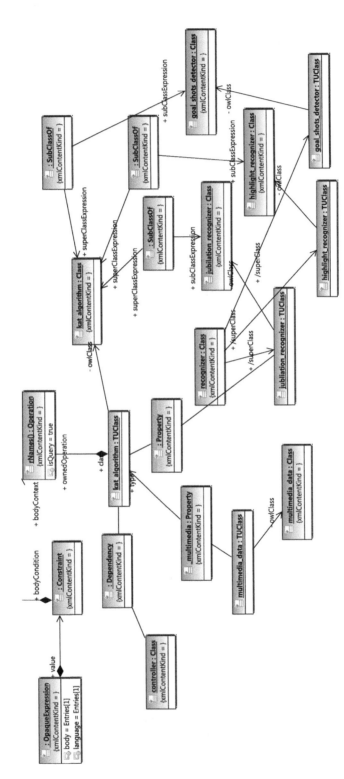

Figure 9.3 Excerpt of a KAT Model (M1).

TABLE 9.2   Evaluation of SPARQLAS Expressions According to the KAT Snapshot.

Context object SPARQLAS expression	alg1	alg2
`?self directType` `   highlight_recognizer`	true	true
`?self directType goal_` `   shots_detector`	false	true

`?self type ?T`	algorithm, description,
	    highlight_recognizer,
	    jubilation_recognizer,
	    method
		algorithm, description,
		    highlight_recognizer,
		    jubilation_
		    recognizer, goal_
		    shots_detector,
		    method

`?self type ?T ?T`
`   subClassOf algorithm`
	highlight_recognizer,
	    jubilation_recognizer
		highlight_recognizer,
		    jubilation_
		    recognizer, goal_
		    shots_detector

`?self directType _:t` `   ?a type _:t`	alg1, alg2	alg1, alg2
`?self directType ?T`	highlight_recognizer	goal_shots_detector

9.3.3   Querying

Table 9.2 lists results of evaluating SPARQLAS expressions considering the snapshot depicted in the Figure 9.4. We take two objects of the snapshot (`alg1`, `alg2`) and bind them to the predefined variable `self`. For example, for the expression `self.owlIsInstanceOf(highlight_recognizer)` where `self` is bound to `alg1`, the result is `true`.

9.4   VALIDATION

Based on the case study, we analyze how TwoUse features reflect development-oriented non-functional requirements according to a quality model covering the following quality factors: maintainability, efficiency (ISO 9126 [80]), reusability, and extensibility [37]. The decision to use UML with OWL does not affect other ISO 9126 quality factors.

Maintainability.   We analyze maintainability with regard to analyzability, changeability, and testability as follows.

Analyzability.   In case of failure in the software, developers have the possibility of checking the consistency of the domain and then use axiom explanation to track down failure, which helps to improve failure analysis efficiency.

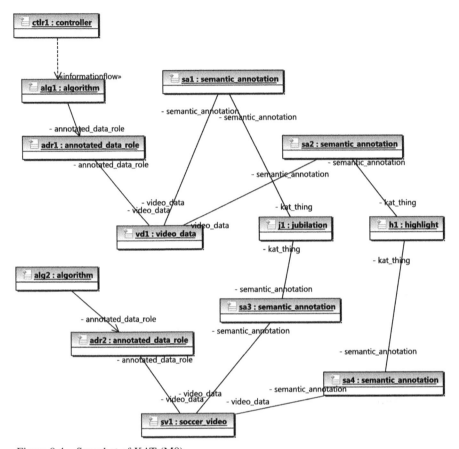

Figure 9.4   Snapshot of KAT (M0).

Changeability. The knowledge encoded in OWL evolves independently of the execution logic, i.e., developers maintain class descriptions in the ontology and not in the software. Since the software does not need recompilation and redistribution, the work time spent to change decreases.

Testability. Developers used queries declared in unit tests to test ontology axioms, enabling test suites to be more declarative.

Reusability. Extending the COMM core ontology allows developers to reuse available knowledge about multimedia content, semantic annotation, and algorithm. Furthermore, developers can reuse the knowledge represented in OWL independently of platform or programming language.

Moreover, developers rely on usage of class descriptions to semantically query the domain. Semantic query plays an important role in large domains like KAT (approx. 750 classes). For example, it is possible to reuse algorithm descriptions applicable to videos. By executing the query

```
1  ?T subClassOf (defines some (annotated_data_role and
   (played_by some video)))
```

using SPARQLAS, developers see that the classes highlight_recognizer, jubilation_recognizer, and goal_shots_detector are candidates to reuse. Such a semantic query is not possible with UML/OCL.

Extensibility. When the application requires it, developers can be more specific by extending existing concepts and adding statements. By adding new statements, developers update the OWL ontology, which does not require generating code if the UML model is not affected. For example, if developers identify that an algorithm works better with certain types of videos, developers extend the algorithm description.

9.4.1 Limitations

By weaving UML and OWL ontologies, TwoUse requires sufficient understanding of developers about class expressions and satisfiability. There is a trade-off between a concise and clear definition of syntax that is unknown to many people as in Table 9.1 versus an involved syntax that people know. From past experiences, we conclude that, in the long term, the higher level expressivity will prevail, as developers are willing to learn a more expressive approach.

Indeed, we have defined multiple notations according to different developers' needs, but this does not prevent them from understanding the semantics of OWL constructs. This shortcoming is minimized in case of ontology-based information systems, since software developers are familiar with OWL.

9.5 CONCLUSION

In this chapter, we show how our approach yields improvements on the maintainability, reusability, and extensibility for designing ontology-based information systems, which corroborates literature on description logics [98]. TwoUse allows developers to raise the level of abstraction of business rules until now embedded in OCL expressions.

CHAPTER 10

ENABLING LINKED DATA CAPABILITIES TO MOF COMPLIANT MODELS

In the software development process, there are standards for general-purpose modeling languages and domain-specific languages, capable of capturing information about different views of systems like static structure and dynamic behavior. In a networked and federated development environment, modeling artifacts need to be linked, adapted, and analyzed to meet information requirements of multiple stakeholders. In this chapter, we present an approach for linking, transforming, and querying MOF-compliant modeling languages on the web of data. We propose the usage of semantic web technologies for linking and querying software models. We apply the proposed framework in a model-driven software.

10.1 INTRODUCTION

In a model-driven architecture, software engineers rely on a variety of languages for designing software systems. As different stakeholders need different views of information, the software development environment needs to encompass a myriad of general-purpose and domain-specific languages with complementary and overlapping applications.

Since it is not feasible to capture all aspects of software into only one single model, contemporary model-driven architectures include numerous notations to serve according to the software development task. The inevitable usage of multiple languages leads to unmanageable redundancy in developing and managing the same information across multiple artifacts and, eventually, information inconsistency. With the growing demand for networked and federated environments, the question arises about what and how existing web standards can help existing modeling standards in fulfilling the requirements of a *web of models*.

Semantic web technologies [4] and linked open data (LOD) principles [16] enable any kind of data to be represented, identified, linked, and formalized on the web. The same data can be adapted for use according to the software engineer's perspective.

The interest in this topic motivated the Object Management Group (OMG) to issue a request for proposals aimed at defining a structural mapping between Meta

Semantic Web and Model-Driven Engineering, First Edition. Fernando Silva Parreiras.
© 2012 Institute of Electrical and Electronics Engineers. Published 2012 by John Wiley & Sons, Inc.

Object Facility (MOF) models and Resource Description Framework (RDF) representations [115]. This mapping should make possible to apply LOD principles to MOF compliant models and to publish MOF compliant models as LOD resources.

In a collaborative environment, developers need to be able to create architectures with information expressed in multiple modeling languages. According to the development phase, developers rely on multiple languages for modeling distinct aspects of the system.

OWL [61] provides a powerful solution for formally describing domain concepts in networked environments. OWL is part of the semantic web stack and is compatible with RDF and with LOD principles. OWL's objective is to provide evolution, interoperability, and inconsistency detection of shared conceptualizations.

Although transformations from the MOF metamodel to OWL have been proposed before, addressing the aforementioned problems requires a coherent framework comprising techniques not only for transforming but for extending, linking, and querying MOF compliant models.

In this chapter, we propose TwoUse as a framework for supporting interrelationships of modeling languages in distributed software modeling environments. We present this chapter as follows: Section 10.2 describes the running example used through the chapter and analyzes the requirements to be addressed. Section 10.3 describes the application of the TwoUse approach. We analyze the approach on Section 10.4 and the related work in Section 10.5. Section 10.6 concludes the chapter.

10.2   CASE STUDY

As a case study, we use the development of the TwoUse toolkit, i.e., "we eat our own dog food." As described in Chapter 7, the TwoUse Toolkit is a model-driven implementation of current OMG and W3C standards for designing ontology-based information systems and model-based OWL ontologies.

TwoUse's development life cycle comprises five phases: requirement specification, analysis, design, code, and management. Figure 10.1 depicts these phases and

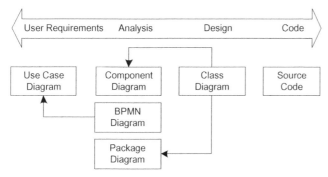

Figure 10.1   Development Life Cycle of the TwoUse Toolkit.

the artifacts generated in each phase. In the requirement specification phase, developers use UML use case diagrams and a domain-specific language for specifying requirements. These requirements are realized by Business Process Model Notation (BPMN) and UML component diagrams in the analysis phase. During the design phase, developers specify metamodels, generations for those metamodels, model transformations, and, in the case of editors, the grammar specification. At the end of the development life cycle, these artifacts are transformed to source code and the dependencies between TwoUse plug-ins are captured by eclipse manifest files. Finally, the management phase controls the development life cycle and provides versioning.

Figures 10.2, 10.3 and 10.4 depict three concrete diagrams and show how they depend on each other. The UML use case diagram depicts use cases from the perspective of two actors: software engineer and ontology engineer (Figure 10.3).

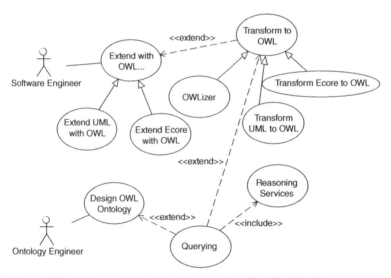

Figure 10.2 Snippets of Use Case Diagram from TwoUse Toolkit.

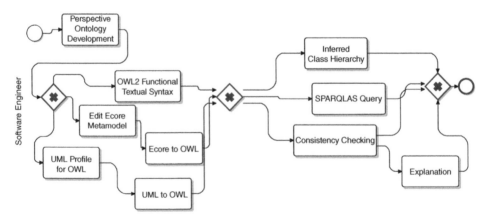

Figure 10.3 Snippets of BPMN Diagram from TwoUse Toolkit.

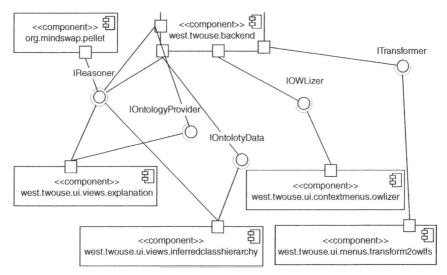

Figure 10.4   Snippets of Component Diagram from TwoUse Toolkit.

Software engineers use the TwoUse toolkit to extend UML or Ecore models with OWL annotations, to transform either of these metamodels into OWL, and subsequently to query them. Ontology engineers use a textual or graphical editor to design an OWL ontology to be queried afterwards.

The BPMN diagram shows the realization of these use cases from the perspective of the software engineer (Figure 10.3). Concretely, software engineers open the perspective "ontology development" to start editing and querying models and metamodels in OWL format.

The component diagram shows the internal structure and dependencies of component in the TwoUse architecture (Figure 10.4).

The TwoUse toolkit development life cycle relies on multiple models to provide viewpoints according to the development phase. For example, testers are interested in the information flow to realize functionalities provided by the system. Software engineers are interested in the impact of changing a given component or task. Other software engineers are interested in a modular view of the system for coordinating deliverables.

10.2.1   Requirements

Based on demand identified in developing the TwoUse toolkit, we identify three fundamental requirements for realizing a linked-open data environment in model-driven engineering:

> **RQ1: Model and metamodel interoperability.** Multiple metamodels may define the same concepts in different ways. Therefore, one needs to extend existing metamodeling frameworks (e.g., EMOF) to include support for primitives for relating different representations, thus allowing for integrated models that conform to heterogeneous metamodels.

RQ2: Techniques for composition of models and metamodels. For semi-automatically integrating modeling languages, one requires alignment techniques that allow for identifying equivalences over multiple languages and represent these equivalences (linking).

RQ3: Integration management. To achieve interoperability of modeling languages, one needs to control all stages of linking modeling languages. Models and metamodels must be *transformed* into the same representation. After the composition takes place developers can create or execute *queries* over artifacts.

Addressing these requirements allows for achieving the following features:

Consistent view over multiple MOF models: Based on an integration of multiple (MOF-based) languages, it is possible to have a consistent view over multiple artifacts.

Query answering: Based on underlying formal semantics and constraints, it is possible to define queries over multiple artifacts. For example, it is possible to answer questions like: What is the effect of updating the plug-in pellet? Which case tests must be executed if this plug-in is updated? Moreover, it enables the identification of the impact of some model components upon others (impact analysis) and thus the identification of cyclic dependencies or other unexpected consequences.

10.3 APPLICATION OF THE TWOUSE APPROACH

In this section, we describe how we exploit the TwoUse approach to address the requirements described in the previous section. We present how to extend and transform modeling languages into OWL. We illustrate how to query and manage links between modeling languages.

In the next subsections, we show how we apply the TwoUse components described in Chapter 7 to realize linked data capabilities to MOF languages. The approach consists of the following components: (1) model extension, (2) model transformation, (3) matching, and (4) querying (please refer to Section 7.3 for the components of the generic architecture).

10.3.1 Model Extension

OWL specifies class expression axioms, object property axioms, and individual axioms that serve to link similar classes and individuals over multiple metamodels and models. Because of OWL 2 expressiveness, it is possible to combine class expressions and axioms to express equivalencies between classes.

Figure 10.5 shows snippets of the UML and BPMN metamodels. From the UML metamodel, it depicts classes of the Use Case package and the Activity package. From the BPMN metamodel, it depicts classes that describe tasks and message edges. A look at both metamodels shows correspondences between the

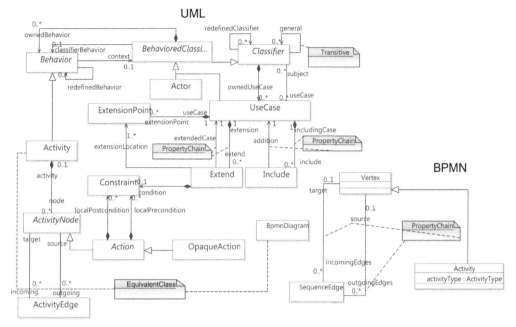

Figure 10.5   Snippet of BPMN Metamodel and UML Metamodel for Use Cases.

LISTING 10.1   Linking Ecore Metamodels with OWL.

```
1  EquivalentClasses (uml:Activity bpmn:BpmnDiagram)
   EquivalentClasses (uml:OpaqueAction ObjectSomeValuesFrom
       (bpmn:activityType bpmn:Task))
   TransitiveObjectProperty (uml:general )
   SubObjectPropertyOf( ObjectPropertyChain (bpmn:outgoingEdges bpmn:target)
       bpmn:sucessorActivities)
5  SubObjectPropertyOf( ObjectPropertyChain (uml:outgoing uml:target)
       uml: sucessorNodes )
   SubObjectPropertyOf( ObjectPropertyChain (uml:include uml:addition)
       uml:includeUseCases )
   SubObjectPropertyOf( ObjectPropertyChain
       (ObjectInverseOf(uml:addition) uml:includingCase)
       uml:includingUseCases )
   EquivalentObjectProperties (uml:sucessorNodes
       bpmn:sucessorActivities)
```

---

activity package and the BPMN metamodel. For example, the UML class `Activity` is equivalent to BPMN class `BpmnDiagram`.

In Listing 10.1, we present examples using OWL 2 syntax of constructs that can serve to link Ecore metamodels with OWL. In Line 1, we describe the equivalence of a UML `Activity` and `BpmnDiagram`. The equivalence of the set of individuals of the class `OpaqueAction` and the set of individuals of the class `Activity` where the property `activityType` is set to `Task` in the BPMN metamodel is defined in Line 2. Lines 3 and 4 characterize the property `general` of the UML metamodel as transitive. In Line 5, we derive a new property in the BPMN metamodel based on a property chain, i.e., a composition of the properties `outgoingEdges` and `target` are properties of `sucessorActivities`. For instance, *outgoingEdges*(*x*, *y*), *target*(*y*, *z*) → *successor Activities*(*x*, *z*). Similarly, a property chain `ancestorNodes` for the UML metamodel is defined in Line 6. The equivalence of the defined property chains is expressed in Line 7.

At the model level, developers can link models elements (metamodel instances) using OWL constructs. The `SameIndividual` axioms allow to define the equality of individuals in order to assert that instances of different metamodels are the same. For example, if we have a UML package called `west.twouse.backend`, we can assert that this package is the same as the Java package with the same name—`SameIndividual(uml:west.twouse.backend java:west.twouse.backend)`.

Additionally, OWL 2 provides constructs to enrich Ecore metamodels and extend its expressiveness. For example, object property axioms aim at characterizing object properties like the definition of sub-property relations and the expression of reflexive, irreflexive, symmetric, asymmetric, and transitive properties.

Another benefit of extending Ecore with OWL is monotonicity, i.e., adding further axioms to a model does not negate existing entailments. We can extend Ecore metamodels with OWL without invalidating any existing assertions. Thus, OWL provides a non-invasive way to integrate the same or similar concepts of different modeling languages.

In order to extend the expressiveness of Ecore metamodels, we use the textual notation defined in the TwoUse approach (Chapter 5).

By extending the Ecore metamodel with OWL, we enable developers with primitives for connecting metamodels like property equivalence, class equivalence, and individual equality, addressing the requirement `RQ1`.

10.3.2   Model Transformation

Based on the mappings between UML class-based modeling and OWL ontology, we develop a generic transformation to transform any Ecore Metamodel/Model into OWL TBox/ABox—OWLizer [163]. Figure 10.6 depicts the conceptual schema of transforming Ecore into OWL.

A model transformation takes a language metamodel and the annotations as input and generates an OWL ontology where the concepts, enumerations, properties, and datatypes (terms) correspond to classes, enumerations, attributes/references, and datatypes in the language metamodel. Additionally, the transformation takes the language model created by the language user and generates assertions in the OWL ontology.

The structural mapping from Ecore-based metamodels and models to OWL makes Ecore models in general data available as federated, accessible, and query-ready LOD resources. Multiple UML models can be transformed into a common representation in OWL ontologies according to this structural mapping. Having

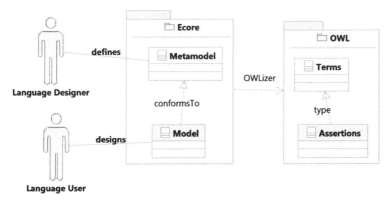

Figure 10.6   Mapping Ecore and OWL.

models represented in OWL ontologies, one might connect these ontologies and process these ontologies in a federated way.

Thus, the resulting OWL representations address the requirement RQ3 defined in Section 10.2.1.

10.3.3   Matching

In a model-driven paradigm, resources that are expressed using different modeling languages must be reconciled before being used. As described previously (see Section 3.5 in Chapter on Ontology Foundations), ontology matching allows for identifying correspondences of elements between two ontologies.

The quality of the correspondences depends on the applied criteria and technique. For example, if we apply only string matching, it generates a false positive correspondence between the UML `Activity` and the BPMN `Activity`. However, if we apply structure-based techniques and analyze the structure of the UML class Action and the BPMN class Activity, we see that both have similar structures (both have one superclass with two associations with the same cardinalities). However, the UML class Action is abstract and the BPMN class Activity is concrete. So, we could assert that the class Activity is a subclass of class Action.

Automatic matching techniques can be seen as support but should be assisted by domain experts, because of false positive matches. For example, the correspondence between `BpmnDiagram` and UML `Activity` is hard to catch automatically.

Ontology matching capabilities address the requirement RQ2 by identifying correspondences in order to link between (meta) models.

10.3.4   Querying with SPARQLAS

As described in Section 6.3, SPARQLAS allows for specifying queries using the OWL syntax for querying OWL ontologies. Listing 10.2 shows a SPARQLAS query about use cases that include other use cases. In this example, we ask about the

LISTING 10.2   Use cases That Includes Some Other Use Case.

```
1 Namespace: uml = <http://www.eclipse.org/uml2/3.0.0/UML#>
  Select ?x
  Where:
      ?x type (UseCase and includeUseCase some UseCase)
```

TABLE 10.1   TwoUse Measurement.

Phase	Artifact	Classes	Instances
User Requirements	Requirements specification	24	212
	UML diagrams	261	174
Analysis	BPMN diagram	24	754
Design	Metamode	23	5370
	Generator specification	20	3374
	Grammar specification	38	7611
	Model transformation	46	8043
Code	Manifest specification	53	2824
Management	Versioning and development life cycle	22	7032

individuals ?x whose type is an anonym class where the transitive property includeUseCase has as a value some use case.

With SPARQLAS, we cover the requirement RQ3 by providing distributed query facilities for models and metamodels that are represented in OWL.

10.4   VALIDATION

In order to validate our approach, we applied it in the TwoUse Toolkit. Table 10.1 presents the list of artifacts that are part of the development process of TwoUse Toolkit and the corresponding metrics. TwoUse Toolkit is a model-driven approach, i.e., each artifact listed below has an Ecore metamodel. For each artifact, we present the number of classes on the metamodel and the number of instances.

Using our approach, we are able to extract information about the Ecore metamodels and models listed in Table 10.1, partially fulfilling requirement RQ3. Our approach for transforming Ecore-compliant metamodels and models captures all Ecore constructs. Thus, transformations from OWL back to Ecore can be done lossless.

After extracting metamodel/model information from TwoUse artifacts, we used ontology matching techniques to identify correspondences between metamodels, fulfilling the requirement RQ2. For Ecore metamodels and models, we have used string distance method that analyzes the similarities between names of elements. Additionally, we have used the class structure alignment method for establishing alignments based on the comparison of class properties.

Ontology matching techniques still generate false positives. Thus, it is necessary that domain experts assist the ontology matching process at the metamodel level (M2) by manually determining which of the identified correspondences should be implemented. At the modeling level (M1), this problem is minimized by alignment rules that query the metamodels. For example, if an instance x of UML metaclass OpaqueAction has the same name as an instance of the BPMN metaclass Activity, then they are the same activity.

Once that domain experts have acknowledged which correspondences should take place, the axioms for realizing the correspondences are generated, fulfilling the requirement RQ2. Listing 10.3 presents sample axioms for linking model and metamodel. Equivalent classes or class expressions are connected by the construct EquivalentClasses, whereas individuals with the same name are connected by the construct SameIndividual.

Finally, we present the specification of queries mentioned at the beginning of this section, fulfilling the requirement RQ3. Listing 10.4 presents the SPARQLAS query for determining which tasks realize the use case Querying. The usage of the transitive property and property chain for includeUseCases simplifies the query.

LISTING 10.3   Sample of Linking Ecore Metamodels with OWL.

```
1  EquivalentClasses (uml:Activity bpmn:BpmnDiagram)
   EquivalentClasses (uml:ActivityNode bpmn:Vertex)
   EquivalentClasses (uml:OpaqueAction ObjectSomeValuesFrom
       (bpmn:activityType bpmn:Task))
   EquivalentDataProperties (uml:name bpmn:name)
5  SameIndividual (uml:west.twouse.reasoner srs:west.twouse.reasoner)
   SameIndividual (mf:west.twouse.reasoner srs:west.twouse.reasoner)
   SameIndividual (uml:ReasoningServices srs:ReasoningServices)
```

LISTING 10.4   Which Tasks Realize Use Case Querying?

```
1  Namespace : = <http://www.eclipse.org/uml2/3.0.0/UML#>
   Select ?name
   Where:  _:u name "Querying" ^^ xsd:string
           _:u includeUseCases ?uc
5          ?uc ownedBehavior ?act
           ?act node ?node
           ?node type OpaqueAction
           ?node name ?name
```

LISTING 10.5 What Use Cases to Test If the Component west.twouse.reasoner Is Updated

```
1  Namespace: uml = <http://www.eclipse.org/uml2/3.0.0/UML#>
   Namespace: srs = <http://west.uni-koblenz.de/SRS#>
   Namespace: mf = <http://west.uni-koblenz.de/EclipseManifest#>
   Select ?name
5  Where:   ?component mf:name "west.twouse.reasoner" ^^ xsd: string
            ?component srs:requirement ?requirement
            ?requirement srs:useCase ?uc
            ?uc uml:name ?name
   Union:
10          ?uc (inverse uml:addition o uml:includingCase) ?iuc
            ?iuc uml:name ?name
```

Moreover, the query works for Activity Diagrams and BPMN Diagrams, since both are integrated.

Listing 10.5 presents an example of querying involving both levels (metamodel M2 and model M1) at the same time. It uses the alignments presented above, i.e., individuals of class UseCase and class Component are the same as individuals of classes UseCase and Component with the same name. Moreover, it uses an anonym property that corresponds to a property chain of the property uml:includingCase and the inverse of the property uml:addition.

10.4.1 Limitations

Since there exist multiple strategies for matching and aligning ontologies, it is possible that false positive matches occur. For example, OWL classes with the same name are matched as equivalent, if one uses a string-based matching technique, although the two concepts are semantically different. Thus, domain experts must be involved to validate the results of matching and alignments.

10.5 RELATED WORK

The integration of software artifacts has been the topic of works including [3, 102]. However, these approaches presented dedicated extractors for specific systems like bug tracking and version control but not for software models. Moreover, neither of these approaches presents formats for publishing data suitable to the linked-data approach, i.e., they do not share the principles of interoperability for connecting federated software models across the web.

Kiefer et al. [89] and Iqbal et al. [79] explore semantic web approaches for transforming software artifacts such as data from version control systems, bug tracking tools, and source code into linked data. Both approaches use artifact-specific extractors and thus work only for a fixed number of software artifacts. We propose a generic approach for transforming and managing any MOF metamodel in a web format.

The OMG ontology definition metamodel [114] specifies mappings between OWL and UML. In this chapter, we present a general approach for mapping arbitrary Ecore models into OWL. We provide the means to express any MOF metamodel in its equivalent OWL.

The OMG Request For Proposal for MOF to RDF Structural Mapping in support of Linked Open Data [115] aims at defining a structural mapping between OMG-MOF models and RDF. This work can be seen as a response to this request. We propose an approach that can serve as a benchmark for future proposals.

10.6 CONCLUSION

In this chapter, we propose an approach to enable analysis, federation, and querying of models expressed in MOF compliant languages, including OMG standards and domain-specific languages. The contribution in this chapter shows that the usage of the Ontology Web Language for specifying metamodels is a viable solution to achieve interoperability and shared conceptualizations. The role of OWL is not to replace MOF or the Object Constraint Language, since OWL addresses distinct requirements, specially concerning networked environments. OWL should complement the spectrum of software modeling languages in a unified architecture.

CONCLUSION OF PART III

In this part, we have analyzed the impact of using OWL constructs and OWL ontology services in software modeling languages (addressing Research Problem III from Section 1.2).

We used class expressions to decouple class selection from OCL expressions embedded in query operations (addressing Research Problem III.A) and improve software design patterns that address variant management.

When applying it in ontology-based information systems, the usage of SPARQLAS4TwoUse for integrating queries over ontologies with operations impacts on maintainability, reusability, and extensibility (addressing Research Problem III.B).

Moreover, the transformation of MOF-based software languages into OWL supports software development by allowing developers to extract software engineering data using SPARQL-like queries over multiple software artifacts (addressing Research Problem III.C).

PART IV

APPLICATIONS IN THE SEMANTIC WEB

CHAPTER 11

MODEL-DRIVEN SPECIFICATION OF ONTOLOGY TRANSLATIONS

The alignment of different ontologies requires the specification, representation, and execution of translation rules. The rules need to integrate translations at the lexical, the syntactic, and the semantic layer requiring semantic reasoning as well as low-level specification of ad-hoc conversions of data. Existing formalisms for representing translation rules cannot cover the requirements of these three layers in one model. We propose a metamodel-based representation of ontology alignments that integrate semantic translations using description logics and lower-level translation specifications into one model of representation for ontology alignments.[1]

11.1 INTRODUCTION

The reconciliation of data and concepts from ontologies and data repositories in the Semantic Web requires the discovery, representation, and execution of ontology translation rules. Although research attention is now devoted to the discovery of alignments between ontologies, a shallow inspection of ontology alignment challenges reveals that there does not exist *one* accessible way of representing such alignments as translation rules [41].

The reason is that alignments must address ontology translation problems at different layers [30, 39]:

1. At the *lexical layer*, it is necessary to arrange character sets, handling token transformations.

2. At the *syntactic layer*, it is necessary to shape language statements according to the appropriate ontology language grammar.

3. At the *semantic layer*, it is necessary to reason over existing ontological specifications and data in both the source and the target ontologies.

---

[1]This chapter contains work from the paper "Model-Driven Specification of Ontology Translations" presented at ER'08 [149].

Semantic Web and Model-Driven Engineering, First Edition. Fernando Silva Parreiras.
© 2012 Institute of Electrical and Electronics Engineers. Published 2012 by John Wiley & Sons, Inc.

For addressing ontology translation problems at the semantic layer, existing frameworks provide reasoning in one or several logical paradigms, such as description logics [19, 65] or logic programming [28, 36, 96]. For addressing ontology translation problems at lexical and syntactic layers, alignment frameworks take advantage of platform-specific implementations, sometimes abstracted into translation patterns [109, 95] or into logical built-ins [96].

Such hybrid approaches, however, fail to provide clarity and accessibility to the modelers that need to see and understand translation problems at semantic, lexical, and syntactic layers. Indeed, modelers need to manage different languages: (1) an ontology translation language to specify translation rules and (2) a programming language to specify built-ins, when the ontology translation language does not provide constructs to completely specify a given translation rule. This intricate and disintegrated manner draws their attention away from the alignment task proper down into diverging technical details of the translation model.

Filling the gap in the ontology translation domain between ontology mapping languages and general purpose programming languages helps to improve productivity, since modelers will not have to be aware of platform-specific details and will be able to exchange translation models, even if they use different ontology translation platforms. Moreover, maintenance and traceability are facilitated because knowledge about mappings is no longer embedded in the source code of programming languages.

We propose a platform-independent approach for ontology translations, based on model-driven engineering (MDE) of ontology alignments. The framework includes a language to specify ontology translations—the Model-Based Ontology Translation Language (MBOTL). In order to reconcile *semantic* reasoning with idiosyncratic *lexical* and *syntactic* translations, we integrate these three translation problems into a representation based on a joint metamodel. The joint metamodel comprises, among others, the OWL 2 metamodel and the OCL metamodel to support specification, representation, and execution of ontology translations.

The chapter is organized as follows: The running example and the requirements for ontology translation approaches are explained in Section 11.2. Our solution is described in Section 11.3, followed by examples in Section 11.4. In Section 11.5 we discuss the requirements evaluation, and in Section 11.6 we present related work. The conclusion, Section 11.7, finishes the chapter with an outlook to future work.

11.2   CASE STUDY

We consider two ontologies of bibliographic references from the test library of the Ontology Alignment Evaluation Initiative (OAEI) [41] to demonstrate the solution presented in this chapter: the reference ontology (#101) and the Karlsruhe ontology (#303). Canonical mappings covered by examples in this chapter and snippets of the source and target ontologies using the Manchester OWL Syntax [73] are shown in Figure 11.1. Please refer to OAEI for complete ontologies.

By examining the mapping between ontology #101 and ontology #303, it becomes clear that translations are required in order to realize the mapping. Individu-

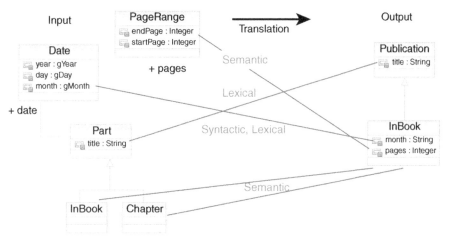

Figure 11.1   Ontology Mapping Challenge for the Running Example.

als of the classes Chapter and InBook in ontology #101 are translated into individuals of the class InBook in the ontology #303. Values of the object property month having a Gregorian month, e.g., "-01", are translated into the equivalent unabbreviated form, e.g., "January". Values of the data property pages in ontology #303 can be calculated by subtracting the value of the data property initialPage from the value of the property endPage in ontology #101.

We define the translation rules explained above by the following logical rules. All variables are treated as universally quantified and prefixed with a question mark. Let *builtin: notShortened* be a built-in function that returns the unabbreviated month, *builtin: toUpper* be a built-in function to capitalize strings, *builtin:—* be a subtractor function, *s* be the namespace prefix of the source ontology #101, and *t* be the namespace prefix of the target ontology #303, the translation rules can be written as follows:

$$t : InBook(?x) \wedge t : month(?x, ?m) \wedge t : title(?x, ?n) \wedge t : pages(?x, ?p) \leftarrow$$
$$(s : InBook(?x) \vee s : Chapter(?x)) \wedge s : month(?x, ?y) \wedge$$
$$builtin : notShortened(?y, ?m) \wedge s : title(?x, ?z) \wedge \quad (11.1)$$
$$builtin : toUpper(?z, ?n) \wedge s : pages(?x, ?w) \wedge s : startPage(?w, ?a) \wedge$$
$$s : endPage(?w, ?e) \wedge builtin : -(?e, ?a, ?p).$$

The translation rule of authors is not trivial either. While in ontology #101 the authors are collected by recursively matching the property first of the class PersonList, in ontology #303 it is a matter of cardinality of the object property author. Let *list:contains* be the built-in able to filter a list structure into object properties, the referred rule can be written as follows:

$$t : Book(?x) \wedge t : author(?x, ?u) \leftarrow$$
$$s : Book(?x) \wedge s : author(?x, ?y) \wedge list : contains(?y, ?u). \quad (11.2)$$

However, built-ins are black boxes that conceal knowledge about algorithms, compromising traceability and maintenance. Therefore, an approach able to specify rules and built-ins without code specifics is required.

From inspecting these examples, we illustrate requirements for a platform-independent ontology translation approach addressing translation problems at the following ontology translation layers proposed by Corcho and Gómez-Pérez [30] based on Euzenat [39]: the lexical layer, the syntactic layer, the semantic layer, and the pragmatic layer. Since the pragmatic layer addresses the meaning of representation in a given context, it is similar to the semantic layer from the point of translation decisions. In this chapter, we refer to both layers as semantic layer.

1. The lexical layer deals with distinguishing character arrangements, including:

    (a) *Transformations of element identifiers.* These are required when different principles are applied to named objects, for example, when transforming the value of the data property `title` into capital letters.

    (b) *Transformations of values.* These are necessary when source and target ontologies use different date formats, for example, when transforming a Gregorian month into an unabbreviated form.

2. The syntactic layer covers the anatomy of the ontology elements according to a defined grammar. The syntactic layer embraces:

    (a) *Transformations of ontology element definitions.* These are needed when the syntax of source and target ontologies are different, e.g., when transforming from OWL RDF syntax into OWL XML syntax.

    (b) *Transformations of datatypes.* These involve the conversion of primitive datatypes, e.g., converting string datatype to date datatype.

3. The semantic layer comprises transformations dealing with the denotation of concepts. We consider the following aspects:

    (a) *Inferred knowledge.* Reasoning services are applied to deduce new knowledge, e.g., inferring properties from class restrictions.

    (b) *Transformations of concepts.* This takes place when translating ontology elements using the same formalism, e.g., translating a concept from Karlsruhe's OWL ontology for bibliographic references into one or more concepts in the INRIA's OWL ontology.

The translation problems are classified in non-strict layers, e.g., one rule commonly addresses more than one translation problem. For example, in Rule 2, the built-in `toUpper` solves a translation problem at the lexical layer, the translation of months happens at the syntactical layer and is achieved by the built-in `notShortened` and, finally, the translation of the union of individuals of the classes `Chapter` and `InBook` in ontology #101 into individuals of the class `InBook` in ontology #303 appears at the semantic layer.

An orthogonal classification of ontology translation problems is given by Dou *et al.* [36]. From their point of view, ontology translation problems comprise dataset translation, ontology-extension generation, and querying. This chapter concentrates

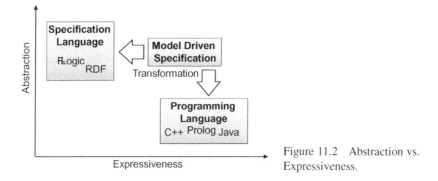

Figure 11.2 Abstraction vs. Expressiveness.

on dataset translation, i.e., translation of instances, leaving the model-driven engineering of the remaining problems for future work.

11.3 APPLICATION OF THE TWOUSE APPROACH

The proposed ontology translation approach relies on advances in model-driven engineering (MDE) with support for ontology reasoning services [20]. We define here the Model-Based Ontology Translation Language (MBOTL) comprising (1) a textual concrete syntax used to write translation rules, (2) an integrated metamodel as abstract syntax to represent the translation rules as models, (3) an extensible model library to provide built-in constructs, and (4) model transformations yielding translational semantics.

Figure 11.2 relates MBOTL with existing approach with respect to abstraction and expressiveness. Languages for specifying translation rules like F-logic and RDF abstract from platform details, but they are not as powerful as programming languages. The usage of a domain specific language for ontology translation (MBOTL) provides the right trade-off between abstraction and expressiveness.

11.3.1 Concrete Syntax

While visual notations are effective in communicating models, textual notations are preferable to express more complex structures. The following subsections present the anatomy of the translation rules, alluding to the requirements presented in Section 11.2.

11.3.1.1 Dealing with Translation Problems at Semantic Layer In order to extract information from the source ontology, we need a query language able to determine which datasets are to be translated. We use OCL expressions [116] to formulate queries. Indeed, OCL has been used in MDE for specifying constraints and queries that are side effect free operations. As OCL is originally designed for UML or MOF, we provide a transformation from OCL to SPARQL.

Ontology translation problems at the semantic layer are treated by querying individuals of the source ontology using OCL queries and matching target individuals. These assumptions have been used by model transformation languages like OMG MOF Query/View/Transformation (QVT) [113] and the Atlas Transformation Language (ATL) [82]. We base MBOTL upon the ATL concrete syntax to specify ontology translations.

The example depicted in the Figure 11.3 illustrates the concrete syntax. A rule Conference2Conference is defined for translating individuals of the class Conference in ontology #101 into individuals of the class Conference in ontology #303.

In OCL, a dot-notation is used to navigate through properties. In the scope of our extension of OCL, a property can be an OWL data property, an OWL object property, a predefined operation, or a helper. A helper is a user defined side effect free query operation belonging to a defined class in one of the given ontologies.

For example, in the expression s.location, s is a reference to an individual of the class Conference with location resulting in a value of the class Address. The navigation can also end with an operation evaluation, as depicted in the Figure 11.3, where the operation concat is used to concatenate the properties city and country.

11.3.1.2 Addressing Translation Problems at Lexical and Syntactic Layers Ontology translation problems at lexical and syntactic layers are supported by employing operations or helpers. For example, for the type string, the operation toUpper() returning a string object with capital letters is available. Thus, the evaluation of s.title.toUpper() capitalizes the value of the property title.

The operation toUpper() is an example of predefined operation. The set of predefined operations is available in the OCL library (M1 layer). These operations are applicable to any type in OCL. Additionally, it is possible to specify *ad hoc* operations, the so-called helpers.

11.3.2 Metamodels

The textual concrete syntax for ontology translation specification presented in the previous section has an integrated metamodel as equivalent abstract syntax. The integrated metamodel consists of the following metamodels: MOF metamodel [111], OCL metamodel [116], OWL metamodel [114], and part of the ATL metamodel [82].

```
                             Matched Rule
                            ⌒⌒⌒⌒⌒⌒⌒
1        rule Conference2Conference {
              from              Ontology Element
                                ⌒⌒⌒⌒⌒⌒⌒⌒
3    In Pattern / s : _101!Conference
                       \ Variables
5            to       /
                   / t : _303!Conference (  Property Expression
                                            ⌒⌒⌒⌒⌒⌒⌒⌒⌒
7  Out Pattern/      location <- s.location.city.concat(', ')
                           \       .concat(s.location.country),
9                       ...    \ Operation Expression
                   ),
11     }                        \ Assignment Operator
```

Figure 11.3 Example of a Translation Rule.

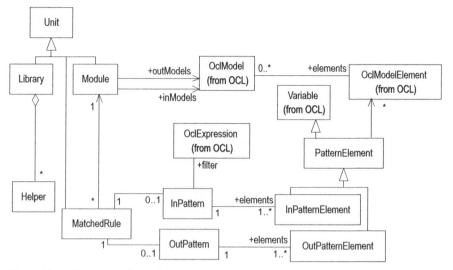

Figure 11.4   Fragment of the ATL Metamodel.

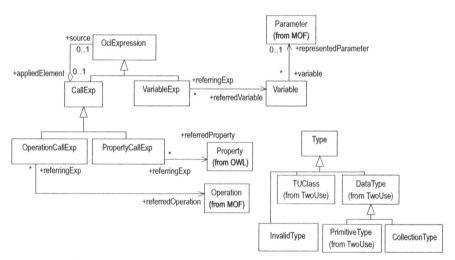

Figure 11.5   Snippet of the Package `Type` and Package `Expressions` of the OCL Metamodel.

The translation metamodel (Figure 11.4) allows for describing translations between two ontologies by a model. A translation is characterized as a `Module` relating source ontologies (`inModels`) and target ontologies (`outModels`). A `MatchedRule` is a specific translation rule that has a pattern for the input model (`inPattern`) and a pattern for the output model (`outPattern`). The `InPattern` has one or more elements that are OCL variables (`Variable`). Variables are bound to model elements (`OclModelElement`). The `InPattern` has an `OclExpression` acting as query to refine individuals of the `OclModelElement`.

Since each expression in OCL has a type, we need a type metamodel (Figure 11.5). The expression evaluation produces a value of type of the expression. The type `TUClassAdapter` is the particular composition of the OWL class with the MOF class. This composition allows for applying side effect-free operations into individuals of OWL classes.

Figure 11.5 depicts additionally another part of the integrated metamodel, namely the package `Expressions` of the extended OCL metamodel. The class `OclExpression` enables MBOTL to define the abstract syntax for OCL expressions. The integration with the OWL metamodel is accomplished by expressions of the type `PropertyCallExp`. Such expression allows for navigating through OWL properties, as explained in Section 11.3.1.

The operation call expressions (`OperationCallExp`) support the declaration of built-in operations and helpers. An operation call expression evaluates to the result of a class operation, providing that such operation is side effect free. This resource is particularly relevant in the scope of ontology translation, i.e., it enables queries to invoke built-in reasoning operations or helpers.

11.3.3   Model Libraries

The model libraries define a number of datatypes, class identifiers, and operations that must be included in the implementation of MBOTL. These constructs are instances of an abstract syntax class. The foundation library exists at the M1 level, where the abstract syntax (metamodel) exists at M2 level. The foundation library is composed of the XML Schema Datatypes library, the RDF library, the OWL library, and the OCL library.

An example of M1 object of the extended OCL library is the construct `oclAny`. All types inherit the properties and operations of `oclAny`, except collection types. This invariant allows for attributing predefined operations to classes. The OCL library is based on the standard OMG OCL library [116].

11.3.4   Semantics

The semantics of MBOTL is defined by the semantics of the languages comprising the integrated metamodel (Section 11.3.2).

MBOTL is translated into a target language (SPARQL and Java). Regarding the target languages, the semantics of SPARQL is described by entailment regimes, whereas the semantics of Java can be defined by providing an Abstract State Machine [63]. More specifically, the SPARQL basic graph pattern is described according to an entailment regime. Indeed, SPARQL-DL [154] provides an entailment regime for OWL-DL.

11.3.5   Ontology Translation Process

In order to guide the user from the ontology translation specification until the running code, the ontology translation process covers the following steps:

1. *Specification of Ontology Translation.* The ontology translation rules and helpers are specified by the user using MBOTL.

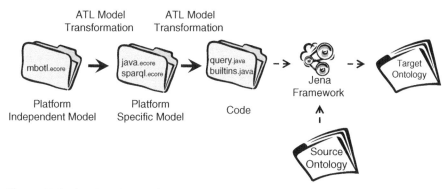

Figure 11.6   Ontology Translation Process.

2. *Specification of Model Transformations.* In order to have a running implementation of ontology translation, the ontology translation specification model is transformed into models for a given platform. The model transformation specification mapping the MOBTL model onto platform-specific models must be specified here. Our framework provides model transformations from MOBTL into SPARQL and Java as target platforms. Notice that other target platforms like F-Logic and Java can be considered.

3. *Transformation into Target Platform.* Three transformations take place at this step. Firstly, the ontology translation specification in the concrete syntax (MOBTL file) is injected into a model conforming with the integrated metamodel, i.e., the ontology translation specification model. The second transformation is responsible for generating models according to the target metamodels, e.g., SPARQL and Java metamodels. Thirdly, SPARQL queries in the SPARQL concrete syntax and Java code are extracted from the SPARQL and Java MOF-based models.

11.3.6   Implementation

The implementation comprises (1) the environment to specify ontology translations and (2) transformations into ontology translation engines in order to realize ontology translation. Figure 11.7 depicts a screen shot of the MBOTL implementation on TwoUse toolkit.

Taking the ontology translation specification model as a source model, we use the Atlas Transformation Language [82] framework to define model transformations into models for an ontology translation platform (2). We use SPARQL and Java as target languages and the Jena framework as a ontology translation solution. The Jena framework includes an API for OWL ontologies and reasoners, as well as a SPARQL engine.

Elements of the ontology translation specification model concerning translation problems at the semantic layer are transformed by ATL into SPARQL CONSTRUCT queries. The SPARQL engine can be extended using custom SPARQL

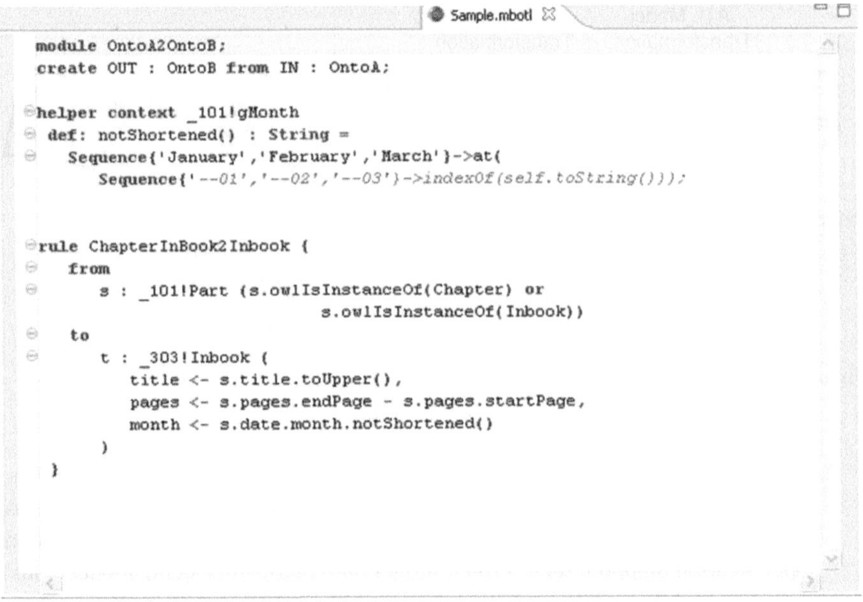

```
                                          Sample.mbotl ⊠                          ⊟
   module OntoA2OntoB;
   create OUT : OntoB from IN : OntoA;

 helper context _101!gMonth
   def: notShortened() : String =
     Sequence{'January','February','March'}->at(
        Sequence{'--01','--02','--03'}->indexOf(self.toString()));


 rule ChapterInBook2Inbook {
   from
       s : _101!Part (s.owlIsInstanceOf(Chapter) or
                              s.owlIsInstanceOf(Inbook))
   to
       t : _303!Inbook {
          title <- s.title.toUpper(),
          pages <- s.pages.endPage - s.pages.startPage,
          month <- s.date.month.notShortened()
        )
    }
```

Figure 11.7   Screenshot of MBOTL.

filter functions—as foreseen as an extension hook in the SPARQL standard, but also using so-called *predicate functions*. Predicate functions are not matched against the knowledge base like normal RDF predicates, but evaluated in Java code. Filter and predicate functions are used to handle translation problems at the lexical and syntactic layer. These functions are defined in the ontology translation specification model and have the Java code automatically generated by the ATL transformation.

The next section illustrates our approach by addressing the translation problems presented in Section 11.4, specifying the translation rules and transforming the ontology translation specification into SPARQL and Java code.

11.4   EXAMPLES

This section presents rules integrating translation problems at semantic, syntactic, and lexical layers, according to the problems presented in Section 11.2.

Example 1: Semantic, Syntactic, and Lexical Translations. The classes Chapter and InBook in ontology #101 are translated into the class InBook in the ontology #303. The translation rule uses a helper to transform a Gregorian month, e.g., "-01", into its equivalent unabbreviated form, e.g., "January". This helper is applicable only to the gMonth datatype. Using MBOTL, we can specify both the rule and the helper—and hence lexical, syntactical and semantical translations—

LISTING 11.1   Semantic, Syntactic, and Lexical Translations with MBOTL.

```
1 helper context _101 ! gMonth
  def: notShortened() : String =
    Sequence{'January','February','March'}->at (
        Sequence{'-01','-02','-03'}->indexOf(self.toString())))
5
  rule ChapterInBook2Inbook {
    from
      s : _101!Part (s.owlIsInstanceOf (Chapter) or
                              s.owlIsInstanceOf(Inbook))
10    to
      t : _303!Inbook (
          title <- s.title.toUpper(),
          pages <- s.pages.endPage - s.pages.startPage,
          month <- s.date.month.notShortened(),
15    )
  }
```

LISTING 11.2   SPARQL Query Corresponding to `ChapterInBook2Inbook`.

```
1CONSTRUCT {?x rdf:type _303:Inbook. ?x _303:title ?y.
          ?x _303:pages ?z. ?x _303:month ?w}
  WHERE {
    ?x rdf:type _101:Part.
5   {?x rdf:type _101:Chapter UNION ?x rdf:type _101:Inbook}
    ?x _101:title ?u. ?u userdef:toUpper ?y.
    ?x _101:pages [rdf:type _101:Page;
                    _101:startPage ?w; _101:endPage ?u].
    ?z userdef:difference (?u ?w).
10  ?x _101:date [rdf:type _101:Date; _101:month ?m].
    ?m userdef:notShortened ?w.
  }
```

using an integrated framework. The helper is shown on top of Listing 11.1, followed by the translation rule.

After specifying mappings with MBOTL, we transform MBOTL specification into suitable languages for execution. Our implementation uses SPARQL queries for semantic mappings and Java code for syntactic translations.

In this example, the rule `ChapterInBook2Inbook` is transformed into a SPARQL query (Listing 11.2), whereas the helper `notShortened` is transformed into Java code (Listing 11.3). The Java code extends a suitable SPARQL engine, in this case Jena.

LISTING 11.3   Automatically Generated Java Code for the Function `notShortened`.

```
 1 public class NotShortened extends PFuncSimple {
       /** Implements Sequence {'January', 'February', 'March'} */
       private List colLit1() {
          List /*(String)*/ myList = new ArrayList(/*String*/);
 5        myList.add ( "January" );
          myList.add ( "February" );
          myList.add ( "March" );
          return myList;
       }
10
       /** Implements Sequence {'—01', '—02', '—03'} */
       private List colLit2() {
          List /*(String)*/ myList = new ArrayList(/*String*/);
          myList.add ( "-01" );
15 myList.add ( "-02" );
          myList.add ( "-03" );
          return myList;
       }
20 private QueryIterator execFixedSubj(Node subject,
             Node object,  Binding binding,
           ExecutionContext execCxt) {
       /** Implements the built-in notShortened() : String */
25     return new QueryIterSingleton (
          colLit1().size() > colLit2().indexOf(this.toString())
          ?((String)colLit1().get(colLit2().indexOf(this.toString())))
          : "", execCxt);
       }
30 }
```

In Lines 1 and 2 of Listing 11.2, the pattern in the target ontology is specified. It is filled with variable bindings obtained from the pattern in Lines 4–11. Variables in SPARQL are denoted with a question mark. In Line 5 we see the disjunction of chapter and book. In Lines 7–8, the start and end page properties of the complex "Page" concept in the source ontology is matched. They are used to compute the simpler page length in the target ontology using a predicate function in Line 9. Analogously, the abbreviated date is matched and mapped in Lines 10–11.

As an example of the translation of a helper, we show a part of the Java code resulting from transforming `notShortened` into a Jena predicate function in Listing 11.3.

Example 2: Semantic and Syntactic Translation of Complex Structures.   In the ontology #101, the class `Article` has the property `author` with the range of type `PersonList`. `PersonList` has a property `first` with the range of type `Person` and a property `rest` with the range of type `PersonList`.

TABLE 11.1   Satisfying Ontology Translation Requirements.

Requirement (Section 11.2)	Use Case	Implementation
1.(a)	Converting to capital letters	Listing 11.1, Line 12
1.(b)	Converting date formats	Listing 11.1, Line 14
2.(b)	Converting gMonth to String	Listing 11.1, Line 14
3.(a)(b)	Union of Chapter and InBook	Listing 11.1, Line 8–9

This rule relies on a helper, able to match elements recursively. In this case, the helper algorithm must add the current value of the property first to the collection of authors and verify whether the value of the property rest is nil, returning in this case the collection. Otherwise, the helper is invoked until value nil is found.

As we can see from the examples, helpers are used for lexical and syntactical translations (Example 1) and semantic translations (Example 2).

11.5   ANALYSIS

In response to the requirements deduced in Section 11.2, Table 11.1 shows use cases according to each requirement and where to find the corresponding examples in this chapter.

Translation problems of lexical nature, e.g., converting a string to an uppercase string, are managed by using predefined OCL operations applied to specific types of objects, in this example a string type. It is also possible to write functions, i.e., helpers, to perform *ad hoc* operations. For example, the helper notShortened (Listing 11.1) allows for converting date formats, i.e., replacing a value of gMonth type to the unabbreviated form.

Translation problems inherent in the syntactic layer are handled distinctly. For example, datatype conversions are achieved by invoking predefined operations, e.g., toString() (Listing 11.1).

Translation problems at the semantic layer, regarding datasets of ontologies with different vocabularies but the same formalism, is demonstrated by the running example. In Listing 11.1, the individuals of the class Chapter in ontology #101 and the individuals of the class InBook are translated into individuals of the class InBook in ontology #303.

Limitations.   Our approach has restrictions reflected by the ATL metamodel. With ATL, it is possible to realize only unidirectional translations. A bidirectional translation must be accomplished by two unidirectional translations.

Moreover, at the current state of development, it is not possible to validate or to reason over translation models. In other words, it is not possible to test the translation model without transforming it into the target platform (SPARQL and Java).

11.6   RELATED WORK

Since related work has been done in the field of ontology alignment, we group works according to semantic, syntactic, and lexical layers.

Among works covering lexical and syntactic translations, Model transformation languages like OMG Query/View/Transformation (QVT) [113] and Atlas Transformation Language (ATL) [82] allow for defining how to transform MOF-based models using declarative and imperative constructs. Nevertheless, they do not support the OWL metamodel and do not provide description logic constructs. Our contribution extends the ATL solution by integrating with the OWL metamodel and providing such constructs.

The work of Atzeni *et al.* [8] is based on a metamodel approach with models described in terms of the constructs they involve, taken from a given set of predefined ones. However, the work is in the scope of databases and does not support reasoning at the semantic layer.

Among works covering semantic reasoning capabilities, C-OWL [19] and the ontology mapping system proposed by Haase and Motik [65] are formal solutions for ontology mapping with description logic expressiveness. The mappings are based on subsumption relationships of concepts between ontologies. Notwithstanding, the usage of built-ins to express lexical and syntactic translation problems is not possible. A metamodeling-based approach of Haase and Motik [65] is provided by Brockmans *et al.* [22]. Although the usage of built-ins in mapping rules is allowed, the latter approach does not provide the means do specify built-ins without recourse to programming languages, whereas MBOTL allows for specifying *ad hoc* functions by helpers.

Among works covering lexical, syntactic, and semantic translations, MAFRA [109] and RDFT [95] are frameworks enabling dataset translations. Nonetheless, both are based on RDF schema and neither provide the expressiveness of OWL nor support reasoning capabilities of description logic inference engines.

OntoMorph [28] and the framework proposed by Dou [36] for ontology translation rely on first-order logic (FOL) expressiveness to specify translation rules. Our approach counts on the decidable subset of FOL, the description logic $\mathcal{SHOIN}$ (D), with complete and sound automated reasoning services for addressing semantic translation problems. Moreover, while the first solution relies on PowerLoom and the latter on Web-PDDL, we propose a platform independent model-based translation language, flexible enough to cope with different knowledge representation systems.

OntoMap [96] is a mapping solution allowing for visual specification of mappings, with a limited number of translation functions. Snoogle [133] is an ontology translation tool that enables the use of SWRL rules to express translations and alignments between geospatial ontologies. While in both approaches it is possible to use custom plug-ins, the user has to write functions using Java and the Jena framework. In contrast, our approach allows for specifying mapping rules and functions in a platform-independent and integrated way.

Corcho and Gómez-Pérez [29] propose ODEDialect, a set of declarative languages to specify ontology translations. However, it is a platform-specific approach based on Java that exposes users to the complexity of programming languages, whereas MBOTL allows modelers to concentrate on business logics instead.

11.7 CONCLUSION

This chapter presents a solution for ontology translation specification that aims at being more expressive than ontology mapping languages and less complex and fine-grained than programming languages. The solution is comprised of a concrete syntax, an integration metamodel covering OWL, MOF, OCL, and ATL metamodels, and model transformations from MOBTL into SPARQL and Java. We validate our solution against canonical ontology translation problems organized in three layers—lexical, syntactic, and semantic.

CHAPTER 12

AUTOMATIC GENERATION OF ONTOLOGY APIS

When developing application programming interfaces of ontologies that include instances of ontology design patterns, developers of ontology-based information systems usually have to handle complex mappings between descriptions of information given by ontologies and object-oriented representations of the same information. In current approaches, annotations on API source code handle these mappings, leading to problems with reuse and maintenance. We propose a domain-specific language to tackle these mappings in a platform-independent way—*agogo*. Agogo provides improvements on software engineering quality attributes like usability, reusability, maintainability, and portability.[1]

12.1 INTRODUCTION

Upper level ontologies and domain ontologies comprise occurrences of a variety of ontology design patterns (OPs) [52]. These ontologies are generally large and densely axiomatized. Therefore, in comparison with generic solutions like RDF or OWL APIs, the development of dedicated application programming interfaces (APIs) eases the adoption of this kind of ontologies.

When developing such dedicated APIs, developers of ontology-based information systems face the challenge of mapping descriptions of complex relations or entities to object-oriented (OO) representations thereof. For example, core ontologies such as COMM [6], X-COSIMO [50], or Event-Model-F [140] represent complex objects, e.g., a multimedia annotation, a conversation among participants, or an event decomposition. Such objects are not represented by a single instance of a class but by ontology design patterns involving a number of connected (linked) instances.

The task of implementing object manipulation functionality becomes complex as well. For example, the specification of creation or deletion of multimedia objects is spread out in a number of connected (linked) data instances using decompositions, descriptions, and segments.

---

[1]This chapter contains work from the paper "APIs *a gogo*: Automatic Generation of Ontology APIs" presented at ICSC'09 [153].

Semantic Web and Model-Driven Engineering, First Edition. Fernando Silva Parreiras.
© 2012 Institute of Electrical and Electronics Engineers. Published 2012 by John Wiley & Sons, Inc.

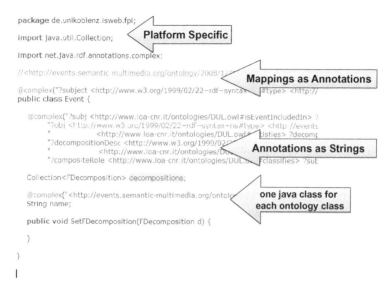

```
package de.unikoblenz.isweb.fpi;

import java.util.Collection;

import net.java.rdf.annotations.complex;

//<http://events.semantic-multimedia.org/ontology/2008/1/

@complex("?subject <http://www.w3.org/1999/02/22-rdf-synta  #type> <http://
public class Event {

    @complex("?subj <http://www.loa-cnr.it/ontologies/DUL.owl#isEventIncludedIn> ?
        "?obj <http://www.w3.org/1999/02/22-rdf-syntax-ns#type> <http://events
        "                <http://www.loa-cnr.it/ontologies/DUL.owl  #decomp
        "?decompositionDesc <http://www.w3.org/1999/02
        "                <http://www.loa-cnr.it/ontologies/Do
        "?compositeRole <http://www.loa-cnr.it/ontologies/DUL.ow  #classifies> ?sut

    Collection<FDecomposition> decompositions;

    @complex("<http://events.semantic-multimedia.org/ontolo
    String name;

    public void SetFDecomposition(FDecomposition d) {

    }

}
```

Platform Specific

Mappings as Annotations

Annotations as Strings

one java class for
each ontology class

Figure 12.1   Limitations of Current Approaches.

Specifying interfaces for manipulating ontologies should provide constructs that enable handling of complex structures defined by ontologies. Accordingly, such constructs need to map from a single programming object to multiple RDF statements.

Current approaches store annotations as plain text on API source code to handle these mappings. These approaches have the following disadvantages (Figure 12.1):

- Low level of abstraction. When it comes to complex mappings between ontology classes and OO classes, current approaches require developers to deal with platform-specific details like database connection, data validation, and deviating attention from the mappings.

- No portability. The APIs are tightly coupled to programming languages and cannot be easily ported to other programming platforms.

- Low reuse rate. Mappings between ontology classes and OO classes are in the form of annotations. These annotations are stored as plain text, and to be reused, they have to be copied instead of being referred.

- Hard maintenance. Changes of mappings on the ontology usually imply changing all occurrences of a given Java annotation, since mappings are stored as annotations and must be copied to be reused.

Indeed, addressing these issues has been one of the objectives of the field of model-driven engineering (MDE) [88], i.e., to develop and manage abstractions of the solution domain towards the problem domain in software design. Considering the expansion and usage of MDE techniques, we investigate the following problems in this chapter: What MDE techniques address the aforementioned issues? What are the results of applying these techniques in ontology API development?

Tackling the aforementioned problems results in improving the usability, maintainability, and portability of ontology API specifications. This enables developers to concentrate on the mappings instead of taking care of problems inherent in programming. By considering mappings as first-order objects rather than as annotations, developers can keep track of mapping ontology elements like classes and properties. Finally, introducing an abstraction from the programming language allows developers to generate APIs for different programming languages or domain-specific APIs.

We extend the TwoUse approach and introduce *agogo*, an approach that provides a development environment for API developers to handle complex mappings, to define and to reuse complex OPs, and to automatically generate ontology API code. Moreover, we present results of comparing *agogo* with existing ontology API code, showing drastic reduction in size.

We organize this chapter as follows: After introducing the challenges and benefits of *agogo*, we analyze current approaches in Section 12.5. We derive requirements based on our experience in developing APIs for core ontologies (COMM [6], X-COSIMO [50], and Event-Model-F [140]) in Section 12.2. Section 12.3 presents the techniques and artifacts used by *agogo* to tackle these requirements. We describe how *agogo* uses these techniques and artifacts by example in Section 12.3.2. In Section 12.4, we analyze how the *agogo* approach allows for improving quality of ontology APIs based on the quality characteristics introduced in this section. Finally, Section 12.6 concludes this chapter.

12.2   CASE STUDY

From the set of ontology design patterns found in the COMM ontology, we use the Semantic Annotation Pattern to illustrate the solution presented in this chapter. The basic rationale applies to any other pattern used in COMM, X-COSIMO [50], and Event-Model-F [140]. Figure 12.2 illustrates the semantic annotation pattern as

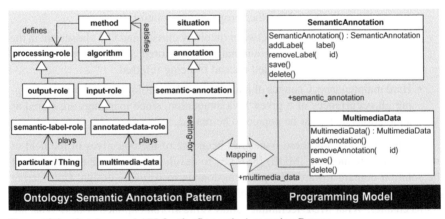

Figure 12.2   Ontology and API for the Semantic Annotation Pattern.

defined by the COMM ontology and the desired classes of the API in the programming model.

The pattern describes the annotation of a multimedia item with some label, e.g., the annotation of a part of a photo with a label pointing to a person—Carsten (not included in the Figure 12.2). This association is embodied through a `semantic-annotation` that satisfies a `method` (e.g., algorithms for image recognition) that defines a `semantic-label-role` as well as an `annotated-data-role`. The `multimedia-data` has to play the `annotated-data-role`, which identifies the part of the image that is annotated. The depicted particular has to play the `semantic-label-role`, e.g., the instance `Carsten`.

The COMM API comprises mappings between such patterns and Java objects. For instance, objects of the class `SemanticAnnotation` represent instantiations of the pattern `semantic-annotation`. The mapping is achieved by implementing the intended behavior for create, read, update, and delete operations (CRUD) that affect the knowledge base accordingly:

Create: The construction of a *new* object, i.e., an object representing data that is *not yet present* in the knowledge base, needs to result in the correct and complete instantiation of an ontology pattern.

Read: The construction of an object based on *existing* data in the knowledge base. Although similar from an application programming interface point of view, the underlying operation in the knowledge base is fundamentally different. In this case, the knowledge base is queried for the instance of a pattern, and all involved resources and statements required to fully instantiate the object.

Update: The update of an object needs to result in the replacement of information in the knowledge base. Thereby, developers need to implement distinct update behaviors. For example, the class `MultimediaData` implements a method to add a `SemanticAnnotation`. This method either adds a semantic label to an existing `SemanticAnnotation` for the image or creates a new instance of a `SemanticAnnotation`.

Delete: The deletion of an object has different implications. For instance, the deletion of `SemanticAnnotation` results in the deletion of the *relation* between the image and Carsten as expressed by the instance of the pattern. In another scenario, developers may want to delete the image and Carsten as well or to delete the representation of Carsten.

Based on our experience in developing the core ontologies COMM, X-COSIMO, and Event-F and their APIs, we have identified problems and derived the following requirements:

RQ1. Emphasis on domain concepts. When programming ontology APIs, developers have to deal with aspects inherent in programming languages like database access coding or data validation coding. For example, for each mapping, developers have to write code for handling access to the knowledge base. These tasks divert developers' attention from the specification of ontology APIs.

Moreover, currently, developers have to redundantly implement programming code for validating the correct instantiation of objects, e.g., code that checks whether all required information is available in an object. In our example, the Java class `SemanticAnnotation` needs to provide code that checks whether all information for a correct instantiation of the *Semantic Annotation Pattern* is available. The instantiation of this pattern without both the part of the image and the depicted person makes no sense.

RQ2. Patterns as first-class citizens. Currently, when specifying standard behaviors for CRUD operations, developers have no choice but tangling the specification over the classes that implement the pattern. Thus, developers cannot reuse these operations across software projects or programming languages.

RQ3. Support for debugging. The ontology API code consists of complex queries. Such queries are typically represented as strings and are not always recognized by programming languages or programming environments during compile time. This makes debugging particularly hard for two reasons: First, the programming environment gives no hints for syntax errors during compile time. Accordingly, developers can track syntax errors only at runtime. Second, even at runtime, semantic errors are hard to recognize. For instance, the following SPARQL-query has the correct syntax but does not return any results due to the mistyped concept name *semantic-an(n)otation*: *"select ?s where {?s a comm: semantic-anotation}"*

RQ4. Change management. As the programming code references ontology concepts that the programming environment ignores, refactoring code in case of ontology changes is difficult. For instance, if a developer changes the ontology concept `semantic-annotation` to `Annotation`, associations in the programming code (e.g. annotations, query strings, URI strings) need to be updated manually.

RQ5. Generation of APIs for the same ontology or for different platforms. Currently, mappings cannot be reused in other programming languages, since they are implemented by programming code and specific means provided by a programming language, e.g., Java annotations.

The problems that motivate these requirements impair the development of ontology APIs by retarding their availability, affecting the adoption of the respective ontologies. Moreover, having families of APIs for a given ontology or APIs for different platforms is implausible due to the effort needed.

To enforce the importance of these requirements, we analyze the current COMM API. The current COMM ontology has 702 classes while its API has 34 packages, 294 classes, 1823 functions, and 11597 non-commenting source statements (NCSSs).

12.3   APPLICATION OF THE TWOUSE APPROACH

agogo is an application of the TwoUse approach for automatically generating OWL APIs on demand. To tackle the problems presented in the previous section, *agogo* relies on technologies regularly applied in model-driven development: metamodeling, concrete syntax, and model transformations.

Agogo's metamodel and concrete syntax constitute a domain-specific language (DSL) that provides an abstraction layer over programming languages, encapsulating redundant data validation, or implementation behavior. The DSL simplifies the process of specifying ontology APIs by focusing on domain concepts (RQ1).

Moreover, the usage of metamodels allows for defining concepts in a structured way, improving maintainability (RQ4). For example, elements of the ontology API specification are maintained as single units instead of being stored in annotations.

The definition of constraints on concepts in the *agogo* metamodel improves design time checking, i.e., it enables API developers to validate API specifications against these constraints, minimizing errors at runtime (RQ3).

The concrete syntax for ontology API specification enables users to model patterns as first-class citizens (RQ2). For example, developers specify CRUD operations and patterns using SPARQL syntax independently from the class definition. Furthermore, the concrete syntax allows for identifying missing references and for helping to find errors before code generation.

Model transformations allow for code generation to eventually more than one platform, overcoming the restriction on programming language (RQ5). Additionally, model transformations ease the creation of families of APIs. It enables developers to release a subset of the COMM API for lightweight applications, if required.

12.3.1   Key Domain Concepts

The *agogo* metamodel extends the TwoUse metamodel and defines the concepts of an ontology API specification and corresponds to the abstract syntax of *agogo* DSL. The definition of the concepts of an ontology API specification in a metamodel raises the abstraction level and allows API developers to work exclusively with relevant constructs. For example, developers handle mappings, patterns, and operations without considering implementation issues.

In the following, we describe *agogo* key concepts. Figure 12.3 depicts how these concepts are related in the *agogo* metamodel.

Classes. The construct `Class` defines the associations between platform specific classes and ontology classes. The property `ontoElement` associates classes to patterns or ontology classes.

Patterns. When a platform specific class does not correspond directly to a single ontology class but to an occurrence of an ontology design pattern (OP), the concept of pattern applies. The construct `QueryPattern` describes OPs using SPARQL queries [126]. It is possible to define patterns for classes, properties and operations.

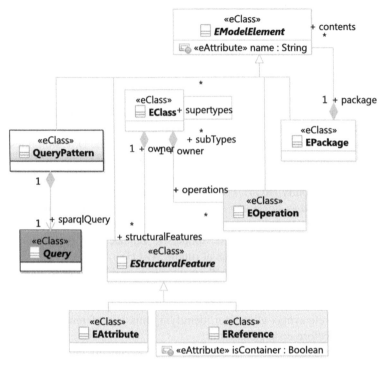

Figure 12.3   Snippet of the *agogo* Metamodel.

Operations. CRUD operations (Create, Read, Update, and Delete) are defined in ontology APIs to enable manipulation of ontology classes. Using SPARQL-like syntax, these operations as well as patterns are defined in a platform independent way.

Imports. Developers may group patterns for classes, properties, and operations into packages and make them available or reuse them in another API specification.

The *agogo* metamodel extends the TwoUse metamodel that and reuses existing metamodels for SPARQL, OWL 2, and Ecore.

Metamodel Constraints.   Together with the *agogo* metamodel, we define constraints used by the syntax checker to enforce valid ontology API specifications. This functionality allows for identifying errors before generating ontology APIs.

In Listing 12.1, we exemplify these constraints with two OCL constraints. In the first constraint, we enforce that all variables passed as parameter to an operation are used in the body of the query.

In the second constraint, we enforce that every pattern associated to a property must include the variable ?obj in the select statement. The predefined variable ?obj points to the range of a property in the OO representation.

LISTING 12.1   Constraints on the *agogo* Metamodel.

```
1  context Operation
   inv inv1:self.ontoElement.SPARQLQuery.whereClause
     .variables.includesAll(self.parameters);

5  context Property
   inv inv2: self.ontoElement.SPARQLQuery
     .variables.varname. includes ("obj");
```

LISTING 12.2   An Example of Using *agogo* Basic Constructs.

```
1  PREFIX rdf: <http://www.w3.org/1999/02/22-rdf-syntax-ns#>
   PREFIX core: <http://comm/core.owl#>
   PREFIX dvl: <http://comm/dolce-very-lite.owl#>
   PREFIX edns: <http://comm/extended-dns-very-lite.owl#>
5  PREFIX agogo: <http://uni-koblenz/agogo#>

   PACKAGE <http://comm.agogo#> {

     IMPORT <http://comm-lite.agogo#>;
10
     CLASS SemanticAnnotation TO core:semantic-annotation {
       PROPERTY label^^dvl:particular TO prop_label;
       . . .
```

12.3.2   *agogo* Concrete Syntax by Example

In this section, we demonstrate the main components of the *agogo* textual syntax and exemplify them with the running example. In this chapter, we concentrate on how *agogo* supports patterns as first-class citizens, CRUD operations, support for debugging, and change management.

To improve user experience, we have based the definition of the *agogo* textual syntax on the SPARQL syntax [126]. For example, for prefix declaration and specification of patterns, we use the SPARQL constructs.

Listing 12.2 presents the basic constructs of the *agogo* syntax like PACKAGE, IMPORT, CLASS, and PROPERTY in exemplary fashion. We group API specifications into packages, which contain all model elements. The construct IMPORT allows for reusing classes and patterns definitions.

The construct CLASS specifies the mappings between ontology concepts and OO representations. The reserved word TO points to a pattern declaration or directly to a SPARQL query that represents a pattern. The construct PROPERTY follows the same rationale. In Listing 12.2, the property label is of type dvl:particular and points to the pattern prop label, defined in Listing 12.3.

LISTING 12.3   Patterns as First-Class Citizens.

```
1  PATTERN prop label {
     SELECT   ?obj
     WHERE
       { ?subj   edns:satisfies   ?method .
5        ?method  rdf:type         edns:method ;
                  edns:defines    ?slr ;
                  edns:defines    ?adr .
         ?slr  rdf:type   core:semantic-label-role .
         ?adr  rdf:type   core:annotated-data-role .
10       ?obj   edns:plays      ?slr .
         ?data  edns:plays      ?adr ;
                rdf:type        core:multimedia-data .
         ?subj  edns:setting-for  ?obj ;
                edns:setting-for  ?data .
15     }
     }
```

To detach pattern specifications from class specifications, patterns must be first-class citizens, i.e., their declarations must not be associated to class declarations.

The definition of patterns is an essential point in our approach. To represent a pattern, we need to represent how ontology classes and relations compose this pattern. A user-friendly way of doing it is by using the SPARQL syntax. By using the SPARQL SELECT construct, developers describe the pattern structure.

In Listing 12.2, we declare that the OO class SemanticAnnotation maps onto the ontology class core:semantic-annotation and that the OO class SemanticAnnotation has a property of name label of type dvl:particular. Next, we specify how the values of the property label are matched. To have the labels of a semantic annotation, we need to navigate through the structure of the Semantic Annotation Pattern (Figure 12.2).

Listing 12.3 shows the declaration of a query pattern for the property label. The pattern is a SPARQL query that describes the structure of the Semantic Annotation Pattern. In the clause WHERE, the structure of the pattern is represented. In the clause WHERE, we have all classes and relations that need to be created, read, updated, and deleted when dealing with the property label. The SPARQL query in Listing 12.3 is comparable with the classes and relations composing the pattern in the Figure 12.2.

The definition of patterns includes the usage of two predefined variables: ?subj and ?obj. The variable ?subj identifies the OO class, i.e., in this case, the class SemanticAnnotation, while the variable ?obj refers to the values or the property label.

For example, this pattern will match the labels associated to the class semantic-annotation, e.g., the particular Carsten (see Section 12.2). In other words, the domain of the pattern `prop_label` is the ontology class `semantic-annotation` and the range is the class `particular` (see declaration in Listing 12.2).

Model transformations are responsible for generating automatically CRUD (Create/Read/Update/Delete) operations for each OO property based on the pattern specification. Although CRUD operations are generated automatically, in some cases, developers may want to customize operations. For example, developers may want to customize an insert operation to use existing individuals.

To specify Read operations, we use the standard construct `SELECT`, and to specify custom CRUD operations, we use SPARQL Update [144] syntax[2]. Listing 12.4 shows the definition of the customized operation `addLabel`. The operation uses an existing instance of the class `method-:method1`. For each variable in the INSERT clause, one new individual is created in the ontology (except variables `?subj` and `?obj`).

Model transformations take specifications of CUD and generate corresponding programming language code. For example, the usage of variables (Listing 12.4, Lines 4–6) leads to the generation of statements to create a new instance of the class `semantic-annotation-role` (`?slr`).

Developers may declare patterns anonymously, i.e., developers may associate patterns directly with properties or classes. Listing 12.5 shows the specification of a pattern associated with the property `semantic annotation`.

The definition of the SPARQL syntax together with the SPARQL metamodel allows for identifying non-well-formed SPARQL statements. Consequently,

LISTING 12.4   Definition of an Operation Using SPARQL Update Syntax.

```
1  OPERATION addLabel (? obj ) {
      INSERT DATA
      {
         :method1     edns:defines     ?slr.
5        ?slr         a core:semantic-label-role.
         ?obj         edns:plays       ?slr .
         ?subj        edns:setting-for ?obj.
      }
      WHERE
10    {
         ?subj         edns:satisfies   :method1.
      }
   };
```

[2]*agogo* does not require a SPARQL Update engine. We use the SPARQL Update syntax only to generate appropriate code.

LISTING 12.5   Mapping a Property onto a Pattern.

```
1 CLASS MultimediaData TO core:multimedia-data {
  PROPERTY semantic-annotation ^^ core:semantic-annotation TO {
    SELECT ?obj
    WHERE
5    {?obj    edns:setting-for ?subj ;
            rdf:type core:semantic-annotation ;
                edns:satisfies        ?method .
      ?method  rdf:type        edns:method ;
                edns:defines         ?adr .
10    ?adr rdf:type core:annotated-data-role .
      ?subj    edns:plays        ?adr .
    }
  };
```

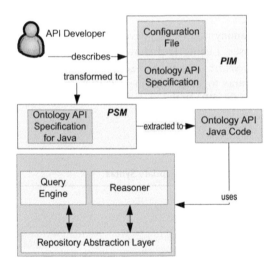

Figure 12.4   Architecture of the *agogo* Approach.

developers may check for syntax errors at design time. Moreover, by integrating the OWL 2 metamodel into the *agogo* metamodel, *agogo* allows for enforcing the ontology as schema for the specification. If developers mistype names of classes or individuals, the syntax checker identifies that there is no corresponding element in the ontology for that name. This functionally helps to identify typos at design time.

12.3.3   Implementation

agogo consists of a model-driven process composed of model transformations, models, and metamodels. Figure 12.4 depicts the *agogo* architecture and the embed-

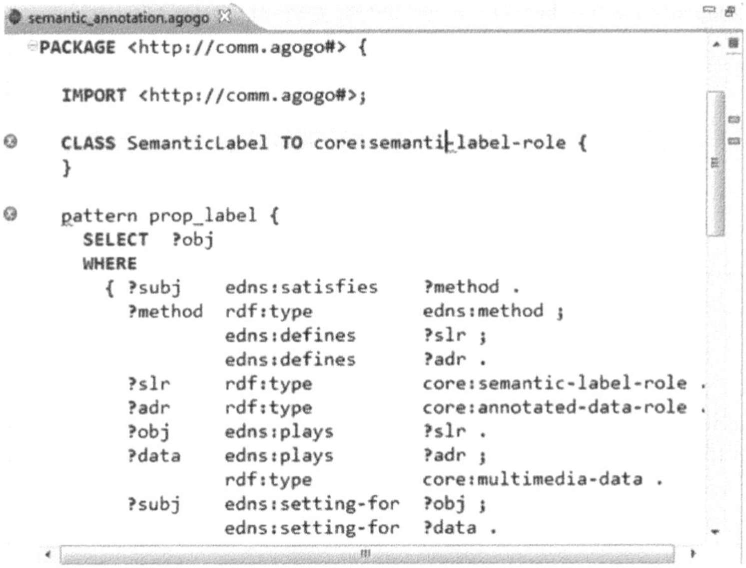

```
● semantic_annotation.agogo ⊠                                    ⊟ ⌐
  ⊝PACKAGE <http://comm.agogo#> {                              ▲ ▦

    IMPORT <http://comm.agogo#>;

⊗   CLASS SemanticLabel TO core:semanti|label-role {
    }

⊗   pattern prop_label {
      SELECT  ?obj
      WHERE
        { ?subj    edns:satisfies    ?method .
          ?method  rdf:type          edns:method ;
                   edns:defines      ?slr ;
                   edns:defines      ?adr .
          ?slr     rdf:type          core:semantic-label-role .
          ?adr     rdf:type          core:annotated-data-role .
          ?obj     edns:plays        ?slr .
          ?data    edns:plays        ?adr ;
                   rdf:type          core:multimedia-data .
          ?subj    edns:setting-for  ?obj ;
                   edns:setting-for  ?data .
◄ └                          ⫼                          ► ▼
```

Figure 12.5   Screenshot of *agogo* Implementation.

ded MDA process. Developers use *agogo* textual syntax to specify ontology API specifications. These specifications are injected to platform-independent models (PIMs). We use EFMText [70] for defining *agogo* textual syntax and Ecore [164] for defining the *agogo* metamodel.

Model transformations take the PIM and a configuration file as input. The configuration file contains directives for code generation like names of classes and identifiers. Consequently, model transformations produce platform-specific models (PSMs) as output, which are then extracted to programming code. To specify model transformations, we use the Atlas Transformation Language (ATL) [82].

The usage of a PIM enables developers to detach the ontology API specification from programming code. Consequently, model transformations for different programming platforms may be specified, allowing code generation for multiple platforms.

We have implemented *agogo* as part of the TwoUse Toolkit. Figure 12.5 shows a screen shot of the semantic annotation example design using the agogo DSL. By referring to non-existing classes or using misspelled reserve words, the editor raises an error.

12.4   ANALYSIS

In this section, we analyze how *agogo*'s functionalities affect the quality of ontology API specifications. In the following, we consider four quality characteristics of ontology API specification according to ISO 9126 [80].

TABLE 12.1 Comparison of Size between *agogo* and the Current COMM API in Two Cases.

	agogo		Current COMM API	
	Case 1	Case 2	Case 1	Case 2
Packages	1	1	4	15
Classes	2	5	19	101
NCSS	50	70	461	3928

Q1. Usability. One cognitive dimension of usability analysis is the abstraction level [58]. With *agogo*, developers concentrate on constructs related to the problem domain, e.g., `map` and `pattern`, raising the abstraction level.

Raising the abstraction level influences productivity. To demonstrate this impact, we have conducted an exploratory evaluation of the size of both *agogo* API specifications and Java API specifications of the running example based on the current COMM API.

As metric for size, we consider the number of non-commenting source statements (NCSSs) [121]. Table 12.1 summarizes the comparison of size between *agogo* and the current COMM API in two cases.

In *Case1*, we consider a specification with only two classes: `SemanticAnnotation` and `SemanticLabel`. The current COMM API requires coding 19 Java Classes and more than 400 NCSSs. With *agogo*, developers concentrate on coding 50 NCSSs in two classes.

To have an idea of the effort of extending or taking a subset of the COMM API, we consider the addition of the class `MultimediaData` in *Case2*. Although including the class `MultimediaData` implies implementing another OP—the object decomposition—the size of the ontology API increases drastically to approximately. nine times the original size.

Based on this exploratory analysis, even if developers have in *agogo* half of the productivity ratio they have in Java, because the *agogo* specification is smaller than the Java specification, the effort for producing NCSSs in Java is still higher. In other words, developers are more productive with *agogo*, with benefits increasing as the API grows due to the possibilities for reuse and improved maintenance.

Q2. Reusability. By defining patterns as first-class citizens, developers may reuse patterns on further mappings. Moreover, complete libraries can be reused to generate derived APIs. For example, API developers may want to have multiple ontology APIs according to the complexity, e.g., COMM lite and COMM full.

Q3. Maintainability. *agogo* defines constructs as metamodel concepts instead of parsing strings of text. Consequently, structured models are easier to maintain than plain text.

TABLE 12.2   Correlating *agogo* Requirements with Quality Attributes.

Requirement	Artifact	Example	Quality Attribute
RQ1	MM, CS	Figure 12.3, List. 12.2	Q1
RQ2	MM, CS	List. 12.2, List. 12.3	Q2
RQ3	MM, CS	Figure 12.3, List. 12.1	Q3
RQ4	MM, CS	List. 12.5	Q3
RQ5	T	—	Q4

When the ontology changes, developers change the ontolgy API specification and automatically regenerate the ontology API. The syntax checker assists developers with tasks like renaming and raises errors for missing references.

Moreover, constraint validation and syntax checking take place at design time, and not only at runtime as by existing approaches. The developer counts on a syntax checker for pattern specifications.

Q4. Portability. Providing that model transformations are available, it is possible to generate APIs for multiple programming languages. Developers describe ontology APIs once and model transformations use the specification to generate ontology APIs for multiple platforms.

agogo may be seen as an abstraction layer over existing approaches for generating ontology APIs (Section 12.5). As *agogo* does not mandate a specific programming language, developers may specify model transformations for transforming *agogo* API specifications into programming code for the platform of choice.

Nevertheless, developers need to bear in mind the effort of specifying the model transformations. To achieve abstraction from programming code, the model transformations have to handle the gap between the *agogo* API specification and the programming language. The initial effort in developing these model transformations needs to be considered when deciding to provide ontology APIs in a given programming language.

To track how the *agogo* approach addresses the requirements of Section 12.2 and affects ontology API quality characteristics, we present a traceability matrix in Table 12.2. It relates *agogo* requirements, the artifacts that tackle these requirements (metamodel (MM), concrete syntax (CS), and transformations (T)), examples, and their relations to quality attributes. As one may notice, by establishing a domain-specific notation for designing ontology APIs, we improve the quality characteristics above, corroborating the literature on domain-specific languages [99].

12.5   RELATED WORK

Ontology engineers count on a variety of solutions for specifying ontology APIs. In the following, we analyze these approaches according to the abstraction level.

Generic solutions for developing ontology APIs are the Jena API [178] and the Sesame API [24]. However, these approaches are triple-based, i.e., developers have to work with methods such as getSubject and getObject. Low abstraction level and high complexity are aggravated when dealing with big ontologies.

RDFReactor [172] and [85] are "plain" RDFS—Java/OO mapping approaches. These approaches do not provide support for complex mappings implied by ontology design patterns, i.e., developers have to program one java class for each ontology class. Moreover, when the ontology changes, developers have to manually change ontology API code.

A solution with higher abstraction level is ActiveRDF [118]. ActiveRDF relies on annotations to specify mappings for Ruby programs. As we have seen, annotations are hard to maintain and to debug. Moreover, these applications force API developers to commit to one programming language.

12.6 CONCLUSION

This chapter presents an application of TwoUse for designing mappings between complex ontology descriptions and object oriented representations—*agogo*. The solution comprises a domain-specific language and model transformations to generate API programming code.

agogo improves productivity on ontology API specification and enables developers with functionalities infeasible until now. Additionally, *agogo* accomplishes improvements in reusability and maintainability.

CHAPTER 13

USING TEMPLATES IN OWL ONTOLOGIES

Integrating model-driven development and semantic web resulted in metamodels and model-driven tools for the semantic web. However, these metamodels or tools do not provide dedicated support for dealing with templates in ontology engineering. Templates are useful for encapsulating knowledge and modeling recurrent sets of axioms. We propose an extension of existing metamodels and tools to support ontology engineers in modeling ontology templates. Our approach allows ontology engineers to keep template specifications as first-class citizens, reducing complexity and increasing reusability in ontology engineering. We demonstrate our approach with templates for ontology design patterns.[1]

13.1 INTRODUCTION

As OWL ontologies becomes more complex, approaches that use abstraction to encapsulate complexity emerge. For example, ontology engineers may use macros and annotations to represent ontology design patterns (ODPs) [52], key artifacts for reuse in ontology engineering.

Nevertheless, these approaches do not consider abstraction mechanisms as first-class citizens to encapsulate complexity. For instance, the development of ODPs relies on the usage of macros [173] or annotations [78] to represent the structure of these patterns. Ontology engineers should be able to encapsulate reusable sets of axioms that capture modeling practices in templates. In other words, ontology engineers need declarative specifications of templates and tools to test these specifications and realizations.

The usage of templates is a well-known technique to encapsulate complexity in generative programming, leading OMG to add support for templates in UML [117]. For ontology engineers, the main advantages of using templates are increase in productivity, since ontology engineers rely on well-known reusable pieces to design the ontology; and increase in reliability, since templates comprise reliable sets of axioms developed by domain experts.

---

[1]This chapter contains work from the paper "A Model-Driven Approach for Supporting Ontology Design Patterns" [148].

Semantic Web and Model-Driven Engineering, First Edition. Fernando Silva Parreiras.
© 2012 Institute of Electrical and Electronics Engineers. Published 2012 by John Wiley & Sons, Inc.

Providing declarative specifications of templates and support for template realization enables ontology engineers to handle templates as first-class citizens instead of having template descriptions embedded in ontologies as annotations or using preprocessing macros. Moreover, a dedicated approach for handling templates enables ontology engineers to explore the full expressiveness of template declarations and to analyze template realization scenarios.

Current approaches [78, 173, 158] have limited expressiveness and are tool-oriented instead of generic, i.e., they do not allow ontology engineers to choose freely tools and representation notations for templates. Moreover, current ontology metamodels and model-driven tools do not provide these constructs [114, 23, 106].

Templates should be first-class citizens in a higher abstract level than annotations, i.e., in the ontology metamodel. Such an approach allows the following: (1) to extend the usage of templates to other OWL-related languages like SWRL [76], SAIQL [93], or SPARQL-DL [154]; (2) to use different modeling notations, including graphical languages; and (3) to extend the usage of templates beyond individuals, classes, and properties to literals and class expressions.

The contribution of this chapter is twofold: (1) we present an approach for modeling ontology templates applicable to different OWL metamodels and extensible to SWRL, SPARQL-DL, and SAIQL; (2) we introduce graphical notations containing dedicated constructs to specify templates and to bind them with domain ontologies, enabling ontology engineers to design and test templates as first-class citizens.

We present our approach in this chapter as follows. Section 13.2 gives a scenario motivating template design. We give an example of our approach and describe the graphical notations and the main constructs of our approach in Section 13.3. Section 13.4 presents application scenarios of ontology templates. Section 13.5 presents an analysis of existing approaches, and Section 13.6 concludes the chapter.

13.2 CASE STUDY

As a running example, we consider an ontology for capturing music records as domain ontology. For this domain ontology, we want to reuse existing knowledge from three resources: ontology design patterns (ODP), SWRL rules, and domain closure.

To represent the role of performers, we use the *AgentRole* ontology design pattern [52] from the ontology design pattern collection. The intention of this ODP is to represent agents and their roles. A `Role` is a subclass of the class `Concept`, i.e., a `Role` is a specialization of `Concept`. An `Agent` is a specialization of the class `Object`. The property `hasRole` assigns `Roles` to `Objects`, whereas the inverse property `isRoleOf` assigns `Objects` to `Roles`.

Additionally, we want to propagate the genre of a musical group to a record, i.e., we want to assert that the style of the record is the same as the style of the group. Thus, we reuse a SWRL rule (in this case a description logic rule) to move the property values from one individual to a related individual.

Furthermore, we want to consider the knowledge about genres as complete. In general, OWL models realize the open-world assumption (OWA), i.e., the represented knowledge base is considered as incomplete. However, in certain applications, it is more appropriate to consider a knowledge base as complete. If complete knowledge is assumed, the set of all individuals in the knowledge base must be equivalent to the set of individuals declared.

The following knowledge base (TBox and ABox) describes a simple domain ontology about music records. *Beatles* and *RollingStones* are instances of *Group*. A *Group* has *Performer* as a member. A *Performer* plays a role in a *Group*. The *Group* belongs to a *Genre* and produces *Records*. In our knowledge base, there are only four genres: *Rock, Blues, Country,* and *Samba*.

$$Group \sqsubseteq \exists hasMember.Performer \sqcap \exists hasStyle.Genre$$
$$\sqcap \exists creatorOf.Record \tag{13.1}$$

$$Record \sqsubseteq \exists stylePeriod.Style \tag{13.2}$$

$$Performer \sqsubseteq \exists hasRole.Position \tag{13.3}$$

$$Genre(Rock, Blues, Country, Samba), Record(LetItBleed) \tag{13.4}$$

$$Group(RollingStones), Performer(Mick), Position(Vocalist) \tag{13.5}$$

$$hasRole(Mick, Vocalist), creatorOf(RollingStones, LetItBleed) \tag{13.6}$$

$$hasMember(RollingStones, Mick) \tag{13.7}$$

$$hasStyle(RollingStones, Rock), Group(Beatles) \tag{13.8}$$

$$hasStyle(Beatles, \neg Blues), hasStyle(Beatles, \neg Country) \tag{13.9}$$

$$hasStyle(Beatles, \neg Samba) \tag{13.10}$$

Based on this knowledge base, a user may be looking for all rock bands as described by the following description logic query: $\exists hasStyle.\{Rock\}$. If we consider an incomplete knowledge base, the result of this query contains only the individual *RollingStones*. If we assume a complete knowledge base though, the result also includes the group *Beatles*.

There are multiple strategies for closing the domain of a class. In this chapter, we only make the class *Genre* equivalent to the set of existing individuals of the class *Genre*, i.e., *Rock, Blues, Country, Samba*.

Additionally, we want to assert that the genre of a record is the same as the genre of the group:

$$Performer(?a) \land Genre(?s) \land Record(?c) \land hasStyle(?a?s)$$
$$\rightarrow creatorOf(?a, ?c) \rightarrow stylePeriod(?c, ?s) \tag{13.11}$$

For other ontologies, ontology engineers want to reuse these resources, since these resources represent modeling guidelines and best practices identified by domain experts. Thus, it makes sense to encapsulate these axioms, identifying generic pieces, i.e., to create a *template*. We consider templates as parameterized generic sets of axioms that can be combined with different specifications to produce a variety of artifacts like domain ontologies and queries.

A possibility is to use inheritance to encapsulate reusable axioms and define a super class of *Genre* that is equivalent to a list of existing individuals of this type, and the SWRL rule to propagate the genre to records. However, this super class and rule are reusable for other types of art like poetry, painting, and acting and work only for music.

In summary, the usage of a template has the following advantages:

- Templates work as interfaces to encapsulate axioms and expose only the constructs to be used as parameters. Thus, ontology engineers know exactly which concepts and roles are needed for applying the ontology design pattern.

- Ontology engineers can reuse repeatedly templates in other ontologies or in other pieces of the same ontology.

- Ontology engineers bind and unbind templates to exploit different results, e.g., using the open world or closed domain assumption.

- Templates are reliable, since ontology experts derive templates from well-known sets of axioms.

- Templates realize macros when inheritance is not enough.

13.3 APPLICATION OF THE TWOUSE APPROACH

In this section, we describe the application of TwoUse and the main constructs of our metamodel extension and the different notations.

Figure 13.1 depicts the result of applying TwoUse into the running example to add support for templates in OWL ontologies. It uses the UML profile for OWL with package templates. A template `agent-role` represents the agent role ODP. This template has the two parameters—Agent and Role—to be bound in order to adopt this pattern.

A template `closed-domain` defines a class X that is equivalent to a list of individuals {}. Class X and class expression {} are template parameters and are bound to the class `Genre` and to the class expression {`Rock Blues Country Samba`}of the ontology `music records`.

Finally, the third template shows an ontology with a SWRL rule asserting that the genre of an artist is the same as the genre of a record. When realizing these template bindings, the result is set of axioms (1–11) presented in Section 13.2.

13.3.1 Extending the OWL Metamodel with Templates

In this section, we use the TwoUse integration and apply the idea of package templates of UML into OWL and extend it to different OWL-related languages like SWRL [76] and query languages like SPARQL-DL Abstract Syntax [154] and SAIQL [93].

UML [117] allows software developers to design templates of packages and classes. With templates, software developers describe reusable structures with unbound parameters. In order to use these templates, developers have to bind

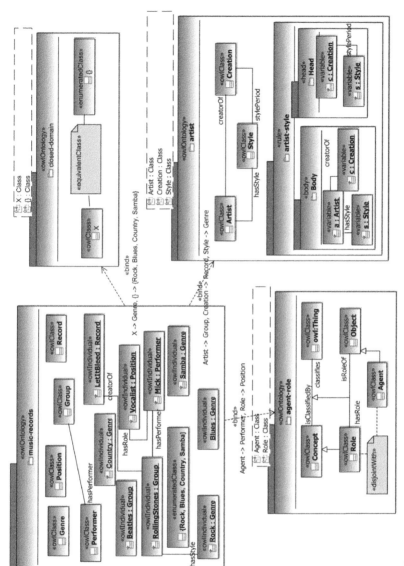

Figure 13.1 Modeling the Running Example with OMG UML Profile for OWL and UML Profile for SWRL.

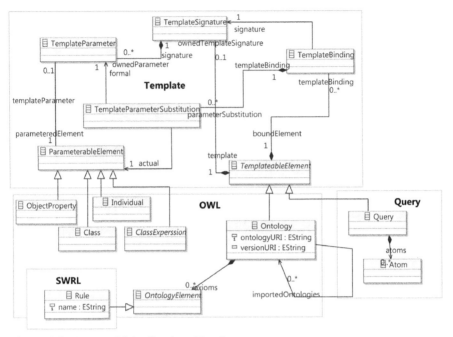

Figure 13.2   Metamodel for Ontology Templates.

package templates to actual classes or properties to create real structures. By binding template parameters to actual values, developers apply, for example, software design patterns to a software model.

While UML package templates allow classes, interfaces, and datatypes as parameterable elements, we define ontology templates as templateable elements and allow classes, properties, datatypes, literals, and class expressions as parameterable elements.

In the following, we explain each of these metamodel elements as addressed in our solution and present the relationships between them in Figure 13.2.

- *TemplateableElement:* A templateable element is an element that can option-ally be defined as a template. When a template is used, a *template binding* is created describing the replacement of template parameters with actual param-eters. Examples of templateable elements are ontologies and queries.

- *Ontology:* The class `Ontology` specializes `TemplateableElement` to specify an ontology template. We apply the same rationale to queries (`SPARQLDL::Query` and `SAIQL::Query`). For example, in Figure 13.1, `closed-domain`, `artist`, and `agent-role` are ontology templates.

- *TemplateSignature:* A template signature wraps the set of template parameters for a templateable element. In Figure 13.1, the signature of `closed-domain` is a bundle containing the parameters X, and { }.

- *TemplateParameter:* A template parameter exposes a parameterable element as a template parameter of a template. For example, in the template signature `closed-domain`, `X`, and `{}` are representations of the parameterable elements with the same names.

- *ParameterableElement:* A parameterable element is an element that can be exposed as a template parameter for a template or be specified as an actual parameter in a binding of a template. In Figure 13.2, we show only some parameterable elements like ObjectProperty, Class, and Individual. Other parameterable elements include DataProperty, ClassExpression, and Literal. For example, in Figure 13.1, the class `X` and the class expression `{}` are template parameters while the class `Genre` and the class expression `{Rock Blues Country Samba}` are actual parameters in the template binding.

- *TemplateBinding:* A template binding represents a relationship between a templateable element and template parameters. A template binding specifies the substitutions of actual parameters for the template parameters of the template. In Figure 13.1, the template binding is represented on top of the ontology `music-record ontology` by the symbol `->`.

- *TemplateParameterSubstitution:* A template parameter substitution relates the actual parameter(s) to a template parameter as part of a template binding.

The metamodel for ontology templates depicted in Figure 13.2 is independent of the ontology metamodel. Although we have considered the OWL 2 metamodel for our implementation, implementers can use any OWL metamodel of choice or other ontology metamodels like RDF. Implementers must then specialize the class `ParameterableElement` with the elements that can be used as parameters, e.g., `RDFClass`.

To write description logic rules, ontology engineers rely on the structure provided by the SWRL metamodel, which connects with the OWL metamodel through the class `Rule`.

In order to have query templates, we specialize the class `TemplateableElement` with the class `Query` and the class `ParameterableElement` with variables. Thus, we can specify templates of queries and give variables as parameters. We discuss query templates in Section 13.3.4.

13.3.2 Semantics of Templates

We treat templates as generators, i.e., templates for generating axioms. Thus, reasoners cannot inspect the contents of templates until a transformation *realizes* the template bindings by generating an effective OWL ontology.

One issue when creating templates is to ensure that they are consistent, i.e., that there exists at least one possible valid binding. A mechanism for doing this is to realize the template by automatically generating an ontology and the respective bindings. Thus, the effective OWL ontology can be tested with any standard reasoning for satisfiability and consistency.

The template mechanics do not add to the complexity of the OWL ontology. The complexity of the effective OWL ontology is composed of the complexity of

Algorithm: RecursiveBinding(TemplateableElement E, List$\langle TemplateableElement \rangle$ $Templates$)
Input: A templateable element E (ontology or query) and a set of TemplateableElements ($Templates$)
Output: Templateable Element (ontology or query) $Result$
begin
 1: **if** List == null **then**
 2:     **Return** E
 3: **else if** List.tail() == null **then**
 4:     **Return** List.head()
 5: **else**
 6:     TemplateableElement $RecursiveResult$ = RecursiveBinding(E, List.tail());
 7:     TemplateableElement $Result$ = list.head()
 8:     /* Bind the Template (list.head) to $RecursiveResult$ */
 9:     **for all** Param : Result.TemplateBinding **do**
10:         **for all** Substitution : Param.parameterSubstitution **do**
11:             Substitute template parameters in $Result$ by actual parameters of $RecursiveResult$
12:         **end for**
13:     **end for**
14:     Import $RecursiveResult$ to $Result$
15:     **Return** Result
16: **end if**
end

Figure 13.3 The Template Binding Realization Algorithm.

the template and the complexity of the ontology bound to the template. For example, if the template definition has expressivity $\mathcal{SHON}$ and the ontology bound to the template has expressivity $\mathcal{ALCIQ}$, the effective ontology would have expressivity $\mathcal{SHOINQ}$.

The outcome of realizing the template bindings is an effective OWL ontology that can be normally checked by reasoners. When realizing template bindings, actual parameters replace template parameters, and the remaining elements are copied. Consequently, the template definition is not part of the effective ontology document (the generated one), but of the implicit ontology document based on our approach. The implicit ontology document contains all axioms defined by the ontology engineers and the template definitions.

The realization of template bindings takes place when transforming the implicit ontology document into an effective ontology document. Figure 13.3 depicts in abstract language the transformation realizing the template bindings of actual parameters of a templateable element (ontology or query) and the template parameters of at least one template.

The recursive algorithm RecursiveBinding (Figure 13.3) guarantees that all binds of an eventual template chain take place, since templates can be connected to other templates. The input of the algorithm is a templateable element E, e.g., the music record ontology. The second input parameter is the set of all templates that generate the output element (ontology or query). For the templates, the type list is used, since in case of multiple connected templates, the ordering of the binding of the template parameters is significant.

The first case (line 1,2) occurs if no template is given. The second case (line 3,4) is the end of the recursion. In the third case, the binding and generation is realized. The next template (first element of the template list) is bound with the previous (recursive) template bindings and generations, which is templateable element *RecursiveResult*. The binding and generation is in lines 9–14. The template parameters are substituted by the actual parameter of *RecursiveResult* according to the parameter substitution (lines 9–11). After the binding, the *RecursiveResult* (ontology or query) is imported or included to the bound template (*Result*). The result, i.e., the effective ontology is a set of axioms, like axioms (1–7) presented in Section 13.2.

13.3.3   Notations for Templates in OWL

TwoUse provides an abstraction independent of concrete syntax, i.e., it is possible to provide multiple notations for modeling ontology templates. In Figure 13.1, we show the running example modeled using the OMG UML Profile for OWL and the UML Profile for SWRL [21]. It relies on package templates natively supported by UML.

Figure 13.4 shows the same example using the OWL 2 graphical notation. We have implemented a graphical notation based on [1] that uses the OWL 2 metamodel as concrete syntax.

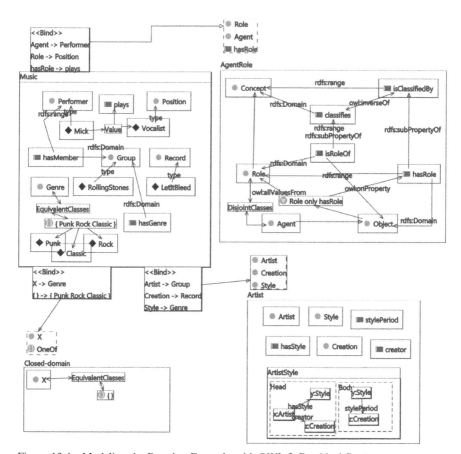

Figure 13.4   Modeling the Running Example with OWL 2 Graphical Syntax.

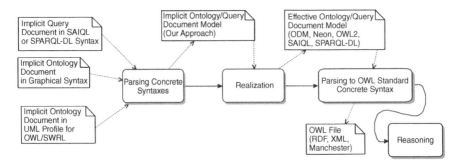

Figure 13.5   Ontology Development with Templates.

LISTING 13.1   Artists of a Given Style.

```
1 Prefix: owl = <http://www.w3.org/2002/07/owl#>
  IRI <http://ArtistsStyle#>
  Parameters: ?artist type owl:Class, ?style owl:oneOf
  Select ?x
5 Where (
      ?x type (?artist and (hasStyle some ?style))
  )
```

A model transformation takes a diagram in one of the supported notations (OWL 2 graphical syntax or UML Profile for OWL/SWRL) and parses it into an implicit ontology document model based on our approach. The realization step takes the output and generates the effective ontology document model, which is later parsed into OWL standard syntax. Figure 13.5 describes these steps.

13.3.4   Query Templates

In this section, we show how ontology engineers can benefit from query templates. Taking the running example, we analyze a simple query about artists belonging to a set of genres.

Since there exist different types of Artists (musician, painter, actor), it is useful to write the query once and set artist and style as parameters. Listing 13.1 depicts this query using SPARQLAS with templates.

Lines 4–5 of Listing 13.1 show the declaration of two parameters for the query template: `?artist` and `?style`. Each of these parameters has a specific type associated to it: `owl:Class` and `owl:oneOf` (from the default namespace).

It is possible to reuse this query for search for music groups popular in the USA. Thus, Users need to bind the parameter `?artist` to the class `Group` of ontology `Ontology1261152793434` and the parameter `?style` to the list {`Rock Blues Country`}. Listing 13.2 depicts these bindings.

LISTING 13.2   Groups and Styles Popular in the USA.

```
1  Prefix: = <http://Ontology1261152793434.owl#>
   Prefix: q = <http://ArtistsStyleInUSA#>
   Bind: (q:artist Group) (q:style {Rock Blues Country})
```

LISTING 13.3   Effective Query.

```
1  Prefix: = <http://Ontology1261152793434.owl#>
   Select ?x
   Where (
      ?x type (Group and (hasStyle some {Rock Blues Country}))
5  )
```

Realizing these bindings produce the query presented in Listing 13.3.

It is clear here that abstraction plays an important role. Users can reuse knowledge encoded in query templates and combine the results. We apply the same rationale illustrated with SPARQLAS into SAIQL queries [93].

13.4   ANALYSIS

The requirements of using templates in OWL ontologies and SPARQLAS are based in our experience in building core ontologies in the past years [6, 140, 139] and in modeling software artifacts with OWL. In this section, we analyze the application of our approach.

Many Versions of Ontologies.   We can, at the low maintenance cost of a template binding, generate many versions of an ontology. For example, it is possible to have two versions of the artist ontology: one with the open-world assumption and another with the closed-domain assumption on class Genre. In some domains like software engineering, it is usual to assume complete knowledge. We can generate variations of ontologies simply by changing the bindings.

Ontology Design Patterns.   Ontology design patterns (ODPs) are key artifacts for reuse in ontology engineering. Applying templates in ODPs demands specialized support for ODP constructs.

We have applied our approach in the development of domain ontologies that use core ontologies: the COMM ontology [6], the Event-Model-F ontology [140], and the M3O ontology [139]. We are able to model all ODPs of these ontologies (three of COMM, six of Event-Model-F, four of M3O), which pointed at advantages and limitations of our approach.

Introducing templates raises the level of abstraction by allowing ontology engineers to identify the requirements for using a given ODP. For example, in the COMM ontology, the semantic annotation design pattern involves at least 12 concepts and six roles to represent that a multimedia data is annotated with a label. The concepts are grounded by upper-level ontologies like DOLCE. In this case, we use templates for creating an *interface* for semantic annotations, i.e., we expose only two classes—label and multimedia-data—as parameters. In comparison with textual templating systems, the main advantage of our approach is portability. Because we handle templates and macros at the platform-independent level, it is possible to develop plug-ins for multiple ontology editors like Protégé or NeOn Toolkit.

13.4.1   Limitations

The usability of the tool is a fact to consider when working with templates. Although we used existing standards for UML profiles for OWL and SWRL created to popularize OWL among software developers, there is limited tool support for these.

Another issue is transparency. Because templates work as generators, their results are not always apparent. Therefore, using templates requires attention about possible unsatisfiability or inconsistency caused by properties or concepts added to the effective ontology.

13.5   RELATED WORK

Relevant works related to this chapter cover mainly the engineering of ontology design patterns from three perspectives: macros, annotations, and language dependency.

Multiple works cover the engineering of ontology design patterns [78, 173, 158]. Iannone [78] uses a pre-processor language to specify knowledge patterns to allow modeling on a more general pattern level than directly in the OWL ontology. This is a tool-oriented application with procedural constructs like ADD and REMOVE. Our approach is declarative and provides support for multiple notations.

Vrandecic analyzes the usage of macros in ontologies in [173]. These macros allow the specification of design patterns for OWL ontologies. In a preprocessing step, a macro is transformed to a set of axioms in the OWL ontology. However, the authors do not provide a concrete specification language for macros.

In [158] semantic patterns are described in RDF. These semantic patterns are transformed into the target language. The target language is not restricted to a certain language; therefore, the semantic patterns are more general. Although general, this approach does not provide constructs to handle patterns as first-class citizens as our approach does.

Presutti [125] considers the creation of ontology design patterns from existing ontologies. The creation methods that are similar to our approach are the re-engineering from other (conceptual) data models and the extraction method from reference ontologies.

In comparison with related work, we provide an approach that is flexible, since it supports multiple notations (including UML), extensible, as it comprises metamodels for OWL and related languages like SWRL, SPARQL, and SAIQL, and platform independent, since templates are tackled at the modeling level and not at the language-specific level.

13.6   CONCLUSION

In this chapter, we present an approach that raises the level of abstraction in the ontology development process by providing platform-independent specifications of templates. The prime benefit of this approach is that it is based on pre-existing metamodels and profiles and, therefore, enhances the utility of previous work. Moreover, our approach is generic enough to enable model-driven tools to support metamodels of multiple OWL-related languages.

CONCLUSION OF PART IV

In this part, we investigate the support of generative techniques in ontology engineering services and address the abstraction gap between specification languages and programming languages for ontology engineering tasks (Research Question IV from Section 1.2).

Applying the TwoUse approach raises the abstraction level and consequently, influences productivity. With the TwoUse approach, ontology engineers concentrate on domain problems instead of implementation problems. Moreover, the usage of domain-specific languages enables ontology engineers to handle domain concepts as first-class citizens, improving maintainability (and addressing Research Questions IV.A and IV.B).

We use the integration between UML class-based modeling and OWL modeling to extend techniques used in model-driven engineering to ontology engineering to declaratively specify artifacts (Research Question IV.C).

CHAPTER 14

CONCLUSION

This book addresses challenges in composing model-driven engineering and OWL technologies. This work comprises multiple facets of this challenge, namely: (1) classification of existing approaches integrating both paradigms; (2) the specification of a coherent framework for integrated usage of both modeling approaches, comprising the benefits of UML class-based modeling and OWL; and applications of the proposed framework to improve (3) model-driven engineering and (4) ontology engineering.

14.1 CONTRIBUTIONS

This work present contributions of different natures. In the following, we summarize the contributions of this book.

Classification of Approaches Involving MDE and OWL Ontologies. We outline state-of-the-art research on model-driven engineering and ontology technologies. Then, we describe a domain analysis of both paradigms and identify their commonalities and variations. The contribution is a taxonomy to categorize approaches involving ontology technologies and model-driven engineering.

Integration of UML Class-Based Modeling and OWL Ontologies. We propose an integrated use of both modeling approaches in a coherent framework—TwoUse. We present a framework involving multiple notations for developing integrated models and use a SPARQL-like approach for writing query operations. We validate TwoUse's applicability with case studies and conclude that TwoUse achieves enhancements of non-functional software requirements like maintainability, reusability, and extensibility. The contribution is a method for applying ontology technologies in model-driven engineering and for applying model-driven engineering in ontology engineering.

Ontology-Based Software Design Patterns. We deal with problems in common design patterns and propose ontology-based modeling to overcome drawbacks of the strategy pattern, that are also extensible to the abstract factory pattern and other patterns that deal with variant management. The result is an ontology-based software design pattern to be used with design patterns: the Selector Pattern.

Semantic Web and Model-Driven Engineering, First Edition. Fernando Silva Parreiras.
© 2012 Institute of Electrical and Electronics Engineers. Published 2012 by John Wiley & Sons, Inc.

Transformation of Modeling Languages into OWL. In a networked and federated development environment, modeling artifacts need to be linked, adapted, and analyzed to meet the information requirements of multiple stakeholders. We present an approach for linking, transforming, and querying MOF-compliant modeling languages on the web of data. We use the definition of structural mappings between MOF and OWL and propose the usage of semantic web technologies for linking and querying software models.

Framework for Designing Ontology-Based Domain Specific Languages. We address major challenges in the field of domain specific languages with OWL ontologies and automated reasoning in [175]. We applied the TwoUse approach to enable applications of reasoning to help DSL designers and DSL users through the development and usage of DSLs. DSL designers profit by formal representations, an expressive language, and constraint analysis. DSL users profit by progressive verification, debugging support, and assisted programming.

A Language for Specifying Ontology Translations. We address the balance between abstraction and expressiveness that causes ontology mapping frameworks to turn to programming languages when built-in constructs fail in specifying complex rules for dataset translation. The contribution is a platform-independent language that allows modelers to abstract from implementation details while providing expressiveness to address translation problems at the semantic as well as at the syntactical and lexical layer.

Automatic Generation of Ontology APIs. We address the complex mappings between descriptions of information given by ontologies and object-oriented representations of the same information for developing application programming interfaces of ontologies that include instances of ontology design patterns. The contribution is a domain-specific language to tackle these mappings in a platform independent way—*agogo*. Agogo provides improvements on software engineering quality attributes like usability, reusability, maintainability, and portability.

Templates for OWL Ontologies. Metamodels for the semantic web do not provide dedicated support for dealing with templates in ontology engineering. Our contribution is an extension of existing metamodels and tools to support ontology engineers in modeling ontology templates. Our approach allows ontology engineers to keep template specifications as first-class citizens, reducing complexity and increasing reusability in ontology engineering.

The TwoUse Toolkit. The result of implementing the approach is a free open source tool available for use—the TwoUse Toolkit. We address the lack of a framework that allows the integration of multiple W3C and OMG standards at the designing level. The contribution is the implementation of an architecture for designing artifacts using multiple standard languages, turning the focus from code-centric to transformation-centric.

14.2   OUTLOOK

This research has been made possible by intensive work in the last 10 years in the fields of MDE and ontology technologies. There remains a considerable body of research problems that are currently being tackled or that are open for future work.

14.2.1   Ongoing Research

Integrating Linguistic Metamodeling and Ontological Metamodeling.   The integration between OWL modeling and UML class-based modeling covered in this book involves the usage of OWL ontologies for linguistic metamodeling [7]. The alignment between UML class-based modeling and OWL in the metamodeling level requires the transformation of elements of the metamodel into OWL classes and properties and the transformation of elements of the model into OWL individuals and assertions.

In this book, we do not address the usage of OWL for ontological metamodeling as described by Atkinson and Kühne [7]. An integration of both linguistic metamodeling and ontological metamodeling involves the usage of MOF for metamodeling as a language definition tool (linguistic metamodeling) and the usage of OWL for modeling the relationships between concepts and domain types at the same linguistic modeling level.

Walter investigates such an integration with preliminary results in [176, 174].

Modeling and Querying Patterns for MDE in OWL.   In this book, we align constructs of UML class-based modeling and OWL modeling and allow the integration of UML class-based modeling and OWL modeling independently of the modeling level, i.e., at the metamodeling level (language bridge) or at the modeling level (model bridge) [163].

Nevertheless, some modeling approaches require a dedicated transformation of model constructs into OWL. For example, the transformation of business process models into OWL handles the mappings of tasks and gateways into OWL classes [177], whereas the transformation of feature models handles mappings of features and relationships between parent feature and its child features onto OWL classes [130].

Gröner investigates patterns of modeling, querying, and reasoning for MDE in OWL in his ongoing research, with preliminary results in [60, 59].

Linked Data in Software Engineering.   The advent of the semantic web has given a new perspective to aspects of software engineering like collaboration, representation, and interoperability. For example, existing works present the impact of semantic web technologies like RDF(S) and SPARQL on programmer's assistance [79, 180].

Semantic web technologies and Linked Data principles [16] are paving the way for the Web of Data, a global data space that relies on a stack of technologies like URIs, HTTP, and RDF to empower information retrieval. In this context, there is a need for investigation of the impact of applying Linked Data principles and techniques for mining, collecting, and analyzing software engineering data.

Scalability of Ontological Reasoning Technology. The scalability of onto-logical reasoning technology has matured over the last 10 years and current imple-mentations point to the assumption that reasoners will scale to higher efficiency by one or several orders of magnitude. Research on techniques for semantic transforma-tions between OWL profiles [132, 120] is in place to benefit from the most appropri-ate and most efficient technique at each given point in the software development process.

APPENDIX A

A.1 EBNF DEFINITION OF THE CONCRETE TEXTUAL SYNTAX FOR TWOUSE

LISTING A.1 EBNF Syntax for Concrete Syntax.

```
1
  digit = "0" | "1" | "2" | "3" | "4" | "5" | "6" | "7" | "8" | "9" ;
  nonnulldigit = "1" | "2" | "3" | "4" | "5" | "6" | "7" | "8" | "9" ;
  integer = [ "-" ] nonnulldigit { digit }| "0" ;
5 nonnegativeinteger = "0" | nonnulldigit { digit } ;
  name = ( letter | "_" ) { letter | digit | "_" } ;
  letter = "a" .. "z" | "A" .. "Z" ;

  EPackage = { EAnnotation } " package " name [ EDataType ] [ "\"" EDataType
       "\"" ] "{" { EClass }{EPackage } "}" ;
10 EClass = [ "abstract" ]( "interface" | "class" )[ "<" EClass {","
       EClass } ">" ] name [ "\"" name "\"" ][ "extends" EClass {","
       EClass }] { classAnnotation } "{" { EClass | EOperation } "}" ;
   EAttribute = { EAnnotation }(("derived" | "volatile" | "unique"|
       "ordered" | "unsettable" | "changeable" | "transient" | "iD" ) }
       "attribute " ( EClass | EGenericType ) name [ "=" "\"" name "\"" ]
       [ "("integer".."integer")" ] ";" ;
   EParameter = { EAnnotation }{( " ordered " | " unique" ) } EClass name
       [ "(" integer ".." integer ")" ];
   EReference =
     {( "containment" | "derived" | "transient" | "volatile" | "unique"
         | "ordered" | "unsettable" | "changeable" | "resolveProxies" ) }
15 { frontReferenceAnnotation } " reference " ( EClass | EGenericType )
           name [ "=" "\"" name "\"" ][ "(" integer ".." integer ")" ]
           [ "opposite" EReference ] { endReferenceAnnotation } ";" ;
   EOperation = { EAnnotation }{( "ordered" | "unique" ) } " operation "
     ( "void" | EClass ) [ "(" integer ".." integer ")" ][ "<"
     ETypeParameter {"," ETypeParameter } ">" ] name "(" [ EParameter
     {"," EParameter }] ")" [ "throws " EClass {"," EClass }] ";" ;
   EEnum = { EAnnotation } [ " serializable " ] "enum"name"\"" name "\""
       "{" { EEnumLiteral } "}" ;
   EEnumLiteral = { EAnnotation } EDataType ":" name "=" "\""
       EEnumLiteral "\"" ";" ;
   EAnnotation = "(" { "eAnnotations" ":" EAnnotation | "source" ":"
       "\"" name "\"" | "details" ":" "\"" name "\"" "=" "\"" name
       "\"" | "contents" ":" EObject | "references" ":" EReference |
       "eModelElement" ":" EObject } ")" ;
```

                                                              (*Continued*)

Semantic Web and Model-Driven Engineering, First Edition. Fernando Silva Parreiras.
© 2012 Institute of Electrical and Electronics Engineers. Published 2012 by John Wiley & Sons, Inc.

```
20 EObject = "EObject" ;
   EFactory = "EFactory ";
   EStringToStringMapEntry = "cardinality" integer ;
   EDataType = { EAnnotation } [ "serializable" ] " datatype" name "\"" name
       "\"" ;
   ETypeParameter = { EAnnotation } name ;
25 EGenericType = "typed" [ "<" ( ETypeParameter | "?" "extends"
       EGenericType | "?" "super" EGenericType ) ">" ] EClass [ "<"
       ( EGenericType | "?" ) {"," ( EGenericType | "?" ) } ">" ];

   frontReferenceAnnotation = "(" ( "functional" | "inversefunctional" |
       "symmetric" | "asymmetric" | "reflexive" | "irreflexive" |
       "transitive ") ")" ;
   endReferenceAnnotation = "(" ( "equivalentTo" OPE | "subPropertyOf"
       OPE | " domain" CE | "range" CE | "disjointWith" OPE | "inverseOf"
       name | "subPropertyChain" OPE "o" OPE {"o" OPE}) ")" ;
   classAnnotation = "(" (
30                         ( "equivalentTo" | "disjointWith" ) CE {CE}|
                           "subClassOf" CE |
                           "disjointUnionOf" CE CE {CE}
                                         ) ")" ;

35 CE = "(" ([ "not" ] name |
            "not" CE |
            CE "and " CE { "and" CE }|
            CE "or" CE {"or" CE}|
            OPE ( "some" | "only" ) CE |
40          OPE "Self" |
            OPE ( "min" | "max" | "exactly" ) "cardinality"
                nonnegativeinteger CE )
            ")" ;
   OPE = name | "(" "inverse" name ")" ;
```

A.2 EBNF GRAMMAR OF SPARQLAS FUNCTIONAL SYNTAX

LISTING A.2 EBNF Grammar of SPARQLAS Functional Syntax.

```
1
   cardinality = "a nonempty finite sequence of digits between 0 and 9" ;
   lexical = "a nonempty finite sequence of alphanumeric characters
       enclosed in a pair of \" (U+22) characters" ;
   variable = "a nonempty finite sequence of alphanumeric characters
       starting with either a ? (U+3F) character or a $ (U+24)
       character " ;
5  nodeID = "a finite sequence of characters matching the
       BLANK _NODE_LABEL production of SPARQL" ;
   prefix = "a finite sequence of characters matching the PNAME _NS
       production of SPARQL" ;
```

LISTING A.2   *(Continued)*

```
  fullIRI = "an IRI as defined in RFC3987 , enclosed in a pair of <
      (U+3C) and > (U+3E) characters" ;
  abbreviatedIRI = "a finite sequence of characters matching the
      PNAME_LN production of SPARQL" ;

10 IRI = fullIRI | abbreviatedIRI ;

  OntologyDocument = [ QueryIRI ] { Import }{ PrefixDefinition }
      Query ;
  QueryIRI = "IRI" "(" fullIRI ")" ;
  Import = "Import" "(" fullIRI ")" ;
15 PrefixDefinition = "Namespace" "(" [ prefix ] "=" fullIRI ")" ;

  Query = SelectQuery | ConstructQuery | AskQuery | DescribeQuery ;

  SelectQuery = "Select" [ variable { variable }| "*" ] "Where" "(" {
      Atom } ")" ;
20 ConstructQuery = "Construct" "(" { ConstructAtom } ")" "Where" "(" {
      WhereAtom } ")" ;
  AskQuery = "Ask" "Where" "(" { Atom } ")" ;
  DescribeQuery = " Describe " DescribeIRI | "Describe" "Where" "(" {
      Atom } ")" ;

  ConstructAtom = Atom ;
25 WhereAtom = Atom ;
  DescribeIRI = fullIRI ;

  ClassVariable = variable ;
  ObjectPropertyVariable = variable ;
30 DataPropertyVariable = variable ;
  IndividualVariable = variable ;
  LiteralVariable = variable ;

  Class = IRI ;
35 Datatype = IRI ;
  ObjectProperty = IRI ;
  DataProperty = IRI ;
  NamedIndividual = IRI ;
  ConstrainingFacet = IRI ;
40 AnonymousIndividual = nodeID ;
  NamedLiteral = lexical "^^" Datatype ;

  Atom = Assertion | ClassAtom | ObjectPropertyAtom | DataPropertyAtom
      | HasKey | Declaration ;
45 Assertion = ClassAssertion | DirectType | ObjectPropertyAssertion |
      DataPropertyAssertion | NegativeObjectPropertyAssertion |
      NegativeDataPropertyAssertion | SameIndividual |
      DifferentIndividuals ;

  ClassAssertion = ( "ClassAssertion" | "Type" ) "(" Individual
      ClassExpression ")" ;
  DirectType = "DirectType" "(" Individual ClassExpression ")" ;
```

(Continued)

LISTING A.2   *(Continued)*

```
   ObjectPropertyAssertion = ( " ObjectPropertyAssertion " |
        "PropertyValue" ) "(" SourceIndividual ObjectPropertyExpression
        TargetIndividual ")" ;
50 DataPropertyAssertion = ( "DataPropertyAssertion" | "PropertyValue"
        ) "(" SourceIndividual DataPropertyExpression TargetValue ")" ;
   NegativeObjectPropertyAssertion = (
        " NegativeObjectPropertyAssertion " | "NegativePropertyValue" )
        "(" SourceIndividual ObjectPropertyExpression TargetIndividual
        ")" ;
   NegativeDataPropertyAssertion = ( "NegativeDataPropertyAssertion" |
        "NegativePropertyValue" ) "(" SourceIndividual
        DataPropertyExpression TargetValue ")" ;
   SameIndividual = ( "SameIndividual" | "SameAs" ) "(" Individual
        Individual { Individual } ")" ;
   DifferentIndividuals = ( "DifferentIndividuals" | "DifferentFrom" )
        "(" Individual Individual { Individual } ")" ;
55 SourceIndividual = Individual ;
   TargetIndividual = Individual ;
   Individual = NamedIndividual | IndividualVariable |
        AnonymousIndividual ;
   TargetValue = Literal ;
   Literal = LiteralVariable | NamedLiteral ;
60
   ClassAtom = SubClassOf | DirectSubClassOf | StrictSubClassOf |
        EquivalentClasses | DisjointClasses | DisjointUnion ;

   SubClassOf = "SubClassOf" "(" SubClassExpression
        SuperClassExpression ")" ;
   DirectSubClassOf = "DirectSubClassOf" "(" SubClassExpression
        SuperClassExpression ")" ;
65 StrictSubClassOf = "StrictSubClassOf" "(" SubClassExpression
        SuperClassExpression ")" ;
   EquivalentClasses = ( "EquivalentClasses" | "EquivalentTo" ) "("
        ClassExpression ClassExpression { ClassExpression } ")" ;
   DisjointClasses = ( "DisjointClasses" | "DisjointWith" ) "("
        ClassExpression ClassExpression { ClassExpression } ")" ;
   DisjointUnion = "DisjointUnion" "(" DisjointClass
        DisjointClassExpression DisjointClassExpression {
        DisjointClassExpression } ")" ;
   SubClassExpression = ClassExpression ;
70 SuperClassExpression = ClassExpression ;
   DisjointClass = ClassVariable | Class ;
   DisjointClassExpression = ClassExpression ;

   ClassExpression = ClassVariable | Class | ObjectUnionOf |
        ObjectComplementOf | ObjectOneOf | ObjectIntersectionOf |
        ObjectAllValuesFrom | ObjectSomeValuesFrom | ObjectHasValue |
        ObjectMinCardinality | ObjectMaxCardinality |
        ObjectExactCardinality | DataAllValuesFrom | DataSomeValuesFrom
        | DataHasValue | DataMinCardinality | DataMaxCardinality |
        DataExactCardinality ;
```

LISTING A.2   (*Continued*)

```
75
   ObjectUnionOf = ( "ObjectUnionOf" | "Or" ) "(" ClassExpression
      ClassExpression { ClassExpression } ")" ;
   ObjectComplementOf = ( "ObjectComplementOf " | "Not" ) "("
      ClassExpression ")" ;
   ObjectOneOf = ( "ObjectOneOf" | "One" ) "(" Individual { Individual
      } ")" ;
   ObjectIntersectionOf = ( " ObjectIntersectionOf " | "And " ) "("
      ClassExpression ClassExpression { ClassExpression }")" ;
80 ObjectAllValuesFrom = ( "ObjectAllValuesFrom" | " All" ) "("
      ObjectPropertyExpression ClassExpression ")" ;
   ObjectSomeValuesFrom = ( "ObjectSomeValuesFrom" | "Some" ) "("
      ObjectPropertyExpression ClassExpression")" ;
   ObjectHasValue = ( "ObjectHasValue" | "Has" ) "("
      ObjectPropertyExpression Individual ")" ;
   ObjectMinCardinality = ( "ObjectMinCardinality" | "Min " ) "("
      cardinality ObjectPropertyExpression [ ClassExpression ] ")" ;
   ObjectMaxCardinality = ( "ObjectMaxCardinality" | "Max " ) "("
      cardinality ObjectPropertyExpression [ ClassExpression ] ")" ;
85 ObjectExactCardinality = ( "ObjectExactCardinality" | " Exact " ) "("
      cardinality ObjectPropertyExpression [ ClassExpression ] ")" ;
   DataAllValuesFrom = ( " DataAllValuesFrom " | "All" ) "("
      DataPropertyExpression DataRange ")" ;
   DataSomeValuesFrom = ( "DataSomeValuesFrom" | "Some" ) "("
      DataPropertyExpression DataRange ")" ;
   DataHasValue = ( "DataHasValue" | "Has" ) "(" DataPropertyExpression
      Literal ")" ;
   DataMinCardinality = ( "DataMinCardinality" | "Min" ) "("
      cardinality DataPropertyExpression [ DataRange ] ")" ;
90 DataMaxCardinality = ( "DataMaxCardinality" | "Max" ) "("
      cardinality DataPropertyExpression [ DataRange ] ")" ;
   DataExactCardinality = ( "DataExactCardinality" | " Exact" ) "("
      cardinality DataPropertyExpression [ DataRange ] ")" ;

   DataRange = Datatype | DataUnionOf | DataComplementOf | DataOneOf |
      DataIntersectionOf | DatatypeRestriction ;

95 DataUnionOf = ( "DataUnionOf " | "Or" ) "(" DataRange DataRange {
      DataRange } ")" ;
   DataComplementOf = ( " DataComplementOf" | "Not " ) "(" DataRange ")" ;
   DataOneOf = ( " DataOneOf " | "One" ) "(" Literal { Literal } ")" ;
   DataIntersectionOf = ( "DataIntersectionOf" | "And" ) "(" DataRange
      DataRange { DataRange } ")" ;
   DatatypeRestriction = "DatatypeRestriction" "(" Datatype
      FacetRestriction { FacetRestriction } ")" ;
100 FacetRestriction = ConstrainingFacet Literal;

   ObjectPropertyAtom = SubObjectPropertyOf |
      EquivalentObjectProperties | DisjointObjectProperties |
      ObjectPropertyDomain | ObjectPropertyRange |
      InverseObjectPropertyAtom | FunctionalObjectProperty |
```

(Continued)

```
          InverseFunctionalObjectProperty | ReflexiveObjectProperty |
          IrreflexiveObjectProperty | SymmetricObjectProperty |
          AsymmetricObjectProperty | TransitiveObjectProperty ;

      SubObjectPropertyOf = ( "SubObjectPropertyOf" | "SubPropertyOf" )
          "(" SubObjectPropertyExpression SuperObjectPropertyExpression
          ")" ;
105  EquivalentObjectProperties = ( "EquivalentObjectProperties " |
          "EquivalentProperty" ) "(" ObjectPropertyExpression
          ObjectPropertyExpression { ObjectPropertyExpression } ")" ;
      DisjointObjectProperties = ( "DisjointObjectProperties" |
          "DisjointProperty" ) "(" ObjectPropertyExpression
          ObjectPropertyExpression { ObjectPropertyExpression } ")" ;
      ObjectPropertyDomain = ( "ObjectPropertyDomain" | "Domain" ) "("
          ObjectPropertyExpression ClassExpression")" ;
      ObjectPropertyRange = ( "ObjectPropertyRange" | "Range" ) "("
          ObjectPropertyExpression ClassExpression")" ;
      InverseObjectPropertyAtom = ("InverseObjectProperties" |
          "InverseOf" ) "(" ObjectPropertyExpression
          ObjectPropertyExpression ")" ;
110  FunctionalObjectProperty = "FunctionalObjectProperty" "("
          ObjectPropertyExpression ")" ;
      InverseFunctionalObjectProperty = (
          "InverseFunctionalObjectProperty" | "InverseFunctional" ) "("
          ObjectPropertyExpression ")" ;
      ReflexiveObjectProperty = ( "ReflexiveObjectProperty" | "Reflexive"
          ) "(" ObjectPropertyExpression ")" ;
      IrreflexiveObjectProperty = ( "IrreflexiveObjectProperty" |
          "Irreflexive" ) "(" ObjectPropertyExpression ")" ;
      SymmetricObjectProperty = ( "SymmetricObjectProperty" | "Symmetric"
          ) "(" ObjectPropertyExpression ")" ;
115  AsymmetricObjectProperty = ( "AsymmetricObjectProperty" |
          "Asymmetric" ) "(" ObjectPropertyExpression ")" ;
      TransitiveObjectProperty = ( " TransitiveObjectProperty " |
          " Transitive " ) "(" ObjectPropertyExpression ")" ;
      SubObjectPropertyExpression = ObjectPropertyExpression |
          ObjectPropertyChain ;
      SuperObjectPropertyExpression = ObjectPropertyExpression ;
      ObjectPropertyChain = ( "ObjectPropertyChain " | "Chain" ) "("
          ObjectPropertyExpression ObjectPropertyExpression {
          ObjectPropertyExpression } ")" ;
120
      ObjectPropertyExpression = ObjectPropertyVariable | ObjectProperty |
          InverseObjectProperty ;

      InverseObjectProperty = ( "ObjectInverseOf" | "InverseOf" ) "("
          ObjectPropertyExpression ")" ;

125  DataPropertyAtom = SubDataPropertyOf | EquivalentDataProperties |
          DisjointDataProperties | DataPropertyDomain | DataPropertyRange
          | FunctionalDataProperty ;
```

LISTING A.2   (*Continued*)

```
   SubDataPropertyOf = ( "SubDataPropertyOf" | "SubPropertyOf" ) "("
      SubDataPropertyExpression SuperDataPropertyExpression ")" ;
   EquivalentDataProperties = ( "EquivalentDataProperties" |
      "EquivalentProperty" ) "(" DataPropertyExpression
      DataPropertyExpression { DataPropertyExpression } ")" ;
   DisjointDataProperties = ( "DisjointDataProperties" |
      " DisjointProperty " ) "(" DataPropertyExpression
      DataPropertyExpression { DataPropertyExpression } ")" ;
130 DataPropertyDomain = ( "DataPropertyDomain" | "Domain " ) "("
      DataPropertyExpression ClassExpression ")" ;
   DataPropertyRange = ( "DataPropertyRange" | "Range" ) "("
      DataPropertyExpression DataRange ")" ;
   FunctionalDataProperty = "FunctionalDataProperty" "("
      DataPropertyExpression ")" ;
   SubDataPropertyExpression = DataPropertyExpression ;
   SuperDataPropertyExpression = DataPropertyExpression ;
135
   DataPropertyExpression = DataPropertyVariable | DataProperty ;

   HasKey = "HasKey" "(" ClassExpression "(" { ObjectPropertyExpression
      } ")" "(" { DataPropertyExpression } ")" ")" ;
140 Declaration = ObjectPropertyDeclaration | DataPropertyDeclaration |
      NamedIndividualDeclaration | ClassDeclaration ;
   ObjectPropertyDeclaration = "ObjectProperty" "(" ObjectProperty |
      ObjectPropertyVariable ")" ;
   DataPropertyDeclaration = "DataProperty" "(" DataProperty |
         DataPropertyVariable ")" ;
   NamedIndividualDeclaration = "NamedIndividual" "(" NamedIndividual |
      IndividualVariable ")" ;
145 ClassDeclaration = "Class" "(" Class | ClassVariable ")" ;
```

A.3   EBNF GRAMMAR OF SPARQLAS MANCHESTER SYNTAX

LISTING A.3   EBNF Grammar of SPARQLAS Manchester Syntax.

```
1
   cardinality = "a nonempty finite sequence of digits between 0 and 9" ;
   lexical = "a nonempty finite sequence of alphanumeric characters
      enclosed in a pair of \" (U+22) characters" ;
   variable = "a nonempty finite sequence of alphanumeric characters
      starting with either a ? (U+3F) character or a $ (U+24)
      character " ;
5 nodeID = "a finite sequence of characters matching the
      BLANK _NODE_LABEL production of SPARQL" ;
   prefix = "a finite sequence of characters matching the PNAME _NS
      production of SPARQL" ;
   fullIRI = "an IRI as defined in RFC3987 , enclosed in a pair of <
      (U+3C) and > (U+3E) characters" ;
```

(Continued)

```
   abbreviatedIRI = "a finite sequence of characters matching the
       PNAME_LN production of SPARQL" ;

10 IRI = fullIRI | abbreviatedIRI ;

   OntologyDocument = [ QueryIRI ] { Import }{ PrefixDefinition }
       Query ;
   QueryIRI = "IRI" "(" fullIRI ")" ;
   Import = "Import :" fullIRI ;
15 PrefixDefinition = "Namespace:" [ prefix ] fullIRI ;

   Query = SelectQuery | ConstructQuery | AskQuery | DescribeQuery ;
   SelectQuery = " Select " [ variable { variable }| "*" ] "Where:" {
       Atom } ;
20 ConstructQuery = "Construct:" { ConstructAtom } "Where:" { WhereAtom
       };
   AskQuery = "Ask" "Where:" { Atom };
   DescribeQuery = " Describe" DescribeIRI | "Describe" "Where:" { Atom
       };

   ConstructAtom = Atom;
25 WhereAtom = Atom ;
   DescribeIRI = fullIRI ;

   ClassVariable = variable ;
   ObjectPropertyVariable = variable ;
30 DataPropertyVariable = variable ;
   IndividualVariable = variable ;
   LiteralVariable = variable ;

   Class = IRI ;
35 Datatype = IRI ;
   ObjectProperty = IRI ;
   DataProperty = IRI ;
   NamedIndividual = IRI ;
   ConstrainingFacet = IRI ;
40 AnonymousIndividual = nodeID ;
   NamedLiteral = lexical "^^" Datatype ;

   Atom = Assertion | ClassAtom | ObjectPropertyAtom | DataPropertyAtom
       | HasKey | Declaration ;

45 Assertion = ClassAssertion | DirectType | ObjectPropertyAssertion |
       DataPropertyAssertion | NegativeObjectPropertyAssertion |
       NegativeDataPropertyAssertion | SameIndividual |
       DifferentIndividuals ;

   ClassAssertion = Individual "type" ClassExpression ;
   DirectType = Individual " directType " ClassExpression ;
   ObjectPropertyAssertion = SourceIndividual ObjectPropertyExpression
       TargetIndividual ;
```

LISTING A.3   (*Continued*)

```
50 DataPropertyAssertion = SourceIndividual DataPropertyExpression
        TargetValue ;
  NegativeObjectPropertyAssertion = SourceIndividual "not"
        ObjectPropertyExpression TargetIndividual ;
  NegativeDataPropertyAssertion = SourceIndividual "not"
        DataPropertyExpression TargetValue ;
  SameIndividual = Individual "sameAs" Individual | "SameIndividuals"
        "(" Individual Individual { Individual } ")" ;
  DifferentIndividuals = Individual "differentFrom" Individual |
        "DifferentIndividuals" "(" Individual Individual { Individual }
        ")" ;
55 SourceIndividual = Individual ;
  TargetIndividual = Individual ;
  Individual = NamedIndividual | IndividualVariable |
        AnonymousIndividual ;
  TargetValue = Literal ;
  Literal = LiteralVariable | NamedLiteral ;
60
  ClassAtom = SubClassOf | DirectSubClassOf | StrictSubClassOf |
        EquivalentClasses | DisjointClasses | DisjointUnion ;

  SubClassOf = SubClassExpression " subClassOf " SuperClassExpression ;
  DirectSubClassOf = SubClassExpression " directSubClassOf "
        SuperClassExpression ;
65 StrictSubClassOf = SubClassExpression "strictSubClassOf"
        SuperClassExpression ;
  EquivalentClasses = "EquivalentClasses:" ClassExpression ","
        ClassExpression { "," ClassExpression }| ClassExpression
        " equivalentClasses " ClassExpression { "," ClassExpression }|
        ClassExpression " equivalentTo " ClassExpression { ","
        ClassExpression };
  DisjointClasses = " DisjointClasses :" ClassExpression ","
        ClassExpression { "," ClassExpression }| ClassExpression
        " disjointClasses " ClassExpression { "," ClassExpression }|
        ClassExpression " disjointWith " ClassExpression { ","
        ClassExpression };
  DisjointUnion = DisjointClass " DisjointUnionOf :"
        DisjointClassExpression DisjointClassExpression {
        DisjointClassExpression } ;
    SubClassExpression = ClassExpression ;
70 SuperClassExpression = ClassExpression ;
  DisjointClass = ClassVariable | Class ;
  DisjointClassExpression = ClassExpression ;

  ClassExpression = ClassVariable | Class | ObjectUnionOf |
        ObjectComplementOf | ObjectOneOf | ObjectIntersectionOf |
        ObjectAllValuesFrom | ObjectSomeValuesFrom | ObjectHasValue |
        ObjectMinCardinality | ObjectMaxCardinality |
        ObjectExactCardinality | DataAllValuesFrom | DataSomeValuesFrom
        | DataHasValue | DataMinCardinality | DataMaxCardinality |
        DataExactCardinality ;
```

(Continued)

LISTING A.3   *(Continued)*

```
75
   ObjectUnionOf = "(" ClassExpression "or" ClassExpression { "or"
       ClassExpression } ")" ;
   ObjectComplementOf = " not" ClassExpression ;
   ObjectOneOf = "{" Individual { "," Individual } "}" ;
   ObjectIntersectionOf = "(" ClassExpression "and " ClassExpression {
       " and" ClassExpression } ")" ;
80 ObjectAllValuesFrom = ObjectPropertyExpression "only"
       ClassExpression | "(" ObjectPropertyExpression "only"
       ClassExpression ")" ;
   ObjectSomeValuesFrom = ObjectPropertyExpression "some"
       ClassExpression | "(" ObjectPropertyExpression "some"
       ClassExpression ")" ;
   ObjectHasValue = ObjectPropertyExpression "value" Individual | "("
       ObjectPropertyExpression "vaule " Individual ")" ;
   ObjectMinCardinality = ObjectPropertyExpression "min" cardinality [
       ClassExpression ] | "(" ObjectPropertyExpression "min"
       cardinality [ ClassExpression ] ")" ;
   ObjectMaxCardinality = ObjectPropertyExpression "max" cardinality [
       ClassExpression ] | "(" ObjectPropertyExpression "max"
       cardinality [ ClassExpression ] ")" ;
85 ObjectExactCardinality = ObjectPropertyExpression "exactly "
       cardinality [ ClassExpression ] | "(" ObjectPropertyExpression
       " exactly " cardinality [ ClassExpression ] ")" ;
   DataAllValuesFrom = DataPropertyExpression "only" DataRange | "("
       DataPropertyExpression "only" DataRange ")" ;
   DataSomeValuesFrom = DataPropertyExpression " some " DataRange | "("
       DataPropertyExpression "some" DataRange ")" ;
   DataHasValue = DataPropertyExpression " value " Literal | "("
       DataPropertyExpression "value " Literal ")" ;
   DataMinCardinality = cardinality "min " DataPropertyExpression [
       DataRange ] | "(" cardinality "min" DataPropertyExpression [
       DataRange ] ")" ;
90 DataMaxCardinality = cardinality "max" DataPropertyExpression [
       DataRange ] | "(" cardinality "max" DataPropertyExpression [
       DataRange ] ")" ;
   DataExactCardinality = cardinality "exactly" DataPropertyExpression
       [ DataRange ] | "(" cardinality "exactly" DataPropertyExpression
       [ DataRange ] ")" ;

   DataRange = Datatype | DataUnionOf | DataComplementOf | DataOneOf |
       DataIntersectionOf | DatatypeRestriction ;

95 DataUnionOf = "(" DataRange "or" DataRange { "or" DataRange } ")" ;
   DataComplementOf = " DataComplementOf " DataRange | "not" DataRange ;
   DataOneOf = "{" Literal { Literal } "}" ;
   DataIntersectionOf = "(" DataRange "and" DataRange { "and " DataRange
       } ")" ;
   DatatypeRestriction = Datatype "[" FacetRestriction {
       FacetRestriction } "]" ;
100 FacetRestriction = ConstrainingFacet Literal;
```

LISTING A.3 (*Continued*)

```
  ObjectPropertyAtom = SubObjectPropertyOf |
     EquivalentObjectProperties | DisjointObjectProperties |
     ObjectPropertyDomain | ObjectPropertyRange |
     InverseObjectPropertyAtom | FunctionalObjectProperty |
     InverseFunctionalObjectProperty | ReflexiveObjectProperty |
     IrreflexiveObjectProperty | SymmetricObjectProperty |
     AsymmetricObjectProperty | TransitiveObjectProperty ;

  SubObjectPropertyOf = SubObjectPropertyExpression (
     " subObjectPropertyOf " | " subPropertyOf " )
     SuperObjectPropertyExpression ;
105 EquivalentObjectProperties = ( "EquivalentObjectProperties:" |
     "EquivalentProperties:" ) ObjectPropertyExpression ","
     ObjectPropertyExpression { "," ObjectPropertyExpression }|
     ObjectPropertyExpression ( "equivalentObjectProperties "|
     "equivalentTo" ) ObjectPropertyExpression { ","
     ObjectPropertyExpression } ;
  DisjointObjectProperties = ( "DisjointObjectProperties:" |
     "DisjointProperties:" ) ObjectPropertyExpression ","
     ObjectPropertyExpression { "," ObjectPropertyExpression }|
     ObjectPropertyExpression ( "disjointObjectProperties" |
     "disjointWith" ) ObjectPropertyExpression { ","
     ObjectPropertyExpression } ;
  ObjectPropertyDomain = ObjectPropertyExpression (
     "objectPropertyDomain" | "domain" ) ClassExpression ;
  ObjectPropertyRange = ObjectPropertyExpression (
     "objectPropertyRange" | "range" ) ClassExpression ;
  InverseObjectPropertyAtom = ObjectPropertyExpression (
        "inverseObjectProperties" | "inverseOf" )
        ObjectPropertyExpression ;
110 FunctionalObjectProperty = ( "FunctionalObjectProperty" |
     "Functional" ) ObjectPropertyExpression ;
  InverseFunctionalObjectProperty = (
     "InverseFunctionalObjectProperty" | "InverseFunctional" )
     ObjectPropertyExpression ;
  ReflexiveObjectProperty = ( "ReflexiveObjectProperty" | "Reflexive"
     ) ObjectPropertyExpression ;
  IrreflexiveObjectProperty = ( "IrreflexiveObjectProperty" |
        " Irreflexive " ) ObjectPropertyExpression ;
  SymmetricObjectProperty = ( " SymmetricObjectProperty " | "Symmetric"
     ) ObjectPropertyExpression ;
115AsymmetricObjectProperty = ( "AsymmetricObjectProperty" |
     "Asymmetric" ) ObjectPropertyExpression ;
  TransitiveObjectProperty = ( "TransitiveObjectProperty" |
        "Transitive" ) ObjectPropertyExpression ;
  SubObjectPropertyExpression = ObjectPropertyExpression |
     ObjectPropertyChain ;
  SuperObjectPropertyExpression = ObjectPropertyExpression ;
  ObjectPropertyChain = "SubPropertyChain:" ObjectPropertyExpression
     "o" ObjectPropertyExpression { "o" ObjectPropertyExpression } ;
```

(*Continued*)

```
120
   ObjectPropertyExpression = ObjectPropertyVariable | ObjectProperty |
      InverseObjectProperty ;

   InverseObjectProperty = ( " ObjectInverseOf " | " inverseOf " )
      ObjectPropertyExpression ;

125 DataPropertyAtom = SubDataPropertyOf | EquivalentDataProperties |
      DisjointDataProperties | DataPropertyDomain | DataPropertyRange
      | FunctionalDataProperty ;

   SubDataPropertyOf = SubDataPropertyExpression ( "subDataPropertyOf"
      | "subPropertyOf" ) SuperDataPropertyExpression ;
   EquivalentDataProperties = ( "EquivalentDataProperties:" |
      "EquivalentProperties:" ) ObjectPropertyExpression ","
      ObjectPropertyExpression { "," ObjectPropertyExpression }|
      ObjectPropertyExpression ( "equivalentDataProperties" |
      "equivalentTo" ) ObjectPropertyExpression { ","
      ObjectPropertyExpression } ;
   DisjointDataProperties = ( "DisjointDataProperties:" |
      "DisjointProperties:" ) ObjectPropertyExpression ","
      ObjectPropertyExpression { "," ObjectPropertyExpression }|
      ObjectPropertyExpression ( " disjointDataProperties " |
      " disjointWith " ) ObjectPropertyExpression { ","
      ObjectPropertyExpression } ;
130 DataPropertyDomain = DataPropertyExpression ( " dataPropertyDomain " |
      "domain" ) ClassExpression ;
   DataPropertyRange = DataPropertyExpression ( " dataPropertyRange :" |
      "range" ) DataRange ;
   FunctionalDataProperty = ( "FunctionalDataProperty" | "Functional" )
      DataPropertyExpression ;
   SubDataPropertyExpression = DataPropertyExpression ;
   SuperDataPropertyExpression = DataPropertyExpression ;
135
   DataPropertyExpression = DataPropertyVariable | DataProperty ;

   HasKey = "HasKey" "(" ClassExpression "(" { ObjectPropertyExpression
      } ")" "(" { DataPropertyExpression } ")" ")" ;

140 Declaration = ObjectPropertyDeclaration | DataPropertyDeclaration |
      NamedIndividualDeclaration | ClassDeclaration ;

   ObjectPropertyDeclaration = "ObjectProperty:" "(" ObjectProperty |
      ObjectPropertyVariable ")" ;
   DataPropertyDeclaration = "DataProperty:" "(" DataProperty |
      DataPropertyVariable ")" ;
   NamedIndividualDeclaration = "NamedIndividual:" "(" NamedIndividual
      | IndividualVariable ")" ;
145 ClassDeclaration = "Class:" "(" Class | ClassVariable ")" ;
```

A.4   SPARQLAS METAMODEL

See Figure A.1.

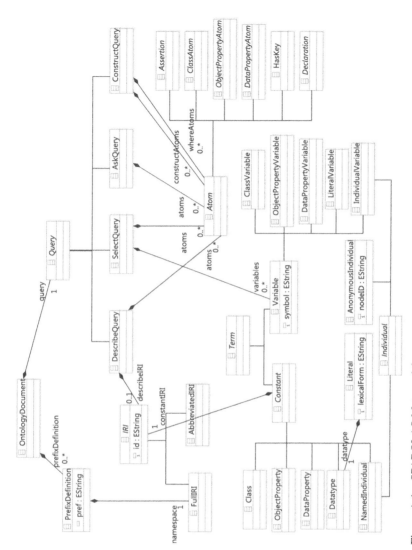

Figure A.1 SPARQLAS Metamodel.

A.5 ECORE TO OWL: TRANSLATION RULES

In this section, we describe the transformation rule for generating OWL ontologies based on the Ecore metamodel.

```
OWL::ClassDeclaration(?x) ← Ecore::EClass(?x)
```

```
OWL::Class(?x) ← Ecore::EClass(?x)
iri(?x,?y) ← name(?x,?y)
```

```
OWL::SubClassOf(?x,?y) ← Ecore::EClass(?x) ∧ Ecore::EClass(?y) ∧
 superClass(?x,?y)
```

```
OWL::Class(?x) ← Ecore::EClass(?x)
OWL::Class(?y) ← Ecore::EClass(?y)
iri(?x,?z1) ← name(?x,?z1)
iri(?y,?z2) ← name(?y,?z2)
```

```
OWL::DataPropertyDeclaration(?y) ← Ecore::EClass(?x) ∧
Ecore::EAttribute(?y)
  ∧ Ecore::EPrimitiveType(?z) ∧ eAttributes(?x,?y) ∧
eAttributeType(?y,?z)
```

```
OWL::DataProperty(?y) ← Ecore::EAttribute(?y)
iri(?y,?z) ← name(?y,?z)
```

```
OWL::ObjectPropertyDeclaration(?y) ← Ecore::EClass(?x)
  ∧ Ecore::EAttribute(?y) ∧ Ecore::EEnum(?z) ∧ eAttributes(?x,?y) ∧
eAttributeType(?y,?z)
```

```
OWL::ObjectProperty(?y) ← Ecore::EAttribute(?y)
iri(?y,?z) ← name(?y,?z)
```

```
OWL::ObjectPropertyDeclaration(?y) ← Ecore::EClass(?x) ∧
Ecore::EReference(?y)
  ∧ Ecore::EClass(?z) ∧ eReferences(?x,?y) ∧ eReferenceType(?y,?z)
```

```
OWL::ObjectProperty(?y) ← Ecore::EReference(?y)
iri(?y,?z) ← name(?y,?z)
```

```
OWL::EquivalentClasses(?v) ← Ecore::EEnum(?v)
```

```
OWL::Class(?w) ← Ecore::EEnum(?v)
iri(?w,?x) ← name(?v,?x)
equivalentClass(?v,?w) ←.
```

```
OWL::ObjectOneOf(?y) ← Ecore::EEnum(?v)
OWL::NamedIndividual(?z) ← Ecore::EEnumLiteral(?z)
oneOfIndividual(?y,?z) ← eLiterals(?v,?z)
equivalentClass(?v,?y) ←.
```

```
OWL::ClassAssertion(?x,?y) ← Ecore::EClass(?x) ∧
  Ecore::EObject(?y) ∧ eClass(?y,?x)

OWL::Class(?x) ← Ecore::EClass(?x)
iri(?x,?z1) ← name(?x,?z1)

OWL::NamedIndividual(?y) ← Ecore::EObject(?y)
iri(?y,?z2) ← name(?y,?z2)
```

```
OWL::ObjectPropertyAssertion(?x,?y,?z) ← Ecore::EObject(?s)
  ∧ Ecore::EObject(?o) ∧ Ecore::EReference(?r) ∧ eGet(?r, ?s,?o)

OWL:ObjectProperty(?r) ← Ecore::EReference(?r)
iri(?r,?n1) ← name(?r,?n1)

OWL::NamedIndividual(?s) ← Ecore::EObject(?s)
iri(?s,?n2) ← name(?s,?n2)

OWL::NamedIndividual(?o) ← Ecore::EObject(?o)
iri(?o,?n3) ← name(?o,?n3)
```

```
OWL::DataPropertyAssertion(?x,?y,?z) ← Ecore::EObject(?s)
  ∧ Ecore::Literal(?l) ∧ Ecore::EAttribute(?r) ∧ eGet(?a, ?s,?l)

OWL:ObjectProperty(?r) ← Ecore::EAttribute(?a)
iri(?a,?n1) ← name(?r,?n1)

OWL::NamedIndividual(?s) ← Ecore::EObject(?s)
iri(?s,?n2) ← name(?s,?n2)

OWL::Literal(?l) ← Ecore::Literal(?l)
```

APPENDIX B

B.1   USE CASES

In the following subsections we describe the use cases of the TwoUse approach. After describing the use cases, we map these use cases onto the requirements in the traceability matrix presented in Section B.2.

B.1.1   Design Integrated Models

Brief Description: This use case covers the creation and visualization of OWL constructs with UML class-based modeling.

Preconditions: None.

Postconditions: An OWL ontology is generated.

Basic Flow:

1. Software engineer `Design Integrated models`.
2. Software engineer saves integrated model.
3. System transforms TwoUse model into OWL.
4. Use case terminates.

Sub flow: Abstract `Design Integrated models`.

B.1.2   Design Integrated UML Class Diagram

Brief Description: This use case covers the creation and visualization of hybrid models using UML as concrete syntax.

Sub flow: `Design Integrated models`

1. Software engineer creates a new UML class diagram.
2. Software engineer use stereotypes of the UML profile for OWL to annotate UML elements.
3. System transforms the hybrid class diagram into a TwoUse model.

Alternate Flows:

1. Software engineer imports existing UML class diagram.

Semantic Web and Model-Driven Engineering, First Edition. Fernando Silva Parreiras.
© 2012 Institute of Electrical and Electronics Engineers. Published 2012 by John Wiley & Sons, Inc.

B.1.3 Design Integrated Ecore Model

Brief Description: This use case covers the creation and visualization of Ecore models using the textual syntax.

Sub flow: `Design Integrated models`

1. Software engineer creates a new Ecore model.

2. Software engineer creates annotations with OWL axioms to Ecore elements.

3. System transforms Ecore model with annotations for OWL into a TwoUse model.

Alternate Flows:

1. Software engineer imports existing Ecore model.

B.1.4 Specify SPARQLAS4TwoUse Query Operations

Brief Description: This use case covers the specification of query operations for classes using SPARQLAS4TwoUse for usage of ontology services in UML class-based modeling.

Preconditions: Integrated model exists.

Postconditions: None.

Basic Flow:

1. Software engineer creates query operations at classes.

2. Software engineer specifies the body of query operations using SPARQLAS4TwoUse.

3. System transforms the hybrid class diagram into a TwoUse model.

4. System generates an OWL ontology from the TwoUse model.

5. System generates a SPARQL query from the SPARQLAS4TwoUse query.

6. Use case terminates.

Alternate Flows: None.

B.1.5 Transform to OWL

Brief Description: This use case covers the transformation of Ecore-based modeling languages. It consists of transforming model and metamodel into individuals and classes in an OWL ontology for usage of ontology services in UML class-based modeling.

Preconditions: A model and its metamodel designed using Ecore technologies exist.

Postconditions: An OWL ontology is generated including elements of the model as individuals and property assertions and the elements of the metamodel as classes and properties.

Basic Flows:

1. Software engineer selects a model for transformation.

2. System creates an OWL ontology.

3. System reads selected model's metamodel and transform it into OWL classes and properties.

4. System reads selected model and transforms it into OWL individuals, class assertions, and property assertions.

5. Use case terminates.

Alternate Flows: None.

B.1.6 Compute Alignments

Brief Description: This use case covers the computation of alignments between two UML class-based models. It consists of transforming models into OWL and applying matching techniques to identify similarities between two models.

Preconditions: Two models exist.

Postconditions: Results of alignments are displayed.

Basic Flows:

1. Software engineer selects two UML class-based models for comparison.

2. System reads the two corresponding OWL ontologies.

3. System computes the alignment between these ontologies.

4. System displays the result.

5. Use case terminates.

Alternate Flows: None.

B.1.7 Browse

Brief Description: This covers the usage of queries and filters for extrating data.

Preconditions: UML class-based modeling exists.

Postconditions: Results are presented.

Basic Flows:

1. Engineer creates new SPARQLAS query.

2. Engineer saves SPARQLAS query.

3. Engineer executes SPARQLAS query.

4. Engineer `Select Model`.

5. System transforms UML class-based model into OWL.

6. System transforms SPARQLAS query into SPARQL query.

7. System uses reasoning systems to classify and realize the ontology and to execute the SPARQL query.

8. System shows query results.

9. Use case terminates.

Alternate Flows: Engineer visualizes inferred class hierarchy.

1. System shows the inferred class hierarchy.

B.1.8   Explain Axioms

Brief Description: This covers the usage of explanation services.

Preconditions: OWL exists.

Postconditions: None.

Basic Flows:

1. Engineer selects axioms for explanation.

2. System generates an explanation for the selected axioms.

3. Use case terminates.

Alternate Flows: None.

Sub flow: Abstract `Select Model`.

B.1.9   Query UML Class-Based Models

Brief Description: This covers the usage of queries over UML class-based modeling.

Sub flow: `Select Model`

1. Software Engineer selects UML class-based model.

2. System transforms UML class-based model into OWL.

B.1.10   Query OWL Ontologies

Brief Description: It extends use case Query.

Sub flow: `Select Model`

1. Software Engineer selects OWL ontology.

B.1.11   Design Ontology Engineering Services

Brief Description: This involves the specification of Ontology Engineering Service.

Preconditions: OWL ontology exists.

Postconditions: None.

Basic Flows:

1. Ontology Engineer `Design Services`.

2. System `Generate Service`.

3. Use case terminates.

Alternate Flows: None.

Extension Point: `Generate Service`.

Sub flow: Abstract `Design Services`.

B.1.12 Design Ontology API

Brief Description: This involves the specification of OWL ontology API.

Sub flow: `Design Services`.

1. Ontology engineer creates OWL ontology API specification.
2. Ontology engineer specifies API using a domain-specific textual language.
3. Ontology engineer saves OWL Ontology API specification.

Alternate Flows: None.

Preconditions: OWL ontology exists.

Postconditions: None.

B.1.13 Design Ontology Translation

Brief Description: This outlines the design of OWL ontology dataset translations.

Sub flow: `Design Services`.

1. Ontology engineer creates OWL ontology dataset translation specification.
2. Ontology engineer specifies OWL ontology dataset translation using a domain-specific textual language.
3. Ontology engineer saves OWL ontology dataset translation specification.

Alternate Flows: None.

Preconditions: Source OWL ontology and Target OWL ontology exist.

Postconditions: None.

B.1.14 Design Ontology Template

Brief Description: This covers the usage of templates in OWL ontologies.

Sub flow: `Design Services`.

1. Ontology engineer imports domain ontology.
2. Ontology engineer specifies ontology templates.
3. Ontology engineer binds templates to domain ontology.

Alternate Flows

1. Ontology engineer uses UML class diagrams for creating templates.
2. Ontology engineer uses the OWL 2 graphical notation for creating templates.

Preconditions: Domain ontology exists.

Postconditions: OWL ontology generated.

B.1.15   Generate Service

Brief Description: This covers the transformation of specification into platform specific artifacts.

Extension Flows: `Generate Service.`

  1. System generates platform specific artifacts for the ontology engineering service.

B.2   CONNECTING USE CASES WITH REQUIREMENTS

Having described the use cases in Section B.1, we have mapped them onto the requirements presented in Section 5.2 in Table B.1, which depicts a traceability matrix and correlates the requirements with the use cases.

TABLE B.1   Mapping Use Cases and Requirements.

Requirements Use Cases	OWL Constructs in UML class-based modeling (5.2.1.1)	Ontology services in UML class-based modeling (5.2.1.2)	MDE support for ontology modeling (5.2.2.1)	Domain modeling for ontology engineering Services (5.2.2.2)
Design integrated models (B.1.1)	X			
Design integrated UML class diagram (B.1.2)	X			
Design integrated Ecore model (B.1.3)	X			
Specify SPARQLAS4TwoUse query operations (B.1.4)		X		
Transform to OWL (B.1.5)		X		
Compute alignments (B.1.6)		X		
Browse (B.1.7)		X	X	X
Query UML class-based models (B.1.9)		X		
Query OWL ontologies (B.1.10)			X	X
Explain axioms (B.1.8)		X		
Design ontology engineering services (B.1.11)			X	X
Design ontology API (B.1.12)				X
Design ontology translation (B.1.13)				X
Design ontology template (B.1.14)			X	
Generate service (B.1.15)			X	

REFERENCES

1. Dean Allemang and James Hendler. *Semantic Web for the Working Ontologist: Effective Modeling in RDFS and OWL*. Morgan Kaufmann Publishers Inc., San Francisco, CA, USA, 2008.

2. Jürgen Angele and Georg Lausen. Ontologies in F-logic. In *Handbook on Ontologies*, International Handbooks on Information Systems, pages 29–50. Springer, 2004.

3. Giuliano Antoniol, Massimiliano Di Penta, Harald Gall, and Martin Pinzger. Towards the Integration of Versioning Systems, Bug Reports and Source Code Meta-Models. *Electr. Notes Theor. Comput. Sci.*, 127(3):87–99, 2005.

4. Grigoris Antoniou and Frank van Harmelen. *A Semantic Web Primer, 2nd Edition*. The MIT Press, Cambridge, MA, USA, 2008.

5. L. Apostel. Towards the formal study of models in a non formal science. *Synthese*, 12:125–161, 1960.

6. Richard Arndt, Raphaël Troncy, Steffen Staab, Lynda Hardman, and Miroslav Vacura. COMM: Designing a Well-Founded Multimedia Ontology for the Web. In *Proceedings of the 6th International Semantic Web Conference and 2nd Asian Semantic Web Conference (ISWC/ASWC 2007), Busan, South Korea, 11–15th November, 2007*, volume 4825 of *Lecture Notes in Computer Science*, pages 30–43. Springer, 2007.

7. C. Atkinson and T. Kuhne. Model-driven development: a metamodeling foundation. *Software, IEEE*, 20(5):36–41, Sept.–Oct. 2003.

8. Paolo Atzeni, Paolo Cappellari, and Philip A. Bernstein. Model-Independent Schema and Data Translation. In *Proceedings of 10th International Conference on Extending Database Technology (EDBT 2006), Munich, Germany, March 26–31, 2006*, volume 3896 of *Lecture Notes in Computer Science*, pages 368–385. Springer, 2006.

9. Franz Baader, Diego Calvanese, Deborah L. McGuinness, Daniele Nardi, and Peter F. Patel-Schneider, editors. *The Description Logic Handbook*. Cambridge University Press, Cambridge, UK, 2003.

10. Kenneth Baclawski, Mieczyslaw M. Kokar, Paul A. Kogut, Lewis Hart, Jeffrey E. Smith, Jerzy Letkowski, and Pat Emery. Extending the Unified Modeling Language for ontology development. *Software and System Modeling*, 1(2):142–156, 2002.

11. Bernhard Beckert, Uwe Keller, and Peter H. Schmitt. Translating the Object Constraint Language into First-order Predicate Logic. In *Proceedings of the Second Verification Workshop (VERIFY 2002), July 25–26, 2002, Copenhagen, Denmark*, volume 02–07 of *DIKU technical report*. DIKU, 2002.

12. Daniela Berardi, Diego Calvanese, and Giuseppe De Giacomo. Reasoning on UML class diagrams. *Artif. Intell.*, 168(1):70–118, 2005.

13. Jean Bézivin. On the unification power of models. *Software and System Modeling*, 4(2):171–188, 2005.

Semantic Web and Model-Driven Engineering, First Edition. Fernando Silva Parreiras.
© 2012 Institute of Electrical and Electronics Engineers. Published 2012 by John Wiley & Sons, Inc.

14. Jean Bézivin, V. Devedzic, D. Djuric, J.M. Favreau, D. Gasevic, and Frédéric Jouault. An M3-Neutral Infrastructure for Bridging Model Engineering and Ontology Engineering. In *Interoperability of Enterprise Software and Applications*, pages 159–171. Springer, 2005.

15. Andreas Billig, Susanne Busse, Andreas Leicher, and Jörn Guy Süss. Platform independent model transformation based on TRIPLE. In *Proceedings of the ACM/IFIP/USENIX International Middleware Conference, Middleware 2004, Toronto, Canada, October 18–20, 2004*, volume 3231 of *Lecture Notes in Computer Science*, pages 493–511. Springer, 2004.

16. Christian Bizer, Tom Heath, and Tim Berners-Lee. Linked Data—The Story So Far. *International Journal on Semantic Web and Information Systems*, 5(3):1–22, 2009.

17. Jean-Paul Bodeveix, Thierry Millan, Christian Percebois, Christophe Le Camus, Pierre Bazex, and Louis Feraud. Extending OCL for verifying UML models consistency. In *Proceedings of the Workshop on Consistency Problems in UML-based Software Development, Workshop at UML 2002, Dresden, Germany, October 1, 2002*, volume 2002:06 of *Research Report*, pages 75–90. Blekinge Institute of Technology, 2002.

18. Harold Boley, Said Tabet, and Gerd Wagner. Design Rationale for RuleML: A Markup Language for Semantic Web Rules. In *Proceedings of the first Semantic Web Working Symposium (SWWS 2001), Stanford University, CA, USA, July 30 -August 1, 2001*, pages 381–401, 2001.

19. Paolo Bouquet, Fausto Giunchiglia, Frank van Harmelen, Luciano Serafini, and Heiner Stuckenschmidt. C-OWL: Contextualizing Ontologies. In *Proceedings of Second International Semantic Web Conference (ISWC 2003), Sanibel Island, FL, USA, October 20–23, 2003*, volume 2870 of *Lecture Notes in Computer Science*, pages 164–179. Springer, 2003.

20. Saartje Brockmans, Robert M. Colomb, Elisa F. Kendall, Evan Wallace, Christopher Welty, Guo Tong Xie, and Peter Haase. A Model Driven Approach for Building OWL DL and OWL Full Ontologies. In *Proceedings of 5th International Semantic Web Conference (ISWC), Athens, GA, USA, November 5–9, 2006*, volume 4273 of *Lecture Notes in Computer Science*, pages 187–200. Springer, November 2006.

21. Saartje Brockmans, Peter Haase, Pascal Hitzler, and Rudi Studer. A Metamodel and UML Profile for Rule-Extended OWL DL Ontologies. In *Proceedings of the 3rd European Semantic Web Conference, ESWC 2006, Budva, Montenegro, June 11–14, 2006*, volume 4011 of *Lecture Notes in Computer Science*, pages 303–316. Springer, 2006.

22. Saartje Brockmans, Peter Haase, and Heiner Stuckenschmidt. Formalism-Independent Specification of Ontology Mappings—A Metamodeling Approach. In *Proceedings of On the Move to Meaningful Internet Systems (OTM 2006), Montpellier, France, October 29–November 3, 2006*, volume 4275 of *Lecture Notes in Computer Science*, pages 901–908. Springer, 2006.

23. Sara Brockmans, Raphael Volz, Andreas Eberhart, and Peter Löffler. Visual Modeling of OWL DL Ontologies Using UML. In *Proceedings of the Third International Semantic Web Conference, ISWC 2004, Hiroshima, Japan, November 7–11, 2004*, volume 3298 of *Lecture Notes in Computer Science*, pages 198–213. Springer, 2004.

24. Jeen Broekstra, Arjohn Kampman, and Frank van Harmelen. Sesame: A Generic Architecture for Storing and Querying RDF and RDF Schema. In *Proceedings of the First International Semantic Web Conference (ISWC 2002), Sardinia, Italy, June 9–12, 2002*, volume 2342 of *Lecture Notes in Computer Science*, pages 54–68. Springer, 2002.

25. Achim D. Brucker and Burkhart Wolff. A Proposal for a Formal OCL Semantics in Isabelle/HOL. In *Proceedings of the 15th International Conference on Theorem Proving in Higher Order Logics (TPHOLs 2002), Hampton, VA, USA, August 20–23, 2002*, volume 2410 of *Lecture Notes in Computer Science*, pages 99–114. Springer-Verlag, 2002.

26. Diego Calvanese, Giuseppe De Giacomo, and Maurizio Lenzerini. On the decidability of query containment under constraints. In *Proceedings of the 17th ACM SIGACT-SIGMOD-SIGART Symposium on Principles of Database Systems, PODS 1998, Seattle, WA, USA, June 1–3, 1998*, pages 149–158. ACM Press, 1998.

27. Diego Calvanese, Giuseppe De Giacomo, and Maurizio Lenzerini. Identification constraints and functional dependencies in description logics. In *Proceedings of the 17th International Joint Conference on Artificial Intelligence, IJCAI 2001, Seattle, WA, USA, August 4–10, 2001*, pages 155–160. Morgan Kaufmann Publishers Inc., 2001.

28. H. Chalupsky. OntoMorph: A Translation System for Symbolic Knowledge. In *Principles of Knowledge Representation and Reasoning Proceedings of the Seventh International Conference (KR 2000), Breckenridge, CO, USA, April 11–15, 2000*, pages 471–482. Morgan Kaufmann, 2000.

29. O. Corcho and A. Gómez-Pérez. ODEDialect: A Set of Declarative Languages for Implementing Ontology Translation Systems. *Journal of Universal Computer Science*, 13(12):1805–1834, 2007.

30. Óscar Corcho and Asunción Gómez-Pérez. A Layered Model for Building Ontology Translation Systems. *Int'l Journal on Semantic Web & Information Systems*, 1(2):22–48, 2005.

31. Stephen Cranefield and Martin K. Purvis. UML as an Ontology Modelling Language. In *Proceedings of the IJCAI-99 Workshop on Intelligent Information Integration, Intelligent Information Integration 1999, Stockholm, Sweden, July 31, 1999*, volume 23 of CEUR *Workshop Proceedings*. CEUR-WS.org, 1999.

32. Krzysztof Czarnecki. Domain Engineering. In John J. Marciniak, editor, *Encyclopedia of Software Engineering*. John Wiley & Sons, Inc., 2002.

33. Stefan Decker, Michael Sintek, Andreas Billig, Nicola Henze, Peter Dolog, Wolfgang Nejdl, Andreas Harth, Andreas Leicher, Susanne Busse, José Luis Ambite, Matthew Weathers, Gustaf Neumann, and Uwe Zdun. TRIPLE—an RDF Rule Language with Context and Use Cases. In *Proceedings of the W3C Workshop on Rule Languages for Interoperability (2005), Washington, DC, USA, April 27–28, 2005*. W3C, 2005.

34. Dragan Djurić, Dragan Gašević, Vladan Devedžić, and Violeta Damjanovic. A UML Profile for OWL Ontologies. In *Proceedings of the Model Driven Architecture, European MDA Workshops: Foundations and Applications, MDAFA 2003 and MDAFA 2004, Twente, The Netherlands, June 26–27, 2003 and Linköping, Sweden, June 10–11, 2004*, volume 3599 of *Lecture Notes in Computer Science*, pages 204–219. Springer, 2005.

35. Francesco M. Donini, Daniele Nardi, and Riccardo Rosati. Description logics of minimal knowledge and negation as failure. *ACM Trans. Comput. Logic*, 3(2):177–225, 2002.

36. Dejinj Dou, Drew Macdermot, and Peishen Qi. Ontology translation on the semantic web. *Journal of Data Semantics*, 2(3360):35–57, 2004.

37. Christof Ebert. Dealing with nonfunctional requirements in large software systems. *Ann. Softw. Eng.*, 3:367–395, 1997.

38. J. Euzenat and P. Shvaiko. *Ontology Matching*. Springer, 2007.

39. Jérôme Euzenat. Towards a Principled Approach to Semantic Interoperability. In *Workshop on Ontologies and Information Sharing at International Joint Conferences on Artificial Intelligence (IJCAI 2001), Seattle, WA, USA, August 4–10, 2001*, pages 19–25, 2001.

40. Jérôme Euzenat. An API for Ontology Alignment. In *The Semantic Web—ISWC 2004: Third International Semantic Web Conference, Hiroshima, Japan, November 7–11, 2004. Proceedings*, volume 3298 of *Lecture Notes in Computer Science*, pages 698–712. Springer, 2004.

41. Jérôme Euzenat, Alfio Ferrara, Laura Hollink, Antoine Isaac, Cliff Joslyn, Véronique Malaisé, Christian Meilicke, Andriy Nikolov, Juan Pane, Marta Sabou, Francois Scharffe, Pavel Shvaiko, Vassilis Spiliopoulos, Heiner Stuckenschmidt, Ondrej Sváb-Zamazal, Vojtech Svátek, Cássia Trojahn dos Santos, George A. Vouros, and Shenghui Wang. Results of the Ontology Alignment Evaluation Initiative 2009. In *Proceedings of the 4th International Workshop on Ontology Matching (OM-2009) collocated with the 8th International Semantic Web Conference (ISWC-2009) Chantilly, VA, USA, October 25, 2009*, volume 551 of *CEUR Workshop Proceedings*. CEUR-WS.org, 2009.

42. Kateryna Falkovych, Marta Sabou, and Heiner Stuckenschmidt. UML for the Semantic Web: Transformation-Based Approaches. In *Knowledge Transformation for the Semantic Web*, volume 95 of *Frontiers in Artificial Intelligence and Applications*, pages 92–106. IOS Press, 2003.

43. James Farrugia. Model-theoretic semantics for the web. In *Proceedings of the International World Wide Web Conference (WWW 2003), Budapest, Hungary, 20–24 May, 2003*, pages 29–38. ACM, 2003.

44. Jean-Marie Favre and Tam Nguyen. Towards a Megamodel to Model Software Evolution Through Transformations. *Electr. Notes Theor. Comput. Sci.*, 127(3):59–74, 2005.

45. Norman E. Fenton and Shari Lawrence Pfleeger. *Software Metrics: A Rigorous and Practical Approach*. PWS Publishing Co., Boston, MA, USA, 1998.

46. Richard Fikes, Pat Hayes, and Ian Horrocks. OWL-QL: A Language for Deductive Query Answering on the Semantic Web. Technical Report KSL 03–14, Stanford University, Stanford, CA, 2003.

47. Richard Fikes and Deborah L McGuinness. An Axiomatic Semantics for RDF, RDF-S, and DAML+OIL. KSL Technical Report KSL-01–01, Stanford University, 2001.

48. R. France, A. Evans, K. Lano, and B. Rumpe. The UML as a formal modeling notation. *Computer Standards & Interfaces*, 19(7):325–334, 1998.

49. David Frankel, Patrick Hayes, Elisa Kendall, and Deborah McGuinness. The Model Driven Semantic Web. In *Proceedings of the 1st International Workshop on the Model-Driven Semantic Web (MDSW2004), Monterey, CA, USA, September 21, 2004*, 2004.

50. Thomas Franz, Steffen Staab, and Richard Arndt. The X-COSIM integration framework for a seamless semantic desktop. In *Proceedings of the 4th International Conference on Knowledge Capture (K-CAP 2007), October 28–31, 2007, Whistler, BC, Canada*, pages 143–150. ACM, 2007.

51. Erich Gamma, Richard Helm, Ralph Johnson, and John Vlissides. *Design patterns: elements of reusable object-oriented software*. Addison-Wesley Professional, Boston, MA, USA, 1995.

52. Aldo Gangemi and Valentina Presutti. Ontology Design Patterns. In *Handbook on Ontologies*, International Handbooks Information System, pages 221–243. Springer, 2009.

53. Dragan Gašević, Dragan Djurić, and Vladan Devedžić. MDA-based Automatic OWL Ontology Development. *Int. J. Softw. Tools Technol. Transf.*, 9(2):103–117, 2007.

54. Birte Glimm, Matthew Horridge, Bijan Parsia, and Peter F. Patel-Schneider. A Syntax for Rules in OWL 2. In *Proceedings of the 6th International Workshop on OWL: Experiences and Directions (OWLED 2009), Chantilly, VA, USA October 23–24, 2009*, volume 529 of *CEUR Workshop Proceedings*. CEUR-WS.org, 2009.

55. Birte Glimm and Chimezie Ogbuji. SPARQL 1.1 Entailment Regimes. W3C Working Draft 1 June 2010, 2010.

56. James Gosling, Bill Joy, Guy Steele, and Gilad Bracha. *Java(TM) Language Specification, The (3rd Edition)*. Addison-Wesley Professional, 2005.

57. Jeff Gray, Kathleen Fisher, Charles Consel, Gabor Karsai, Marjan Mernik, and Juha-Pekka Tolvanen. DSLs: the good, the bad, and the ugly. In *Companion to the 23rd Annual ACM SIGPLAN Conference on Object-Oriented Programming, Systems, Languages, and Applications, OOPSLA 2008, October 19–13, 2007, Nashville, TN, USA*, pages 791–794. ACM, 2008.

58. T. R. G. Green and Marian Petre. Usability analysis of visual programming environments: a "cognitive dimensions" framework. *J. Visual Languages and Computing*, 7(2):131–174, 1996.

59. Gerd Gröner, Fernando Silva Parreiras, and Steffen Staab. Semantic Recognition of Ontology Refactoring. In *The Semantic Web—ISWC 2010, 9th International Semantic Web Conference, ISWC 2010, Shanghai, China, November 7–11, 2010. Proceedings*, volume 6414 of *Lecture Notes in Computer Science*. Springer, 2010.

60. Gerd Gröner and Steffen Staab. Modeling and Query Patterns for Process Retrieval in OWL. In *The Semantic Web—ISWC 2009, 8th International Semantic Web Conference, ISWC 2009, Chantilly, VA, USA, October 25–29, 2009. Proceedings*, volume 5823 of *Lecture Notes in Computer Science*, pages 243–259. Springer, 2009.

61. W3C OWL Working Group. OWL 2 Web Ontology Language Document Overview. W3C Working Draft 27 March 2009.

62. T. R. Gruber. A translation approach to portable ontology specifications. *Knowledge Acquisition*, 5(2):199–220, 1993.

63. Yuri Gurevich. Sequential abstract-state machines capture sequential algorithms. *ACM Trans. Comput. Logic*, 1(1):77–111, 2000.

64. Peter Haase, Jeen Broekstra, Andreas Eberhart, and Raphael Volz. A Comparison of RDF Query Languages. In *Proceedings of the Third International Semantic Web Conference, ISWC 2004, Hiroshima, Japan, November 7–11, 2004*, volume 3298 of *Lecture Notes in Computer Science*, pages 502–517. Springer, 2004.

65. Peter Haase and Boris Motik. A Mapping System for the Integration of OWL-DL Ontologies. In *Proceedings of the First International ACM Workshop on Interoperability of Heterogeneous Information Systems (IHIS'05), CIKM Conference, Bremen, Germany, November 4, 2005*, pages 9–16. ACM Press, 2005.

66. Hans-Jörg Happel and Stefan Seedorf. Applications of Ontologies in Software Engineering. In *Proceedings of the 2nd International Workshop on Semantic Web Enabled Software Engineering, SWESE 2006, Athens, GA, USA, November 6, 2006*, 2006.

67. D. Harel and B. Rumpe. Modeling Languages: Syntax, Semantics and All That Stuff, Part I: The Basic Stuff. Technical report, Jerusalem, Israel, 2000.

68. D. Harel and B. Rumpe. Meaningful modeling: what's the semantics of "semantics"? *Computer*, 37(10):64–72, Oct. 2004.

69. Steve Harris and Andy Seaborne. SPARQL 1.1 Query Language. W3C Working Draft 1 June 2010.

70. Florian Heidenreich, Jendrik Johannes, Sven Karol, Mirko Seifert, and Christian Wende. Derivation and Refinement of Textual Syntax for Models. In *Model Driven Architecture—Foundations and Applications, 5th European Conference, ECMDA-FA 2009, Enschede, The Netherlands, June 23–26, 2009. Proceedings*, volume 5562 of *Lecture Notes in Computer Science*, pages 114–129. Springer, 2009.

71. Tassilo Horn. Model Migration with GReTL. In *Proceedings of Transformation Tool Contest (TTC 2010), Malaga, Spain, 1–2 July, 2010*, volume WP 10-03 of *CTIT Workshop Proceedings Series*. University of Twente, 2010.

72. Matthew Horridge and Sean Bechhofer. The OWL API: A Java API for Working with OWL 2 Ontologies. In Rinke Hoekstra and Peter F. Patel-Schneider, editors, *Proceedings of the 6th International Workshop on OWL: Experiences and Directions (OWLED 2009), Chantilly, VA, USA, October 23–24, 2009*, volume 529 of *CEUR Workshop Proceedings*. CEUR-WS.org, 2009.

73. Matthew Horridge, Nick Drummond, John Goodwin, Alan Rector, Robert Stevens, and Hai Wang. The Manchester OWL Syntax. In *Proceedings of the Workshop on OWL: Experiences and Directions, OWLED 2006, Athens, GA, USA, November 10–11, 2006*, volume 216 of *CEUR Workshop Proceedings*. CEUR-WS.org, 2006.

74. Matthew Horridge and Peter F. Patel-Schneider. OWL 2 Web Ontology Language Manchester Syntax. W3C Working Group Note 27 October 2009.

75. Ian Horrocks, Oliver Kutz, and Ulrike Sattler. The Even More Irresistible SROIQ. In *Proceedings, Tenth International Conference on Principles of Knowledge Representation and Reasoning, Lake District of the United Kingdom, June 2–5, 2006*, pages 57–67. AAAI Press, 2006.

76. Ian Horrocks, Peter F. Patel-Schneider, Harold Boley, Said Tabet, Benjamin Grosof, and Mike Dean. SWRL: A semantic web rule language combining OWL and RuleML. W3C Member submission 21 May 2004.

77. Ian Horrocks and Sergio Tessaris. A Conjunctive Query Language for Description Logic Aboxes. In *Proceedings of the Seventeenth National Conference on Artificial Intelligence and Twelfth Conference on Innovative Applications of Artificial Intelligence, July 30 –August 3, 2000, Austin, TX, USA*, pages 399–404. AAAI Press/The MIT Press, 2000.

78. Luigi Iannone, Alan L. Rector, and Robert Stevens. Embedding Knowledge Patterns into OWL. In *The Semantic Web: Research and Applications, 6th European Semantic Web Conference, ESWC 2009, Heraklion, Crete, Greece, May 31–June 4, 2009, Proceedings*, volume 5554 of *Lecture Notes in Computer Science*, pages 218–232. Springer, 2009.

79. Aftab Iqbal, Oana Ureche, Michael Hausenblas, and Giovanni Tummarello. LD2SD: Linked Data Driven Software Development. In *Proceedings of the 21st International Conference on Software Engineering & Knowledge Engineering (SEKE'2009), Boston, MA, USA, July 1–3, 2009*, pages 240–245. Knowledge Systems Institute Graduate School, 2009.

80. ISO/IEC. *ISO/IEC 9126. Software engineering—Product quality*. ISO/IEC, 2001.

81. Nophadol Jekjantuk, Jeff. Z. Pan, Yuting Zhao, Fernando Silva Parreiras, Gerd Gröner, and Tobias Walter. Report on Querying the Combined Metamodel.

Deliverable EU FP7 STREP MOST ICT216691/UoKL/WP1-D1.2/D/PU/a1, University of Koblenz Landau, January 2009.

82. Frédéric Jouault and Ivan Kurtev. Transforming Models with ATL. In *Proceedings of the Satellite Events at the MoDELS 2005 Conference, MoDELS 2005 International Workshops, Montego Bay, Jamaica, October 2–7, 2005*, volume 3844 of *Lecture Notes in Computer Science*, pages 128–138. Springer, 2006.

83. A. Kalyanpur, B. Parsia, E. Sirin, and J. Hendler. Debugging unsatisfiable classes in OWL ontologies. *Web Semantics: Science, Services and Agents on the World Wide Web*, 3(4):268–293, 2005.

84. Aditya Kalyanpur, Bijan Parsia, Matthew Horridge, and Evren Sirin. Finding All Justifications of OWL DL Entailments. In *Proceedings of the 6th International Semantic Web Conference and 2nd Asian Semantic Web Conference (ISWC/ASWC 2007), Busan, South Korea, 11–15th November, 2007*, volume 4825 of *Lecture Notes in Computer Science*, pages 267–280. Springer, 2007.

85. Aditya Kalyanpur, Daniel Jiménez Pastor, Steve Battle, and Julian A. Padget. Automatic Mapping of OWL Ontologies into Java. In Frank Maurer and Günther Ruhe, editors, *Proceedings of the Sixteenth International Conference on Software Engineering & Knowledge Engineering (SEKE'2004), Banff, Alberta, Canada, June 20–24, 2004*, pages 98–103, 2004.

86. Gerti Kappel, Elisabeth Kapsammer, Horst Kargl, Gerhard Kramler, Thomas Reiter, Werner Retschitzegger, Wieland Schwinger, and Manuel Wimmer. Lifting Metamodels to Ontologies: A Step to the Semantic Integration of Modeling Languages. In *Proceedings of the 9th International Conference of Model Driven Engineering Languages and Systems, MoDELS 2006, Genova, Italy, October 1–6, 2006*, volume 4199 of *Lecture Notes in Computer Science*, pages 528–542. Springer, 2006.

87. Yarden Katz and Bijan Parsia. Towards a Nonmonotonic Extension to OWL. In *Proceedings of the OWLED*05 Workshop on OWL, Experiences and Directions, Galway, Ireland, November 11–12, 2005*, volume 188 of *CEUR Workshop Proceedings*. CEUR-WS.org, 2005.

88. Stuart Kent. Model Driven Engineering. In *Proceedings of the Third International Conference on Integrated Formal Methods (IFM 2002), Turku, Finland, May 1518, 2002*, volume 2335 of *Lecture Notes in Computer Science*, pages 286–298. Springer, 2002.

89. Christoph Kiefer, Abraham Bernstein, and Jonas Tappolet. Mining Software Repositories with iSPARQL and a Software Evolution Ontology. In *Proceedings of the 29th International Conference on Software Engineering Workshops (ICSEW '07), Minneapolis, MN, USA, May 20–26, 2007*.

90. A. G. Kleppe, J. B. Warmer, and W. Bast. *MDA Explained, The Model Driven Architecture: Practice and Promise*. Addison-Wesley, Boston, MA, USA, 2002.

91. Holger Knublauch. Ontology-Driven Software Development in the Context of the Semantic Web: An Example Scenario with Protege/OWL. In *Proceedings of the 1st International Workshop on the Model-Driven Semantic Web (MDSW2004), Monterey, CA, USA, September 21, 2004*.

92. Holger Knublauch, Daniel Oberle, Phil Tetlow, and Evan Wallace. A Semantic Web Primer for Object-Oriented Software Developers. W3c working group note, W3C, Mar. 2006.

93. Alexander Kubias, Simon Schenk, Steffen Staab, and Jeff Z. Pan. OWL SAIQL—An OWL DL Query Language for Ontology Extraction. In *Proceedings of the OWLED*

2007 Workshop on OWL: Experiences and Directions, Innsbruck, Austria, June 6–7, 2007, volume 258 of *CEUR Workshop Proceedings*. CEUR-WS.org, 2007.

94. Ivan Kurtev, Jean Bédézivin, Fréric Jouault, and Patrick Valduriez. Model-based DSL frameworks. In *Proceedings of Object-Oriented Programming Systems, Languages and Applications (OOPSLA 2006), Portland, OR, USA, October 22–26, 2006*, pages 602–616. ACM, 2006.

95. Alexander Maedche, Boris Motik, Nuno Silva, and Raphael Volz. MAFRA—A Mapping Framework for Distributed Ontologies. In *Proceedings of the 13th International Conference on Knowledge Engineering and Knowledge Management (EKAW), Siguenza, Spain, October 1–4, 2002*, volume 2473 of *LNAI*, pages 235–250. Springer, 2002.

96. Andreas Maier, Hans-Peter Schnurr, and York Sure. Ontology-based Information Integration in the Automotive Industry. In *Proceedings of Second International Semantic Web Conference (ISWC 2003), Sanibel Island, FL, USA, October 20–23, 2003*, volume 2870 of *Lecture Notes in Computer Science*, pages 897–912. Springer, October 2003.

97. Jeff McAffer and Jean-Michel Lemieux. *Eclipse Rich Client Platform: Designing, Coding, and Packaging Java(TM) Applications*. Addison-Wesley Professional, 2005.

98. Deborah L. McGuinness and Jon R. Wright. Conceptual modelling for configuration: A description logic-based approach. *AI EDAM*, 12(4):333–344, 1998.

99. Marjan Mernik, Jan Heering, and Anthony M. Sloane. When and how to develop domain-specific languages. *ACM Comput. Surv.*, 37(4):316–344, 2005.

100. J. Miller and J. Mukerji. MDA Guide Version 1.0.1. Technical report, OMG, 2003.

101. Riichiro Mizoguchi and Kouji Kozaki. Ontology engineering environments. In Steffen Staab and Rudi Studer, editors, *Handbook on Ontologies*, International Handbooks Information System, pages 315–336. Springer Berlin Heidelberg, 2009.

102. Audris Mockus and James D. Herbsleb. Expertise browser: a quantitative approach to identifying expertise. In *Proceedings of the 22rd International Conference on Software Engineering, ICSE 2002, 19–25 May 2002, Orlando, FL, USA*, pages 503–512. ACM, 2002.

103. Boris Motik, Ian Horrocks, Riccardo Rosati, and Ulrike Sattler. Can OWL and logic programming live together happily ever after? In *Proceedings of the International Semantic Web Conference (ISWC 2006), Athens, GA, USA, November 5–9, 2006*, volume 4273 of *Lecture Notes in Computer Science*, pages 501–514. Springer, 2006.

104. Boris Motik, Ian Horrocks, and Ulrike Sattler. Bridging the gap between OWL and relational databases. In *Proceedings of the International World Wide Web Conference (WWW 2007), Banff, Canada, May 8–12, 2007*, pages 807–816. ACM Press, 2007.

105. Boris Motik, Peter F. Patel-Schneider, and Bernardo Cuenca Grau. OWL 2 Web Ontology Language: Direct Semantics. W3C Working Draft 02 December 2008.

106. Boris Motik, Peter F. Patel-Schneider, and Ian Horrocks. OWL 2 Web Ontology Language: Structural Specification and Functional-Style Syntax. W3C Recommendation 27 October 2009.

107. Boris Motik, Ulrike Sattler, and Rudi Studer. Query Answering for OWL-DL with rules. *Web Semantics: Science, Services and Agents on the World Wide Web*, 3(1):41–60, 2005.

108. Martin J. O'Connor, Ravi Shankar, Samson W. Tu, Csongor Nyulas, Dave Parrish, Mark A. Musen, and Amar K. Das. Using Semantic Web Technologies for

Knowledge-Driven Querying of Biomedical Data. In *Proceedings of the 11th Conference on Artificial Intelligence in Medicine, AIME 2007, Amsterdam, The Netherlands, July 7–11, 2007*, volume 4594 of *Lecture Notes in Computer Science*, pages 267–276. Springer, 2007.

109. Borys Omelayenko. RDFT: A Mapping Meta-Ontology for Business Integration. In *Proceedings of the Workshop on Knowledge Transformation for the Semantic Web (KTSW 2002) at the 15-th European Conference on Artificial Intelligence (ECAI 2002), Lyon, France, 23 July, 2002*, pages 77–84, 2002.

110. OMG. Human-Usable Textual Notation (HUTN) Specification. OMG Document Number: formal/04-08-01, April 2004.

111. OMG. Meta Object Facility (MOF) Core Specification Version 2.0. OMG Document Number: formal/2006-01-01, January 2006.

112. OMG. Business Process Model and Notation (BPMN) Version 1.2. OMG Document Number: formal/2009-01-03, January 2009.

113. OMG. Meta Object Facility (MOF) 2.0 Query/View/Transformation Specification Version 1.1. Final Adopted Specification ptc/09-12-05, December 2009.

114. OMG. Ontology Definition Metamodel Version 1.0. OMG Document Number: formal/2009-05-01, May 2009.

115. OMG. Request for Proposal MOF to RDF Structural Mapping in Support of Linked Open Data. OMG document AD/2009-12-09, December 2009.

116. OMG. Object Constraint Language Version 2.2. OMG Document Number: formal/2010-02-01, February 2010.

117. OMG. OMG Unified Modeling Language (OMG UML), Superstructure Version 2.3. OMG Document Number: formal/2010-05-05, May 2010.

118. Eyal Oren, Renaud Delbru, Sebastian Gerke, Armin Haller, and Stefan Decker. ActiveRDF: Object-oriented semantic web programming. In *Proceedings of the 16th International Conference on World Wide Web, WWW 2007, Banff, Alberta, Canada, May 8–12, 2007*, pages 817–824. ACM, 2007.

119. Alexander Paar and Walter F. Tichy. Zhi#: Programming Language Inherent Support for XML Schema Definition. In *Proceedings of The Ninth IASTED International Conference on Software Engineering and Applications, SEA 2005, Phoenix, AZ, USA, November 14–16, 2005*, volume 467. ACTA Press, 2005.

120. Jeff Z. Pan, Edward Thomas, and Yuting Zhao. Completeness Guaranteed Approximations for OWL-DL Query Answering. In *Proceedings of the DL Home 22nd International Workshop on Description Logics (DL 2009), Oxford, UK, July 27–30, 2009*, volume 477 of *CEUR Workshop Proceedings*. CEUR-WS.org, 2009.

121. Robert E. Park. Software Size Measurement: A Framework for Counting Source Statements. Technical Report CMU/SEI-92-TR-20, ESC-TR-92-20, Software Engineering Institute, Carnegie Mellon University, September 1992.

122. Fernando Silva Parreiras and Steffen Staab. Using ontologies with UML class-based modeling: The Twouse approach. *Data & Knowledge Engineering*, 69(11):1194–1207, 2010.

123. Peter F. Patel-Schneider and Boris Motik. OWL 2 Web Ontology Language Mapping to RDF Graphs. W3C Recommendation 27 October 2009, 2009.

124. Axel Polleres, François Scharffe, and Roman Schindlauer. SPARQL++ for Mapping Between RDF Vocabularies. In *Proceedings of 6th International Conference on Ontologies, DataBases, and Applications of Semantics, ODBASE 2007, Vilamoura,*

Portugal, November 25–30, 2007, volume 4803 of *Lecture Notes in Computer Science*, pages 878–896. Springer, 2007.

125. Valentina Presutti and Aldo Gangemi. Content Ontology Design Patterns as Practical Building Blocks for Web Ontologies. In *ER 2008, Barcelona, Spain, October 20–24, 2008. Proceedings*, volume 5231 of *Lecture Notes in Computer Science*, pages 128–141. Springer, 2008.

126. Eric Prud'hommeaux and Andy Seaborne. SPARQL Query Language for RDF. W3C Recommendation, Jan 2008.

127. Tirdad Rahmani, Daniel Oberle, and Marco Dahms. An Adjustable Transformation from OWL to Ecore. In *Model Driven Engineering Languages and Systems—13th International Conference, MODELS 2010, Oslo, Norway, October 3–8, 2010, Proceedings, Part II*, volume 6395 of *Lecture Notes in Computer Science*, pages 243–257. Springer, 2010.

128. Alan L. Rector, Nick Drummond, Matthew Horridge, Jeremy Rogers, Holger Knublauch, Robert Stevens, Hai Wang, and Chris Wroe. OWL Pizzas: Practical Experience of Teaching OWL-DL: Common Errors & Common Patterns. In *Proceedings of Knowledge Engineering and Knowledge Management (EKAW 2004), Northamptonshire, UK, 5–8th October, 2004*, volume 3257 of *Lecture Notes in Computer Science*, pages 63–81. Springer, 2004.

129. R. Reiter. A theory of diagnosis from first principles. *Artificial Intelligence*, 32(1):57–95, 1987.

130. Yuan Ren, Gerd Gröner, Jens Lemcke, Tirdad Rahmani, Andreas Friesen, Yuting Zhao, Jeff Z. Pan, and Steffen Staab. Validating Process Refinement with Ontologies. In *Proceedings of the DL Home 22nd International Workshop on Description Logics (DL 2009), Oxford, UK, July 27–30, 2009*, volume 477 of *CEUR Workshop Proceedings*. CEUR-WS.org, 2009.

131. Yuan Ren, Jeff Z. Pan, and Yuting Zhao. Closed World Reasoning for OWL 2 with Negation as Failure. In *Proceedings of the 4th Chinese Semantic Web Symposium (CSWS 2010), August 19–21, Beijing, China, 2010*, 2010.

132. Yuan Ren, Jeff Z. Pan, and Yuting Zhao. Soundness Preserving Approximation for TBox Reasoning. In *Proceedings of the Twenty-Fourth AAAI Conference on Artificial Intelligence, AAAI 2010, Atlanta, GA, USA, July 11–15, 2010*, pages 351–356. AAAI Press, 2010.

133. James Ressler, Mike Dean, Edward Benson, Eric Dorner, and Chuck Morris. Application of Ontology Translation. In *Proceedings of the 6th International Semantic Web Conference and 2nd Asian Semantic Web Conference (ISWC 2007 + ASWC 2007), Busan, Korea, November 11–15, 2007*, volume 4825 of *Lecture Notes in Computer Science*, pages 830–842. Springer, 2007.

134. Mark Richters. A Precise Approach to Validating UML Models and OCL Constraints. PhD thesis, Universität Bremen, 2002.

135. Stephan Roser and Bernhard Bauer. An Approach to Automatically Generated Model Transformations Using Ontology Engineering Space. In *Proceedings of the 2nd International Workshop on Semantic Web Enabled Software Engineering, SWESE 2006, Athens, GA, USA, November 6, 2006*.

136. J. Rothenberg. The nature of modeling. In *Artificial Intelligence, Simulation & Modeling*, pages 75–92. John Wiley & Sons, Inc., New York, NY, USA, 1989.

137. James Rumbaugh, Ivar Jacobson, and Grady Booch. *Unified Modeling Language Reference Manual, The (2nd Edition)*. Addison-Wesley, Boston, MA, USA, 2004.

138. Carsten Saathoff, Simon Schenk, and Ansgar Scherp. KAT: The K-Space Annotation Tool. In *Proceedings of the Third International Conference on Semantic and Digital Media Technologies, SAMT 2008, Koblenz, Germany, December 3–5, 2008.*

139. Carsten Saathoff and Ansgar Scherp. Unlocking the Semantics of Multimedia Presentations in the Web with the Multimedia Metadata Ontology. In *Proceedings of the 19th International Conference on World Wide Web (WWW 2010), Raleigh, NC, USA, April 26–30, 2010*, pages 831–840. ACM, 2010.

140. Ansgar Scherp, Thomas Franz, Carsten Saathoff, and Steffen Staab. F–a model of events based on the foundational ontology dolce+DnS ultralight. In *Proceedings of the 5th International Conference on Knowledge Capture (K-CAP 2009), September 1–4, 2009, Redondo Beach, CA, USA*, pages 137–144. ACM, 2009.

141. David A. Schmidt. *Denotational Semantics: A Methodology for Language Development*. William C. Brown Publishers, Dubuque, IA, USA, 1986.

142. Douglas C. Schmidt. Guest Editor's Introduction: Model-Driven Engineering. *Computer*, 39(2):25, 2006.

143. Mark Schneider. SPARQLAS—Implementing SPARQL Queries with OWL Syntax. In *Proceedings of the 3rd Workshop on Transforming and Weaving Ontologies in Model Driven Engineering (TWOMDE 2010). Malaga, Spain, June 30, 2010.*, volume 604 of *CEUR Workshop Proceedings*. CEUR-WS.org, 2010.

144. Andy Seaborne and Geetha Manjunath. SPARQL Update: A language for updating RDF graphs. W3c member submission 15 july 2008, W3C, 2008.

145. E. Seidewitz. What models mean. *Software, IEEE*, 20(5):26–32, sep. 2003.

146. Alan Shalloway and James Trott. *Design Patterns Explained: A New Perspective on Object-Oriented Design*. Addison-Wesley, Boston, MA, USA, 2002.

147. Fernando Silva Parreiras, Gerd Gröner, and Tobias Walter. Filling the Gap between Semantic Web and Model Driven Engineering: The TwoUse Toolkit. In *Proceedings of the Tools Demonstrations and Consultancy Presentations at 6th European Conference on Modelling Foundations and Applications, ECMFA 2010, Paris, France, June 15–18, 2010, 2010.*

148. Fernando Silva Parreiras, Gerd Gröner, Tobias Walter, and Steffen Staab. A Model-Driven Approach for Using Templates in OWL Ontologies. In *Knowledge Engineering and Knowledge Management by the Masses, 17th International Conference, EKAW 2010, Lisbon, Portugal, October 11–15, 2010. Proceedings*, volume 6317 of *Lecture Notes in Computer Science*. Springer, 2010.

149. Fernando Silva Parreiras, Steffen Staab, Simon Schenk, and Andreas Winter. Model Driven Specification of Ontology Translations. In Qing Lia, Stefano Spaccapietra, and Eric Yu, editors, *Proceedings of Conceptual Modeling—ER 2008, 27th International Conference on Conceptual Modeling, Barcelona, Spain, October 20–24, 2008*, number 5231 in Lecture Notes in Computer Science, pages 484–497. Springer, 2008.

150. Fernando Silva Parreiras, Steffen Staab, and Andreas Winter. On Marrying Ontological and Metamodeling Technical Spaces. In *Proceedings of the European Software Engineering Conference and the ACM SIGSOFT Symposium on the Foundations of Software Engineering (ESEC/FSE 2007), Dubrovnik, Croatia, September 3–7, 2007*, pages 439–448. ACM, 2007.

151. Fernando Silva Parreiras, Steffen Staab, and Andreas Winter. Improving Design Patterns by Description Logics: A Use Case with Abstract Factory and Strategy. In *Proceedings of Modellierung 2008, Berlin, Germany, March 12–14, 2008*, volume 127 of *LNI*, pages 89–104. GI, 2008.

152. Fernando Silva Parreiras and Tobias Walter. Report on the Combined Metamodel. Deliverable EU FP7 STREP MOST ICT216691/UoKL/WP1-D1.1/D/PU/a1, University of Koblenz Landau, July 2008.

153. Fernando Silva Parreiras, Tobias Walter, Steffen Staab, Carsten Saathoff, and Thomas Franz. APIs agogo: Automatic Generation of Ontology APIs. In *Proceedings of the 3rd IEEE International Conference on Semantic Computing (ICSC 2009), Santa Clara, CA, USA, September 14–16, 2009*, pages 342–348. IEEE Computer Society, 2009.

154. Evren Sirin and Bijan Parsia. SPARQL-DL: SPARQL Query for OWL-DL. In *Proceedings of the OWLED 2007 Workshop on OWL: Experiences and Directions, Innsbruck, Austria, June 6–7, 2007*, volume 258 of *CEUR Workshop Proceedings*. CEUR-WS.org, 2007.

155. Evren Sirin, Bijan Parsia, Bernardo Cuenca Grau, Aditya Kalyanpur, and Yarden Katz. Pellet: A practical OWL-DL reasoner. *Journal of Web Semantics*, 5(2):51–53, 2007.

156. Ken Slonneger, Kenneth Slonneger, and Barry Kurtz. *Formal Syntax and Semantics of Programming Languages: A Laboratory Based Approach*. Addison-Wesley Longman Publishing Co., Inc., Boston, MA, USA, 1995.

157. Raymond M. Smullyan. *First-Order Logic*. Dover Publications, 1994.

158. S. Staab, M. Erdmann, and A. Maedche. Engineering Ontologies Using Semantic Patterns. In *17th International Joint Conference on Artificial Intelligence (IJCAI 2001) Workshop on E-business and the Intelligent Web, Seattle, WA, USA, August 4, 2001*, 2001.

159. S. Staab, A. Scherp, R. Arndt, R. Troncy, M. Gregorzek, C. Saathoff, S. Schenk, and L. Hardman. Semantic Multimedia. In *Tutorial Lectures of the 4th International Summer School 2008, Reasoning Web, Venice, Italy, September 7–11, 2008*, volume 5224 of *Lecture Notes in Computer Science*, pages 125–170. Springer, 2008.

160. Steffen Staab, Thomas Franz, Olaf Görlitz, Carsten Saathoff, Simon Schenk, and Sergej Sizov. Lifecycle Knowledge Management: Getting the Semantics Across in X-Media. In *Proceedings of The 16th International Symposium on Methodologies for Intelligent Systems, ISMIS 2006, Bari, Italy, September 27–29, 2006*, volume 4203 of *Lecture Notes in Computer Science*, pages 1–10. Springer, 2006.

161. Steffen Staab and Rudi Studer, editors. *Handbook on Ontologies*. International Handbooks on Information Systems. Springer, 2004.

162. Steffen Staab, Rudi Studer, Hans-Peter Schnurr, and York Sure. Knowledge Processes and Ontologies. *IEEE Intelligent Systems*, 16(1):26–34, 2001.

163. Steffen Staab, Tobias Walter, Gerd Gröner, and Fernando Silva Parreiras. Model Driven Engineering with Ontology Technologies. In *Reasoning Web. Semantic Technologies for Software Engineering, 6th International Summer School 2010, Dresden, Germany, August 30 -September 3, 2010. Tutorial Lectures*, volume 6325 of *Lecture Notes in Computer Science*, pages 62–98. Springer, 2010.

164. David Steinberg, Frank Budinsky, Marcelo Paternostro, and Ed Merks. *EMF: Eclipse Modeling Framework 2.0, 2nd edition*. Addison-Wesley Professional, Boston, MA, USA, 2009.

165. Ragnhild Van Der Straeten, Tom Mens, Jocelyn Simmonds, and Viviane Jonckers. Using Description Logic to Maintain Consistency between UML Models. In *Proceedings of the 6th International Conference of The Unified Modeling Language, Modeling Languages and Applications, UML 2003, San Francisco, CA, USA, October*

20–24, 2003, volume 2863 of *Lecture Notes in Computer Science*, pages 326–340. Springer, 2003.

166. Rudi Studer, V. Richard Benjamins, and Dieter Fensel. Knowledge engineering: principles and methods. *Data Knowl. Eng.*, 25(1–2):161–197, 1998.

167. G. Taentzer. AGG: A graph transformation environment for modeling and validation of software. In *Proceedings of Applications of Graph Transformations with Industrial Relevance (AGTIVE 2003), Charlottesville, VA, USA, September 27—October 1, 2003*, volume 3062 of *Lecture Notes in Computer Science*, pages 446–453. Springer, 2004.

168. Phil Tetlow, Jeff Z. Pan, Daniel Oberle, Evan Wallace, Michael Uschold, and Elisa Kendall. Ontology Driven Architectures and Potential Uses of the Semantic Web in Systems and Software Engineering. W3C Working Draft Working Group Note 2006/02/11, W3C, 03 2006.

169. W. F. Tichy. A Catalogue of General-Purpose Software Design Patterns. In *Proceedings of the 23rd International Conference on Technology of Object-Oriented Languages and Systems, TOOLS 1997, Santa Barbara, CA, USA, July 28–August 1, 1997*, pages 330–339. IEEE Computer Society, 1997.

170. Thanh Tran, Peter Haase, Holger Lewen, Óscar Muñoz-García, Asuncíon Gómez-Pérez, and Rudi Studer. Lifecycle-Support in Architectures for Ontology-Based Information Systems. In *Proceedings of the 6th International Semantic Web Conference and 2nd Asian Semantic Web Conference (ISWC/ASWC 2007), Busan, South Korea, 11–15th November, 2007*, volume 4825 of *Lecture Notes in Computer Science*, pages 508–522. Springer, 2007.

171. Michael Uschold and Robert Jasper. A Framework for Understanding and Classifying Ontology Applications. In *IJCAI-99 Workshop on Ontologies and Problem-Solving Methods: Lessons Learned and Future Trends, Stockholm, Sweden, August 2, 1999*, volume 18 of *CEUR Workshop Proceedings*. CEUR-WS.org, 1999.

172. Max Völkel and York Sure. RDFReactor—From Ontologies to Programmatic Data Access. In *Poster Proceedings of the Fourth International Semantic Web Conference*, 2005.

173. D. Vrandecic. Explicit Knowledge Engineering Patterns with Macros. In *Workshop on Ontology Patterns for the Semantic Web at ISWC 2005, 4th International Semantic Web Conference, ISWC 2005, Galway, Ireland, November 6–10, 2005*, 2005.

174. Tobias Walter. Combining Domain-Specific Languages and Ontology Technologies. In *Proceedings of the Doctoral Symposium at the 12th International Conference on Model Driven Engineering Languages and Systems, MODELS 2009, Denver, CO, USA, October 5, 2009*, volume 2009-566 of *Technical Report*, pages 34–39. School of Computing, Queen's University, 2009.

175. Tobias Walter, Fernando Silva Parreiras, and Steffen Staab. OntoDSL: An Ontology-Based Framework for Domain-Specific Languages. In *Proceedings of the 12th International Conference on Model Driven Engineering Languages and Systems, MODELS 2009, Denver, CO, USA, October 4–9, 2009*, volume 5795 of *Lecture Notes in Computer Science*, pages 408–422. Springer, 2009.

176. Tobias Walter, Fernando Silva Parreiras, Steffen Staab, and Juergen Ebert. Joint Language and Domain Engineering. In *Proceedings of the 6th European Conference on Modelling Foundations and Applications, ECMFA 2010, Paris, France, June 15–18, 2010*, volume 6138 of *Lecture Notes in Computer Science*, pages 321–336. Springer, 2010.

177. Hai H. Wang, Yuan Fang Li, Jing Sun, Hongyu Zhang, and Jeff Pan. Verifying feature models using OWL. *Web Semantics: Science, Services and Agents on the World Wide Web*, 5(2):117–129, 2007.

178. Kevin Wilkinson, Craig Sayers, Harumi Kuno, and Dave Reynolds. Efficient RDF Storage and Retrieval in Jena2. In *Proceedings of the 1st Workshop on Semantic Web and Databases, Co-located with VLDB 2003, Berlin, Germany, September 7–8, 2003.*

179. Edward D. Willink. UMLX: A graphical transformation language for MDA. In *Proceedings of the Workshop on Model Driven Architecture: Foundations and Application MDAFA 2003, Enschede, The Netherlands, June 26–27, 2003*, volume TR-CTIT-03-27 of *Technical Report*, pages 13–24. CTIT Technology University of Twente, 2003.

180. Michael Würsch, Giacomo Ghezzi, Gerald Reif, and Harald Gall. Supporting developers with natural language queries. In *Proceedings of the 32nd ACM/IEEE International Conference on Software Engineering—Volume 1, ICSE 2010, Cape Town, South Africa, 1–8 May 2010*, pages 165–174. ACM, 2010.

181. Yuting Zhao, Jeff Z. Pan, Nophadol Jekjantuk, Jakob Henriksson, Gerd Gröner, and Yuan Ren. Classification of Language Hierarchy and Complexity. Deliverable EU FP7 STREP MOST ICT216691/UNIABDN/WP3-D3.1/D/PU/b1, University of Aberdeen, July 2008.

INDEX

ABox. *See* Assertional box (ABox)
Abstract Factory pattern, 101–103
   compared to TwoUse-based solution, 108
   drawbacks, 103–104
Abstraction
   expressiveness *vs.*, 145
   software engineering and raising level of, 9
Abstract syntax, 14, 15, 47
   TwoUse, 68, 70, 119–120
ActiveRDF, 170
Adaptee classes, 71
Adapter classes, 71
ADD, 182
addAttribute, implementing in class
      TUClassAdapter, 72–73
Adoption, of Selector pattern, 111
AgentRole ontology design pattern, 172
AGG, 17
Agogo, 156, 158, 188
   analysis of ontology API specifications, 167–169
   architecture of, 166–167
   concrete syntax by example, 163–166
   correlating requirements with quality attributes,
      169
   implementation, 166–167
   key concepts, 161–163
   metamodel constraints, 162–163
   snippet, 162
Aligning, 52
Alignments, compute, 208
Analysis plug-ins, 113
Analyzability, 121
Annotations, 182
APIs. *See* Application programming interfaces
      (APIs)
Applicability, Selector pattern, 110
Application programming interfaces (APIs), 156.
      See also Ontology APIs
   OWL, 34
Approximative transformations, 52
Artifacts
   OWL constructs and, 7
   semantic web approaches for transforming,
      134–135
   semantic web technologies and, 112
   TwoUse, 132–133

Artificial intelligence, ontologies and, 21
ASK, 40
Assertional box (ABox), 24, 31, 173
Assertions
   semantics of, 28
   syntax of, 26
ATL. *See* Atlas Transformation Language (ATL)
Atlas Transformation Language (ATL), 17, 52,
      91, 146, 154
   model transformations using, 167
   ontology translation platform and, 149–150
Atlas Transformation Language (ATL)
      metamodel, 146–147
   limitations of, 153
Attributes, 13
Axiomatic semantics, 47
Axioms
   explain, 209
   templates for generating, 177

Bidirectional transformations, 52
Bindings, 180–181
Black box method for single justification, 33
BPMN. *See* Business Process Modeling Notation
      (BPMN)
Browse, 208–209
Built-ins, 144
Business Process Modeling Notation (BPMN),
      15, 126, 127
Business Process Modeling Notation (BPMN)
      metamodel
   model extension, 128–129

Case studies
   automatic generation of ontology APIs,
      158–160
   enabling linked data capabilities for MOF
      compliant models, 124–135
   improving software design patterns with OWL,
      100–104
   model-driven specification of ontology
      translations, 142–145
   modeling ontology-based information systems,
      113–117
   using templates in OWL ontologies, 172–174
Changeability, 122

Semantic Web and Model-Driven Engineering, First Edition. Fernando Silva Parreiras.
© 2012 Institute of Electrical and Electronics Engineers. Published 2012 by John Wiley & Sons, Inc.

Printed and bound by CPI Group (UK) Ltd, Croydon, CR0 4YY

27/10/2024

14580280-0001